A New  & Other from Frommer's!

In our continuing effort to publish the savviest, most up-to-date, and most appealing travel guides available, we've added some great new features.

Frommer's guides now include a new **star-rating system.** Every hotel, restaurant, and attraction is rated from 0 to 3 stars to help you set priorities and organize your time.

We've also added **seven brand-new features** that point you to the great deals, in-the-know advice, and unique experiences that separate travelers from tourists. Throughout the guide, look for:

(Finds	Special finds—those places only insiders know about
(Fun Fact	Fun facts—details that make travelers more informed and their trips more fun
(Kids	Best bets for kids—advice for the whole family
(Moments	Special moments—those experiences that memories are made of
(Overrated	Places or experiences not worth your time or money
(Tips	Insider tips—some great ways to save time and money
(Value	Great values—where to get the best deals

Here's what critics say about Frommer's:

"Amazingly easy to use. Very portable, very complete."

—*Booklist*

"Detailed, accurate, and easy-to-read information for all price ranges."

—*Glamour Magazine*

"Hotel information is close to encyclopedic."

—*Des Moines Sunday Register*

"Frommer's Guides have a way of giving you a real feel for a place."

—*Knight Ridder Newspapers*

Frommer's®

PORTABLE
Venice

4th Edition

by Darwin Porter & Danforth Prince

WILEY

Wiley Publishing, Inc.

Published by:

WILEY PUBLISHING, INC.
909 Third Ave.
New York, NY 10022

ISBN 0-7645-6752-7
ISSN 1092-2032

Editor: Christine Ryan
Production Editor: Bethany André
Photo Editor: Richard Fox
Cartographer: John Decamillis
Production by Wiley Indianapolis Composition Services

For information on our other products and services or to obtain technical
support, please contact our Customer Care Department within the U.S. at
800/762-2974, outside the U.S. at 317/572-3993, or fax 317/572-4002.

Wiley also publishes its books in a variety of electronic formats. Some content that appears in print may not be available in electronic formats.

Manufactured in the United States of America

5 4 3 2 1

Contents

List of Maps

ABOUT THE AUTHORS

A native of North Carolina, **Darwin Porter** was a bureau chief for the *Miami Herald* when he was 21, and later worked in television advertising. A veteran travel writer, he wrote Frommer's first-ever guide to Italy, and he's been a frequent traveler in Italy ever since. He's joined by **Danforth Prince,** formerly of the Paris bureau of the *New York Times,* who has lived and traveled extensively in Italy. This team writes a number of best-selling Frommer guides, notably to Italy, England, France, the Caribbean, Austria, and Germany.

AN INVITATION TO THE READER

In researching this book, we discovered many wonderful places—hotels, restaurants, shops, and more. We're sure you'll find others. Please tell us about them, so we can share the information with your fellow travelers in upcoming editions. If you were disappointed with a recommendation, we'd love to know that, too. Please write to:

Frommer's Portable Venice, 4th Edition
Wiley Publishing, Inc. • 909 Third Ave. • New York, NY 10022

AN ADDITIONAL NOTE

Please be advised that travel information is subject to change at any time—and this is especially true of prices. We therefore suggest that you write or call ahead for confirmation when making your travel plans. The authors, editors, and publisher cannot be held responsible for the experiences of readers while traveling. Your safety is important to us, however, so we encourage you to stay alert and be aware of your surroundings. Keep a close eye on cameras, purses, and wallets, all favorite targets of thieves and pickpockets.

WHAT THE SYMBOLS MEAN

The following abbreviations are used for credit cards:

AE	American Express	DISC	Discover	V	Visa
DC	Diners Club	MC	MasterCard		

FROMMERS.COM

Now that you have the guidebook to a great trip, visit our website at **www.frommers.com** for travel information on nearly 2,500 destinations. With features updated regularly, we give you instant access to the most current trip-planning information available. At Frommers.com, you'll also find the best prices on airfares, accommodations, and car rentals—and you can even book travel online through our travel booking partners. At Frommers.com, you'll also find the following:

- Online updates to our most popular guidebooks
- Vacation sweepstakes and contest giveaways
- Newsletter highlighting the hottest travel trends
- Online travel message boards with featured travel discussions

The Venice Experience

You don't exactly have to get on the next plane to be sure to see Venice while it still exists, but scientists are warning that only a miracle or more advanced engineering than is known in the early 21st century can save one of the world's most fabled cities of art and architecture.

The most recent reports indicate that Venice is sinking faster than had been anticipated. The gloomiest forecast is that the encroaching waters of the Adriatic Sea could devastate Venice within this century, especially if global warming causes waters to rise faster.

What a catastrophe this would be. Surely there is no more preposterous monument to the folly of humankind than La Serenissima, the Serene Republic of Venice, a fantasy city on the sea.

When you arrive and are stunned by all the architectural wonders and riches of Venice, its vivid colors of sienna, Roman gold, and ruby peach, you may think that reports of tide damage are overblown. Once you experience your first flood and see for yourself how close the sea is to sweeping over Venice, you'll most likely change your mind.

Pollution, uncontrolled tides, and just plain old creaky age are eating away daily at the treasures of this fabled city of art. As the debate rages about how to save Venice, with no real solution in sight, the waters keep rising.

Why did those "insane" Venetians build on such swampy islands and not on the dry land, which there was plenty of centuries ago?

In an effort to flee the barbarians, Venetians left dry dock and drifted out to a flotilla of "uninhabitable" islands in the lagoon. For a long time Venice did elude foreign armies intent on burning, looting, and plundering. Eventually, Napoleon and his forces arrived; however, the Corsican's intent was never to destroy Venice.

Foreign visitors have conquered Venice in ways most barbarian armies did not. Some 10 million people visit Venice every year—and that's only counting the visitors who actually spend the night. Since Venice is known as an expensive city and has only a limited

Impressions

When I went to Venice, my dream became my address.
    —Marcel Proust, letter to Mme Strauss (May 1906)

number of accommodations, there are countless day-trippers invading every day all summer long. Few Venetians desire the presence of these day-trippers, because they tend to spend little money. Some Venetian officials, to counter the presence of these nonspenders, have advocated that the city institute an admission charge.

Those who spend the night and actually dine in the restaurants are received with a much warmer embrace by the merchants, hoteliers, and restaurateurs. But even these big spenders are viewed with a certain disdain by Venetians, who'd rather have their city to themselves. However, high prices have forced out many locals, who've fled across the lagoon to dreary Mestre, an industrial complex launched to help boost the regional economy and make it far less dependent on tourism. Mestre, with its factories, helps keep Venice relatively industry-free, though it spews pollution across the city—hardly what the art of Venice needs.

The capital of the Veneto, Venice encompasses some 466 sq. km (180 sq. miles), if Mestre, Marghera, and the islands of the lagoon are counted. Of these square kilometers, about 260 (100 sq. miles) are water. The city is built around some 117 islands or, as is often the case, "islets." Venice is bisected by 177 canals, including its showcase artery, the palazzo-flanked Grand Canal. The islands are joined together by 400 small concrete-and-iron bridges, the most important of which are the Accademia, the Degli Scalzi, and the Rialto, all spanning the Grand Canal. Venice itself is connected to the mainland by a 5km (3-mile) bridge that crosses the Venetian lagoon to Mestre.

What will you find in Venice? Unendurable crowds; dank, dark canals and even danker, claustrophobic alleys; outrageous prices; and a certain sinister quality in the decay. But you'll also find one of the most spectacular cities ever conceived.

1 Frommer's Favorite Venice Experiences

- **Riding the Grand Canal in a Gondola.** Just before sunset, order some delectable sandwiches from Harry's Bar and a bottle of chilled Prosecco, then take someone you love on a gondola ride along the Grand Canal for the boat trip of a lifetime.

- **Sipping Cappuccino on Piazza San Marco.** Select a choice spot on one of the world's most famous squares, order a cup of cappuccino, listen to the classical music, and absorb the special atmosphere of Venice.
- **Sunning on the Lido.** The world has seen better beaches, but few sights equal the parade of flesh and humanity of this fashionable beach on a hot summer day.
- **Contemplating Giorgione's** *Tempest.* If you have time to see only one painting, make it this one at the Accademia. The artist's haunting sense of oncoming menace superimposed over a bucolic setting will stay with you long after you leave Venice.
- **Trailing Titian to the High Renaissance.** Known for his technical skill, use of brilliant color, and robust style, Titian was a master of the High Renaissance. In Venice, you can see some of this great painter's major works (the ones Napoleon didn't haul off to Paris) in the Accademia, Santa Maria Gloriosa dei Frari, and Santa Maria della Salute.

- **Spending a Day on Torcello.** Of all the islands in the lagoon, our favorite is Torcello, the single best day trip from Piazza San Marco. Visit to see Santa Maria Assunta, the first cathedral of Venice and home to splendid 11th- and 12th-century mosaics. But also come to explore the island, wandering around at leisure in a place time seems to have forgotten. Follow your discoveries with a lunch of cannelloni at Locanda Cipriani, and the day is yours.

- **Making a Pub Crawl in Search of *Cicchetti*.** There's no better way to escape the tourists and mingle with locals than wandering Venice's back streets in search of local color, drink, and *cicchetti* (the local version of tapas). By the time you've made the rounds, you'll have had a great time and a full meal—everything from deep-fried mozzarella and artichoke hearts to mixed fish fries and pizza. Finish, of course, with an ice cream at a gelateria. A good place to start a pub crawl is Campo San Bartolomeo near the Rialto Bridge—one of Venice's authentic neighborhoods.

- **Paying a Visit to the World's Greatest Market.** When you tire of Gothic glory and High Renaissance masterpieces, head for the Rialto Market. Here you can sample local life and see what the Venetians are going to have for dinner. Barges, or *mototopi,* arrive throughout the day loaded with the rich produce of the Veneto and other parts. Somehow, blood-red oranges are bloodier here, fresh peas more tender and greener than elsewhere, and red radicchios redder. Of course, you'll get to meet all the sea creatures from the lagoon as well. Sample a pastry fresh from a hot oven at some little hole in the wall, then cap your visit at the stall holders' favorite place, the **Cantina do Mori,** Calle do Mori 429 (© **041-5225401**), where you can belt down a glass of wine made from Tocai grapes. There's been a tavern at this site since 1462.

- **Wandering Around Dorsoduro.** Dorsoduro attracts everybody coming to see the Peggy Guggenheim Collection or the Accademia. But few stick around to explore the neighborhood in any depth. Susanna Agnelli, sister of Gianni Versace, keeps a place here, as do many wealthy industrialists who could afford to live anywhere. Yet parts are so seedy as to look haunted. The most intriguing promenade is the Zattere, running the length of the district along the Giudecca Canal. Take a break at any watering hole; one of our favorites is the **No Name Caffè,** Calle Corfu 1491, between the Accademia and Campo San Barnaba.

- **Visiting the Island of the Dead.** For a Venetian, "the last gondola ride" is to **San Michele,** in a traditional funeral gondola
  decorated with golden angels. San Michele is a walled cemetery
  island shaded by massive cypresses, and there's no place quite
  like it. Celebrities are buried here, but so are ordinary
  Venetians. Time stands still in more ways than one at this
  cemetery. There's no more room here; today Venice has to send
  its dead to the mainland for burial. But poet Ezra Pound, who
  lived in Venice from 1959 until his death in 1972, made it just
  in time. It's reached by vaporetto no. 52, running from Piazza
  San Marco to Murano.

- **Seeing the Sun Rise on the Lagoon.** For us, there's no more
  enthralling experience than to get up before dawn and cross
  the lagoon to San Giorgio Maggiore. Architect Andrea Palladio
  knew exactly what he was doing when he created the church
  on this exact spot. The church faces Piazza San Marco and the
  entrance to the Grand Canal. While the tourist zillions are still
  asleep, waiting to overtake the city, you'll have Venice to yourself as the sun comes up. The architectural ensemble you can
  see in the first glow of dawn, the panorama in all directions as
  the city awakens, ranks as one of the greatest human-made
  spectacles on earth.

- **Experiencing Venice at 2am.** You'll truly know the meaning
  of the word *spectacular* when sitting at 2am on an outdoor seat
  on vaporetto no. 1 as it circles Venice. Only the most die-hard
  night owls will be onboard with you. With its twinkling lights
  and "Titian blue" skies, Venice at this time takes on an aura
  unique in Europe. It's very quiet at this hour (except for the
  sound of the vaporetto's motor). Perhaps a gondola will silently
  glide by. The buildings themselves take on a different mood
  and color, looking like ghostly mansions from another time.
  When you get back home, it may just be that this experience
  lingers longer in your memory than any other.

2 A City of Art

Venice is a city of art. The adornment of its churches, its palazzi, and
its public buildings is unmatched anywhere. Among this wealth of
art, four important painters stand out.

Giovanni Bellini (1430–1516)   Giovanni was the most important
of a family of painters that included his father, Jacopo (1400–70),
and his brother Gentile (1429–1504). His work paved the way for

the later innovations of Giorgione and Titian. He painted religious and mythological subjects, and was a supreme portraitist. He worked in oils rather than the more common tempura, and is known for his luminous color and the harmony of his compositions. Light and color bind the lifelike figures in his paintings to his atmospheric landscapes in a harmonious whole. Giovanni's works can be seen in the Accademia and in the San Zaccaria and Frari churches. Gentile excelled in crowd scenes and panoramas; several of his paintings are in the Accademia.

Titian (1485?–1576)   Tiziano Vecellio, known as Titian, came to Venice while still an adolescent to study in the workshop of Giovanni Bellini. The foremost painter of the Venetian Renaissance and a cosmopolitan man of the world, he socialized with leading academics, writers, and aristocrats of his time. Among his patrons were kings, popes, and emperors. His portraits were prized for their technical mastery and psychological perception; he painted Pope Paul III, Phillip II of Spain, and Francis I of France. As a result, much of his most important work is in museums and collections outside Italy.

The work you should not miss is his *Assumption* in the Frari church. In this picture, the Virgin seems to ascend toward the heights of the apse, surrounded by soaring Gothic tracery windows that flood the space with light. This revolutionary altarpiece (1516–18), filled with movement and drama, was Titian's first major public commission and sent his reputation soaring. As Titian grew older his style of painting became increasingly broad and complex, and he was said to paint more with his fingers than with the brush. The year of his birth is uncertain, but he lived to a great age, and may have been close to 100 years old at the time of his death.

Tintoretto (1518–94)   Jacopo Robusti, known as Tintoretto, came from a humble background (his father was a dyer). Unlike Titian, Tintoretto was not a worldly man, and he only traveled beyond Venice once in his life. A devout man totally absorbed in painting religious subjects, Tintoretto rebelled against traditional representations and re-created religious scenes from new perspectives, working at a furious pace with fluid brushstrokes. His canvases are filled with phantasmagoric light and intense, mystical spirituality. Tintoretto's principal assistants were his two sons and his daughter, Marietta Robusti, whose work can possibly be detected in a few of her father's paintings. Tintoretto is only sparsely represented in museums and collections outside Venice. His paintings are seen in churches and *scuole* (guild houses or fraternities) throughout his home city, particularly the Scuola Grande di San Rocco. Tintoretto also filled the walls of his parish church, the Madonna dell'Orto, with his dynamic, visionary canvases.

Veronese (1528–88)   Paolo Caglieri, as his name of Il Veronese tells us, was not born in Venice. He came to Venice from Verona in 1555, where his talent was quickly recognized. His paintings are characterized by splendor of color and are crowded with figures arranged in sinuous patterns. He painted landscapes and mytholog-ical scenes, and is especially known for his religious feast paintings. In the latter, his approach was to use lavish accessories, fashionable figures, and other secular devices. In 1573 when he was called before the Inquisition to explain the "indecent" content of his *Last Supper,* he valiantly defended his use of artistic license. Ordered to alter the work, he took the pragmatic way out and simply changed the name of the painting to *The Banquet in the House of Levi.* He was a supreme decorator, as can be seen in the Doge's Palace and the church of San Sebastiano.

2

Planning a Trip to Venice

This chapter contains all the nuts-and-bolts information you'll need to plan a trip to Venice, from where to get visitor information to how to get there.

1 Visitor Information & Entry Requirements

VISITOR INFORMATION

THE ITALIAN TOURIST BOARD

For information before you go, contact the **Italian Government Tourist Board.**

In the United States: 630 Fifth Ave., Suite 1565, New York, NY 10111 (© **212/245-4822;** fax 212/586-9249); 500 N. Michigan Ave., Suite 2240, Chicago, IL 60611 (© **312/644-0996;** fax 312/644-3019); 12400 Wilshire Blvd., Suite 550, Los Angeles, CA 90025 (© **310/820-1898;** fax 310/820-6367).

In Canada: 175 Bloor St. E, South Tower, Suite 907, Toronto, ON M4W 3R8 (© **416/925-4882;** fax 416/925-4799).

In the United Kingdom: 1 Princes St., London W1R 8AY (© **020/7408-1254;** fax 020/7493-6695).

USEFUL WEBSITES

On the Web, the Italian National Tourist Board sponsors the site **www.italiantourism.com** or **www.enit.it.** Other useful sites include:

Baby Boomer's Venice (http://europeforvisitors.com/venice) For the post-backpacker/pre-senior-tour set, this guide hits the spot. Navigate Venice's canals and gelato stands with help from a fellow baby boomer, who can tell you where to stay—and where not to stay—and point you to online reservation sites.

Carnival of Venice (www.carnivalofvenice.com) Experience the Carnevale celebration of the city of gondolas. Or explore past carnivals, dating back to the year 1268, in the mask-filled historic section of this online guide to one of Italy's most grand annual events.

Destination: Venice—Red-Alert Checklist

- Did you remember your passport?
- If you are a woman intent on visiting the churches of Venice, have you packed a long skirt or pants and a garment to conceal bare shoulders? Men should also be sure to pack appropriate attire (no shorts allowed in St. Mark's Basilica, among others).
- If you purchased traveler's checks, have you recorded the check numbers and stored the documentation separately from the checks?
- Did you pack your camera and an extra set of camera batteries, and purchase enough film? If you packed film in your checked baggage, did you invest in protective pouches to shield film from airport X-rays?
- Do you have a safe, accessible place to store money?
- Did you bring your ID cards that could entitle you to discounts, such as AAA and AARP cards, or student IDs?
- Did you bring emergency drug prescriptions and extra glasses and/or contact lenses?
- Do you have your credit-card PIN numbers?
- If you have an E-ticket, do you have documentation?
- Did you leave a copy of your itinerary with someone at home?

Travelers also can find information about transportation, city services, and other Venice basics.

In Italy Online (www.initaly.com)   This extensive site helps you find all sorts of accommodations (including villas, apartments, historic homes, and gay-friendly hotels) and includes tips on shopping, dining, driving, and viewing works of art. There's an information-packed section dedicated to each region of Italy, plus a section on books and movies to help enjoy the Italian experience at home. Join the mailing list for monthly updates.

Venice World (www.veniceworld.com)   Modeled after a standard American Web directory, this site lists links to Venice's accommodations, centers for the arts, nightclubs, restaurants, sporting events, travel agencies, Internet service providers, transportation, schools, newspapers, and so forth.

Venezia Net (**www.doge.it**)   Take virtual tours of the Doge's Palace and the Piazza San Marco. Skim through directories of hotels and travel agencies. Find out when you can catch the carnival celebration or the Venice Film Festival.

ENTRY REQUIREMENTS

Citizens of the United States, Canada, Australia, New Zealand, and the Republic of Ireland, as well as British subjects, need only a **valid passport** to enter Italy. You don't need a visa if you aren't going to stay more than 90 days and aren't going to work there.

2 Money

The **euro,** the new single European currency, became the official currency of Italy and 11 other participating countries on January 1, 1999.

However, the euro didn't go into general circulation until early in 2002. The old currency, the Italian lire, disappeared into history on March 1, 2002, replaced by the euro, whose official abbreviation is "EUR." The symbol of the euro is a stylized *E:* €. Exchange rates of participating countries are locked into a common currency fluctuating against the dollar.

For more details on the euro, check out **www.europa.eu.int/euro**.

The relative value of the euro fluctuates against the U.S. dollar, the pound sterling, and most of the world's other currencies, and its value might not be the same by the time you actually travel to Venice. A last-minute check is advised before beginning your trip.

At this writing, the euro and the U.S. dollar were almost on par with one another, exchanging at a rate that was virtually 1 to 1. Because of that, no US dollar equivalents are given for the Euro-denominated prices designated within this travel guide.

Also as of this writing, Great Britain still uses the pound sterling, with 1 euro equaling approximately 65 pence, and £1 equaling approximately 1.66€.

Exchange rates are more favorable at the point of arrival. Nevertheless, it's often helpful to exchange at least some money before going abroad (standing in line at the *cambio* [exchange bureau] in the Milan or Rome airport isn't fun after a long overseas flight). Check with any of your local American Express or Thomas Cook offices or major banks. Or order in advance from the following:

American Express (✆ **800/721-9768;** cardholders only), **Thomas Cook** (✆ **800/223-7373;** www.thomascook.com), or **Capital for Foreign Exchange** (✆ **888/842-0880;** www.afex.com).

It's best to exchange currency or traveler's checks at a bank, and not at a cambio, hotel, or shop. Currency and traveler's checks (for which you'll receive a better rate than cash) can be changed at all principal airports and at some travel agencies, such as American Express and Thomas Cook. Note the rates and ask about commission fees; it can sometimes pay to shop around and ask the right questions.

TRAVELER'S CHECKS

Traveler's checks once were the only sound alternative to traveling with dangerously large amounts of cash—they were as reliable as currency, unlike personal checks, but could be replaced if lost or stolen, unlike cash. But these days, traveler's checks seem less necessary because most larger cities have 24-hour ATMs, allowing you to withdraw small amounts of cash as needed. Many banks, however, impose a fee every time you use a card at an ATM in a different city or bank. If you plan to withdraw money every day, you might be better off with traveler's checks—provided you don't mind showing an ID every time you want to cash a check.

You can get traveler's checks at almost any bank. **American Express** offers checks in denominations of $10, $20, $50, $100, $500, and $1,000. You'll pay a service charge ranging from 1% to 4%. You can also get American Express traveler's checks over the phone by calling ✆ **800/721-9768;** or you can purchase checks online at **www.americanexpress.com**. Amex Gold or Platinum cardholders can avoid paying the fee by ordering over the telephone; Platinum cardholders can also purchase checks fee-free in person at Amex Travel Service locations (check the website for the office nearest you). American Automobile Association members can obtain checks fee-free at most AAA offices.

Visa offers traveler's checks at Citibank branches and other financial institutions nationwide; call ✆ **800/732-1322** (www.visa.com) to locate the purchase location near you. **MasterCard** also offers traveler's checks through **Thomas Cook Currency Services;** call ✆ **800/223-7373** (www.thomascook.com) for a location near you.

If you carry traveler's checks, be sure to keep a record of their serial numbers (separate from the checks, of course), so that you're ensured a refund in case they're lost or stolen.

ATMS

ATMs are linked to a national network that most likely includes your bank at home. Both the **Cirrus** (© **800/424-7787;** www. mastercard.com) and the **PLUS** (© **800/843-7587;** www.visa.com) networks have automated ATM locators listing the banks in Italy that will accept your card. Or just search out any machine with your network's symbol emblazoned on it.

You can also get a cash advance through Visa or MasterCard (contact the issuing bank to enable this feature and get a PIN), but note that the credit-card company will begin charging you interest immediately and many have begun assessing a fee every time you get cash. American Express–card cash advances are usually available only from Amex offices.

Important Note: Make sure the PINs on your bank cards and credit cards will work in Italy. You'll need a **four-digit code** (six digits won't work), so if you have a six-digit code, you'll have to go into your bank and get a new PIN for your trip. If you're unsure about this, contact Cirrus or PLUS (see above). Be sure to check the daily withdrawal limit at the same time.

CREDIT CARDS

Credit cards are invaluable when traveling—a safe way to carry money and a convenient record of all your expenses. You can also withdraw cash advances from your cards at any bank (though you'll start paying hefty interest the moment you receive the cash and you won't receive frequent-flyer miles on an airline credit card). At most banks, you don't even need to go to a teller; you can get a cash advance at an ATM with your PIN.

Note, however, that many banks, including Chase and Citibank, have begun to charge a 2% service fee for transactions in a foreign currency (3% or a minimum of $5 on cash advances).

Almost every credit-card company has an emergency toll-free number you can call if your wallet or purse is stolen. They may be able to wire you a cash advance off your credit card immediately, and in many places, they can deliver an emergency card in a day or two. The issuing bank's number is usually on the back of the credit card (which doesn't help you much if the card was stolen). A toll-free **information directory** at © **800/555-1212** will provide the number for you. Citicorp Visa's U.S. emergency number is © **800/ 336-8472.** **American Express** cardholders and traveler's check holders should call © **800/221-7282,** and **MasterCard** holders should call © **800/307-7309.**

3 When to Go

The best months to visit are April through June and September and October. Summers are hot and muggy and the canals are smelly. Winters are gray and wet but not severe, because the natural barrier of the Lido protects central Venice from much of the fury of the Adriatic. Yet in spite of the weather, many savvy visitors prefer to visit Venice in winter, when the city is emptier (the tourist crowds in summer are practically unbearable).

If you're planning to be in Venice any time from October through March, high boots can be useful. The canals flood frequently because of a combination of the tides and the winds. If a flood is expected, a warning siren will be sounded 1 hour before crest so people can get home. The city puts out *passarelle* (boardwalks) along major routes. The *acqua alta* (high water) lasts only about 2 or 3 hours at a time.

Venice's Average Daily Temperature (°) & Monthly Rainfall (in.)

	Jan	Feb	Mar	Apr	May	June	July	Aug	Sept	Oct	Nov	Dec
Temp. (F)	43	48	53	60	67	72	77	74	68	60	54	44
Temp. (C)	6	9	12	16	19	22	25	23	20	16	12	7
Rain	2.3	1.5	2.9	3.0	2.8	2.9	1.5	1.9	2.8	2.6	3.0	2.1

HOLIDAYS

Offices and shops in Italy are closed on January 1 (New Year's Day), Easter Monday, April 25 (Liberation Day), May 1 (Labor Day), August 15 (Assumption of the Virgin), November 1 (All Saints' Day), December 8 (Feast of the Immaculate Conception), December 25 (Christmas Day), and December 26 (Santo Stefano). Closings are also observed in Venice on April 25, the feast day honoring St. Mark, its patron.

VENICE CALENDAR OF EVENTS

February

Carnevale. At this riotous time, theatrical presentations and masked balls take place throughout Venice and on the islands in the lagoon. The balls are by invitation only (except the Doge's Ball), but the street events and fireworks are open to everyone. Contact the **Venice Tourist Office,** San Marco, Giardinetti Reali, Palazzo Selva, 30124 Venezia (© **041-522-5150**). The week before Ash Wednesday, the beginning of Lent.

May

La Sensa. Municipal authorities conduct a pale reenactment of the once-famed ritual of the Marriage of Venice to the Sea. On the same day, the vast **La Vogalonga** ("Long Row") is held. This is an exciting 32km (20-mile) race to Burano and back, open to all comers. Participants reach the San Marco basin between 11am and 3pm. The Sunday after Ascension Day.

June

Biennale d'Arte (International Exposition of Modern Art). One of the most famous art events in Europe takes place during alternate (odd-numbered) years in the *giardini pubblici* (public gardens). Between June and September.

July

Feast of Il Redentore. This festival commemorates the end of the 1576 plague. Half of Venice picnics aboard boats and gondolas and watches spectacular fireworks. A bridge of boats spans the Giudecca Canal and connects Dorsoduro to Palladio's Church of the Redentore on the island of Giudecca. Third Saturday and Sunday in July.

September

Venice International Film Festival. Ranking after Cannes, this festival brings together stars, directors, producers, and filmmakers from all over the world. Films are shown more or less constantly between 9am and 3am in various areas of the Palazzo del Cinema on the Lido. Though many of the seats are reserved for international jury members, the public can attend virtually whenever it wants, pending available seats. For information, contact the **Venice Film Festival,** c/o the Biennale office, Ca' Giustinian, Calle del Ridotto 1364A, 30124 Venezia. Call ℂ **041-2726501** for details on how to acquire tickets or check out **www. biennale.org**. The projected dates for 2003 are August 30 to September 9.

Regata Storica. This is a maritime spectacular—many gondolas participate in the Grand Canal procession. However, gondolas don't race in the regatta itself. First Sunday in September.

November

Opera season. During a wet and rainy season that attracts the fewest numbers of international visitors, the new opera season begins at PalaFenice, Isola Tronchetto (ℂ **041-786511**). The season lasts until July.

Feast of the Madonna della Salute. For approximately 24 hours, a pontoon bridge spans the Grand Canal to the great baroque church of Santa Maria della Salute for a religious procession commemorating the deliverance of Venice from the plague of 1630 and 1631. November 21.

4 Tips for Travelers with Special Needs
FOR TRAVELERS WITH DISABILITIES

Laws in Italy have compelled rail stations, airports, hotels, and most restaurants to follow a stricter set of regulations about **wheelchair accessibility** to restrooms, ticket counters, and the like. Even museums and other attractions have conformed to the regulations, which mimic many of those presently in effect in the United States. Always call ahead to check on the accessibility in hotels, restaurants, and sights you wish to visit.

With overcrowded streets, more than 400 bridges, and difficult-to-board *vaporetti* (public motorboats), Venice has never been accused of being too user-friendly for those with disabilities. Nevertheless, some improvements have been made. The Venice tourist office distributes a free map called *Veneziapertutti* ("Venice for All"), illustrating what parts of the city are accessible and listing accessible churches, monuments, gardens, public offices, hotels, and restrooms. According to various announcements, Venice in the future will pay even more attention to this issue, possibly adding retractable ramps operated by magnetic cards.

Moss Rehab ResourceNet (www.mossresourcenet.org) is a great source for information, tips, and resources relating to accessible travel. You'll find links to a number of travel agents who specialize in planning trips for travelers with disabilities here and through **Access-Able Travel Source** (www.access-able.com), another excellent online source. You'll also find relay and voice numbers for hotels, airlines, and car-rental companies on Access-Able's user-friendly site, as well as links to accessible accommodations, attractions, transportation, tours, local medical resources and equipment repairers, and much more.

You can join the **Society for the Advancement of Travelers with Handicaps** (SATH), 347 Fifth Ave., Suite 610, New York, NY 10016 (© **212/447-7284;** fax 212/725-8253; www.sath.org) to gain access to their vast network of connections in the travel industry. It provides information sheets on destinations and referrals to tour operators who specialize in travelers with disabilities. Its quarterly magazine, *Open World,* is full of good information and resources.

You may also want to join a tour catering to travelers with disabilities. One of the best operators is **Flying Wheels Travel** (© **507/451-5005;** www.flyingwheelstravel.com), offering various escorted tours and cruises, with an emphasis on sports, as well as private tours in minivans with lifts. Other reputable operators are **Accessible Journeys** (© **800/TINGLES** or 610/521-0339; www.disabilitytravel.com), for slow walkers and wheelchair travelers; **The Guided Tour** (© **215/782-1370**); and **Directions Unlimited** (© **800/533-5343**).

FOR GAYS & LESBIANS

Since 1861, Italy has had liberal legislation regarding homosexuality, but that doesn't mean it has always been looked on favorably in this Catholic country. Homosexuality is much more accepted in the north than in the south, and many of Venice's beaches have a vibrant gay scene.

As a companion to this guide, you may want to pick up *Frommer's Gay & Lesbian Europe,* with helpful chapters on Rome, Florence, Venice, and Milan.

If you want help planning your trip, the **International Gay & Lesbian Travel Association** (**IGLTA;** © **800/448-8550** or 954/776-2626; www.iglta.org) can link you with the appropriate gay-friendly service organization or tour specialist. With around 1,200 members, it offers quarterly newsletters, marketing mailings, and a membership directory that's updated quarterly. Members are kept informed of gay and gay-friendly hoteliers, tour operators, and airline and cruise-line representatives.

Out and About (© **800/929-2268** or 212/645-6922; www.out andabout.com) has been hailed for its "straight" reporting about gay travel. It offers a monthly newsletter packed with good information on the global gay and lesbian scene, and its website features links to gay and lesbian tour operators and other gay-themed travel links. *Out and About*'s guidebooks are available at most major bookstores and through **A Different Light Bookstore** (© **800/343-4002** or 212/989-4850; www.adlbooks.com).

Other general-type U.S. gay and lesbian travel agencies include **Family Abroad** (© **800/999-5500** or 212/459-1800) and **Above and Beyond Tours** (© **800/397-2681**). In the United Kingdom, try **Alternative Holidays** (© **020/7701-7040;** fax 020/7708-5668; info@alternativeholidays.com).

FOR SENIORS

One of the benefits of age is that travel often costs less. Always bring an ID card, especially if you've kept your youthful glow. Also mention the fact that you're a senior when you first make your travel reservations, since many airlines and hotels offer discount programs for senior travelers.

Members of **AARP** (© 800/424-3410; www.aarp.org) get discounts on hotels, airfares, and car rentals. AARP offers members a wide range of special benefits, including *Modern Maturity* magazine and a monthly newsletter. If you're not already a member, do yourself a favor and join.

If you want something more than the average vacation or guided tour, try **Elderhostel** (© 877/426-8056; www.elderhostel.org) or the University of New Hampshire's **Interhostel** (© 800/733-9753), both variations on the same theme: educational travel for senior citizens. On these escorted tours, the days are packed with seminars, lectures, and field trips, and the sightseeing is all led by academic experts. The courses in both programs are ungraded, involve no homework, and often focus on the liberal arts. They're not luxury vacations but are fun and fulfilling.

FOR STUDENTS

If you're planning to travel outside the U.S., you'd be wise to arm yourself with an **international student I.D. card,** which offers substantial savings on rail passes, plane tickets, and entrance fees. It also provides you with basic health and life insurance and a 24-hour help line. The card is available for $22 from the **Council on International Educational Exchange,** or CIEE (www.ciee.org). The CIEE's travel branch, **Council Travel Service** (© 800/226-8624; www.counciltravel.com), is the biggest student travel agency in the world. If you're no longer a student but are still under 26, you can get a **GO 25 card** from the same people, which entitles you to insurance and some discounts (but not on museum admissions). **STA Travel** (© 800/781-4040; www.statravel.com) is another travel agency catering especially to young travelers, although their bargain-basement prices are available to people of all ages.

CTS's **U.K. office** is at 28A Poland St. (Oxford Circus), London WIV 3DB (© 020/7437-7767); the **Italy office** is at Via Genova 16, 00184 Roma (© 06-47880476). In Canada, **Travel CUTS,** 200 Ronson St., Suite 320, Toronto, ONT M9W 5Z9 (© 800/667-2887 or 905/361-2022; www.travelcuts.com), offers similar services.

5 Getting There

All roads lead not necessarily to Rome but, in this case, to the docks on mainland Venice. The arrival scene at the unattractive Piazzale Roma is filled with nervous expectation; even the most veteran traveler can become confused. Whether arriving by train, bus, car, or airport limo, everyone walks to the nearby docks (less than a 5-min. walk) to select a method of transport to his or her hotel. The cheapest way is by *vaporetto,* the more expensive by gondola or motor launch (see "Getting Around" in chapter 3).

Warning: If your hotel is near one of the public vaporetto stops, you can sometimes struggle with your own luggage until you reach the hotel's reception area. In any event, the one time-tested piece of advice for Venice-bound travelers is that excess baggage is bad news, unless you're willing to pay dearly to have it carried for you to the docks. Porters can't accompany you and your baggage on the vaporetto. Pack light!

BY PLANE

High season on most airlines' routes to Italy is usually June to the beginning of September. This is the most expensive and most crowded time to travel. **Shoulder season** is April through May, early September through October, and December 15 to 24. **Low season** is November 1 to December 14 and December 25 to March 31.

FROM NORTH AMERICA   There are no direct flights from the United States to Venice; all flights go via Rome or Milan.

Flying time to Rome from New York, Newark, and Boston is 8 hours; from Chicago, 10 hours; and from Los Angeles, 12½ hours. Flying time to Milan from New York, Newark, and Boston is 8 hours; from Chicago, 9¼ hours; and from Los Angeles, 11½ hours.

American Airlines (© 800/433-7300; www.aa.com) offers daily nonstop flights to Rome from Chicago's O'Hare. **Delta** (© 800/221-1212; www.delta.com) also flies from New York's JFK to Milan, Rome, and Venice; separate flights depart every evening for both destinations. **United** (© 800/538-2929; www.united.com) has service to Milan only from Dulles in Washington, D.C. **US Airways** (© 800/428-4322; www.usairways.com) offers one flight daily to Rome out of Philadelphia (you can connect through Philadelphia from most major U.S. cities). And **Continental** (© 800/525-0280; www.flycontinental.com) flies twice daily to Rome from its hub in Newark.

Air Canada (© 800/247-2262; www.aircanada.ca) flies out of Toronto daily for both Milan and Rome.

British Airways (© 800/AIRWAYS; www.british-airways.com), **Virgin Atlantic Airways** (© 800/862-8621; www.virgin-atlantic. com), **Air France** (© 800/237-2747; www.airfrance.com), **Northwest/KLM** (© 800/374-7747; www.klm.nl), and **Lufthansa** (© 800/645-3880; www.lufthansa.com) offer some attractive deals for anyone interested in combining a trip to Italy with a stopover in, say, Britain, Paris, Amsterdam, or Germany.

Alitalia (© 800/223-5730 in the United States, 514/842-8241 in Canada; www.alitaliausa.com) is the Italian national airline, with nonstop flights to Rome from different North American cities, including New York (JFK), Newark, Boston, Chicago, and Miami. Nonstop flights into Milan are from New York (JFK), Newark, and Los Angeles. From Milan or Rome, Alitalia can easily book connecting domestic flights if your final destination is elsewhere in Italy. Alitalia participates in the frequent-flyer programs of other airlines, including Continental and US Airways.

Tips All About E-Ticketing

Only yesterday **electronic tickets (E-tickets)** were the fast and easy ticket-free alternative to paper tickets. E-tickets allowed passengers to avoid long lines at airport check-in, all the while saving the airlines money on postage and labor. With the increased security measures in airports, however, an E-ticket no longer guarantees an accelerated check-in. You often can't go straight to the boarding gate, even if you have no bags to check. You'll probably need to show your printed E-ticket receipt or confirmation of purchase, as well as a photo I.D., and sometimes even the credit card with which you purchased your E-ticket. That said, buying an E-ticket is still a fast, convenient way to book a flight; instead of having to wait for a paper ticket to come through the mail, you can book your fare by phone or on the computer, and the airline will immediately confirm by fax or e-mail. In addition, airlines often offer frequent-flier miles as incentive for electronic bookings.

> ### ⟨*Tips*⟩ Travel Planning & Booking Sites
>
> Keep in mind that because several airlines are no longer willing to pay commissions on tickets sold by online travel agencies, these agencies may add a $10 surcharge to your bill if you book on that carrier—or neglect to offer those carriers' schedules.
>
> The list of sites below is selective, not comprehensive. Some sites may have evolved or disappeared by the time you read this.
>
> - **Travelocity** (www.travelocity.com or www.frommers.travelocity.com) and **Expedia** (www.expedia.com) are among the most popular sites, each offering an excellent range of options. Travelers search by destination, dates, and cost.
> - **Orbitz** (www.orbitz.com) is a popular site launched by United, Delta, Northwest, American, and Continental airlines.
> - **Qixo** (www.qixo.com) is another powerful search engine that allows you to search for flights and accommodations from some 20 airline and travel-planning sites (such as Travelocity) at once. Qixo sorts results by price.
> - **Priceline** (www.priceline.com) lets you "name your price" for airline tickets, hotel rooms, and rental cars. For airline tickets, you can't say what time you want to fly—you have to accept any flight between 6am and 10pm on the dates you've selected, and you may have to make one or more stopovers. Tickets are nonrefundable, and no frequent-flyer miles are awarded.

FROM THE UNITED KINGDOM   Operated by the European Travel Network, **www.discount-tickets.com** is a great online source for regular and discounted airfares to destinations around the world. You can also use this site to compare rates and book accommodations, car rentals, and tours. Click on "Special Offers" for the latest package deals.

British newspapers are always full of classified ads touting slashed fares to Italy. One good source is *Time Out*. London's *Evening*

Standard has a daily travel section, and the Sunday editions of almost any newspaper will run many ads. Although competition is fierce, one well-recommended company that consolidates bulk ticket purchases and then passes the savings on to its consumers is **Trailfinders** (*℗* **020/7937-5400** in London). It offers access to tickets on such carriers as SAS, British Airways, and KLM.

CEEFAX, a British TV information service included on many home and hotel TVs, runs details of package holidays and flights to Italy and beyond. Just switch to your CEEFAX channel and you'll find a menu of listings that includes travel information.

Both **British Airways** (*℗* **0345/222-111** in the U.K.; www.british-airways.com) and **Alitalia** (*℗* **020/8745-2000;** www. alitalia.it/english/index.html) have frequent flights from London's Heathrow airport to Rome, Milan, Venice, Pisa (the gateway to Florence), and Naples. Flying time from London to these cities is from 2 to 3 hours. British Airways also has one direct flight a day from Manchester to Rome. **Virgin Atlantic** doesn't serve Italy at all.

ARRIVING AT THE VENICE AIRPORT   After landing in Rome, Milan, or another Italian gateway city, you can take a flight on **Alitalia** (see above) to Venice. *A word to the wise:* Alitalia allows smoking on its aircraft.

You'll land at Venice's **Aeroporto Marco Polo** (*℗* **041-2606111** for flight arrival and departure information) at Mestre. The **Cooperativa San Marco** (*℗* **041-5222303**) operates a *motoscafo* (shuttle boat) service departing from the airport and taking visitors to Piazza San Marco in about an hour (with a stop at the Lido after about 30 minutes). The fare is 80€ for up to six passengers.

If you've got some extra lire to spend, you can arrange for a **private water taxi** by calling *℗* **041-5415084.** The cost to ride to the heart of Venice is 80€.

It's much less expensive to take a **bus** from the airport, a trip of less than 8km (5 miles) costing 2.70€. The bus takes you across the Ponte della Libertà to the Stazione Santa Lucia, Venice's train station, at Piazzale Roma. From there you can make connections to most parts of Venice, including the Lido.

NEW AIR TRAVEL SECURITY MEASURES

In the wake of the terrorist attacks of September 11, 2001, the airline industry began implementing sweeping security measures in airports. Expect a lengthy check-in process and extensive delays.

Tips What You Can Carry On—and What You Can't

The Transportation Security Administration (TSA), the government agency that now handles all aspects of airport security, has new restrictions for carry-on baggage, not only to expedite screening but to prevent weapons from passing through airport security. Passengers are now limited to bringing just one carry-on bag and one personal item onto the aircraft (previous regulations allowed two carry-on bags and one personal item). For more information, go to the TSA's website, **www.tsa.gov**. The agency has released an updated list of items passengers are not allowed to carry on an aircraft:

Not permitted: knives, box cutters, corkscrews, straight razors, metal scissors, golf clubs, baseball bats, pool cues, hockey sticks, ski poles, ice picks.

Permitted: nail clippers, nail files, tweezers, eyelash curlers, safety razors (including disposables), syringes (with proof of medical need), walking canes, umbrellas (must be inspected first).

The airline you fly may have **additional restrictions,** so call ahead to avoid problems.

Although regulations vary from airline to airline, you can expedite the process by taking the following steps:

- **Arrive early.** Arrive at the airport at least 2 hours before your scheduled flight.
- **Try not to drive your car to the airport.** Parking and curbside access to the terminal may be limited. Call ahead and check.
- **Don't count on curbside check-in.** Some airlines and airports have stopped curbside check-in altogether, whereas others offer it on a limited basis. For up-to-date information on specific regulations and implementations, check with the individual airline.
- **Be sure to carry plenty of documentation.** A government-issued photo ID (federal, state, or local) is now required. You may need to show this at various checkpoints. With an E-ticket,

you may be required to have with you printed confirmation of purchase, and perhaps even the credit card with which you bought your ticket (see "All About E-Ticketing," above). This varies from airline to airline, so call ahead to make sure you have the proper documentation. And be sure that your ID is **up-to-date;** an expired driver's license, for example, may keep you from boarding the plane altogether.

- **Know what you can carry on—and what you can't.** Travelers in the United States are now limited to one carry-on bag, plus one personal bag (such as a purse or a briefcase). The Transportation Security Administration (TSA) has also issued a list of newly restricted carry-on items; see the box "What You Can Carry On—and What You Can't," below.

- **Prepare to be searched.** Expect spot-checks. Electronic items, such as a laptop or cellphone, should be readied for additional screening. Limit the metal items you wear on your person.

- **It's no joke.** When a check-in agent asks if someone other than you packed your bag, don't decide that this is the time to be funny. The agents will not hesitate to call an alarm.

- **No ticket, no gate access.** Only ticketed passengers will be allowed beyond the screener checkpoints, except for those people with specific medical or parental needs.

FLYING FOR LESS: TIPS FOR GETTING THE BEST AIRFARE

Passengers within the same airplane cabin are rarely paying the same fare. Business travelers who need to purchase tickets at the last minute, change their itinerary at a moment's notice, or get home for the weekend pay the premium rate. Passengers who can book their ticket long in advance, who can stay over Saturday night, or who are willing to travel on a Tuesday, Wednesday, or Thursday after 7pm will pay a fraction of the full fare. Here are a few other easy ways to save:

- Airlines periodically lower prices on their most popular routes. Check the travel section of your Sunday newspaper for advertised discounts or call the airlines directly and ask if any **promotional rates** or special fares are available. You'll almost never see a sale during the peak summer vacation months of July and August, or during the Thanksgiving or Christmas seasons; but in periods of low-volume travel, you should pay no more than $400 for a domestic cross-country flight. If your schedule is flexible, say so, and ask if you can secure a cheaper fare by staying an extra day, by flying midweek, or by flying at less-trafficked hours. If you already hold a ticket when a sale breaks, it may even pay to exchange your ticket, which usually incurs a $100 to $150 charge.

Note: The lowest-priced fares are often nonrefundable, require advance purchase of 1 to 3 weeks and a certain length of stay, and carry penalties for changing dates of travel.

• **Consolidators,** also known as bucket shops, are a good place to find low fares, often below even the airlines' discounted rates. Basically, they're just big travel agents who get discounts for buying in bulk and pass some of the savings on to you. Before you pay, however, be aware that consolidator tickets are usually nonrefundable or come with stiff cancellation penalties.

We've gotten great deals on many occasions from **Cheap Tickets** ⚐ (© 800/377-1000; www.cheaptickets.com). **Council Travel** (© 800/2COUNCIL; www.counciltravel. com) and **STA Travel** (© 800/781-4040; www.sta-travel.com) cater especially to young travelers, but their bargain-basement prices are available to people of all ages. Other reliable consolidators include **Lowestfare.com** (© 888/278-8830; www.lowestfare.com); **Cheap Seats** (© 800/451-7200; www.cheapseatstravel.com); and **1-800/FLY-CHEAP** (www. flycheap.com).

Frommers.com: The Complete Travel Resource

For an excellent travel-planning resource, we highly recommend **Frommers.com** (www.frommers.com). We're a little biased, of course, but we guarantee that you'll find the travel tips, reviews, monthly vacation giveaways, and online-booking capabilities thoroughly indispensable. Among the special features are our popular **Message Boards,** where Frommer's readers post queries and share advice (sometimes even our authors show up to answer questions); **Frommers.com Newsletter,** for the latest travel bargains and inside travel secrets; and Frommer's **Destinations Section,** where you'll get expert travel tips, hotel and dining recommendations, and advice on the sights to see for more than 2,500 destinations around the globe. When your research is done, the **Online Reservation System** (www.frommers.com/book_a_trip) takes you to Frommer's favorite sites for booking your vacation at affordable prices.

- Look into **courier flights.** These companies hire couriers to hand-deliver packages or mail, and use your luggage allowance for themselves; in return, you get a deeply discounted ticket—for example, $300 round-trip to Europe in winter. Flights often become available at the last minute, so check in often. **Halbart Express** has offices in New York (© 718/656-8189), Los Angeles (© 310/417-9790), and Miami (© 305/593-0260). **Jupiter Air** (www.jupiterair.com) has offices in New York (© 718/656-6050), Los Angeles (© 310/670-5123), and San Francisco (© 650/697-1773).
- Join a travel club such as **Moment's Notice** (© 718/234-6295;** www.moments-notice.com) or **Sears Discount Travel Club** (© **800/433-9383,** or 800/255-1487 to join; www.travelersadvantage.com), which supply unsold tickets at discounted prices. You pay an annual membership fee to get the club's hotline number. Of course, you're limited to what's available, so you have to be flexible.

BY TRAIN

Trains from all over Europe arrive at the **Stazione Venezia–Santa Lucia** (© 041-785111). To get there, all trains must pass through (though not necessarily stop at) a station marked VENEZIA-MESTRE. Don't be confused: Mestre is a charmless industrial city and the last stop on the mainland. Occasionally trains end at Mestre, in which case you'll have to catch one of the frequent 10-minute shuttle trains connecting Mestre with Venice; when booking your ticket, confirm that the train's final destination is *Stazione Santa Lucia.*

Travel time from Rome is about 5¼ hours; from Milan, 3½ hours; from Florence, 4 hours; and from Bologna, 2 hours. The best and least expensive way to get from the station to the rest of town is to take a vaporetto, which departs near the main entrance to the station (see "Getting Around" in chapter 3).

RAIL PASSES

An **Italian Railpass** (known in Italy as a **BTLC Pass**) allows non-Italian citizens to ride as much as they like on Italy's entire rail network. Buy the pass in the United States or at main train stations in Italy, have it validated the first time you use it at any rail station, and ride as frequently as you like within the time validity. At press time, an 8-day pass costs $330 first class and $222 second, a 15-day pass $417 first class and $276 second, a 21-day pass $484 first class and $320 second, and a 30-day pass $579 first class and $389 second. All passes have a $15 issuing fee per class.

With the Italian Railpass and each of the other special passes, a supplement must be paid to ride on certain rapid trains, designated **ETR-450** or **Pendolino trains.** The rail systems of Sardinia are administered by a separate entity and aren't included in the Railpass or any of the other passes.

You can buy these passes from any travel agent or by calling ℰ **800/848-7245.** You can also call ℰ **800/EURAIL** or **800/ EUROSTAR.**

Eurailpasses are also available from the North American offices of **Rail Europe** (ℰ **800/4-EURAIL;** www.raileurope.com). No matter what everyone tells you, Eurailpasses can be bought in Europe as well (at the major train stations), but are more expensive. Rail Europe can also give you information on the rail-and-drive versions of the passes.

A warning: Many irate readers have complained about train service in Italy—they've found the railroads dirty, overcrowded, unreliable, and with little regard for schedules. As you may have heard, strikes plague the country, and you never know as you board a train when it will reach your hoped-for destination. A sense of humor (and a flexible itinerary) might be your best defense against aggravation and irritating delays.

BY BUS

Buses from mainland Italy arrive in Venice at Piazzale Roma. For information about schedules, call the **ACTV office** at Piazzale Roma (ℰ **041-5287886**). If you're coming from a distant city in Italy, it's better to take the train. But Venice has good bus connections with nearby cities like Padua. A one-way fare between Padua and Venice costs 3.30€. The cheapest way to reach the heart of Venice from the bus station is by vaporetto (see "Getting Around" in chapter 3).

BY CAR

Venice has *autostrada* (expressway) links with the rest of Italy, with direct routes from such cities as Trieste (driving time: 1½ hr.), Milan (3 hr.), and Bologna (2 hr.). Bologna is 150km (93 miles) southwest of Venice, Milan 264km (164 miles) west of Venice, and Trieste 115km (71 miles) east. Rome is 523km (324 miles) southwest.

If you arrive by car, there are several multitiered **parking areas** at the terminus where the roads end and the canals begin. One of the most visible is the **Garage San Marco,** Piazzale Roma (ℰ **041-5232213**), near the vaporetto, gondola, and motor-launch docks. You'll be charged 26€ per day, maybe more, depending on the size of your car. From spring to fall, this municipal car park is nearly always filled. You're more likely to find parking on the **Isola del Tronchetto** (℃ **041-5207555**), which costs 18€ a day. From Tronchetto, take vaporetto no. 82 to Piazza San Marco. If you have heavy luggage, you'll need a water taxi. Parking is also available on the mainland at Mestre.

6 Escorted Tours & Independent Package Tours

The biggest operator of escorted tours is **Perillo Tours** (℃ **800/ 431-1515** or 201/307-1234 in the United States; www.perillotours. com), family operated for three generations—perhaps you've seen the TV commercials featuring the "King of Italy," Mario Perillo, and his son. Since it was founded in 1945, it has sent more than a million travelers to Italy on guided tours. Perillo's tours cost much less than you'd spend if you arranged a comparable trip yourself. Accommodations are in first-class hotels, and guides tend to be well qualified and well informed.

Another contender is **Italiatour,** a company of the Alitalia Group (℃ **800/845-3365;** www.italiatourusa.com), offering a wide variety of tours through all parts of Italy. It specializes in packages for independent travelers (not tour groups) who ride from one destination to another by train or rental car. In most cases, the company sells prereserved accommodations, which are usually less expensive than if you had reserved them yourself. Because of the company's close link with Alitalia, the prices quoted for air passage are sometimes among the most reasonable on the retail market.

Trafalgar Tours (℃ **800/854-0103;** www.trafalgartours.com) is one of Europe's largest tour operators, offering affordable guided tours with lodgings in unpretentious hotels. Check with your travel agent for more information on these tours (Trafalgar takes calls only from agents).

One of Trafalgar's leading competitors is **Globus/Cosmos Tours** (℃ **800/338-7092;** www.globusandcosmos.com). Globus has first-class escorted coach tours of various regions lasting from 8 to 16 days. Cosmos, a budget branch of Globus, sells escorted tours of about the same length. Tours must be booked through a travel agent, but you can call the toll-free number for brochures. Another competitor is **Insight Vacations** (℃ **800/582-8380;** www.insight vacations.com), which books superior first-class, fully escorted motor-coach tours lasting from 1 week to a 36-day grand tour.

Finally, **Abercrombie & Kent** (© **800/323-7308** in the U.S., or **0845/0700-610** in the U.K.; www.abercrombiekent.com or www.abercrombiekent.co.uk) offers a variety of luxurious premium packages. Your overnight stays will be in meticulously restored castles and exquisite Italian villas, most of which are four- and five-star accommodations. Several trips are offered, including tours of the Lake Garda region and the southern territory of Calabria. The company's website is **www.abercrombiekent.com.**

The oldest travel agency in Britain, **Cox & Kings** (© **020/7873-5000;** www.coxandkings.co.uk) specializes in unusual, if pricey, holidays. Their Italy offerings include organized tours through the country's gardens and sites of historic or aesthetic interest, opera tours, pilgrimage-style visits to sites of religious interest, and food- and wine-tasting tours. The staff is noted for its focus on tours of ecological and environmental interest.

 FAST FACTS: Venice

American Express   The office is at Salizzada San Moisè, San Marco 1471 (© **041-5200844;** vaporetto: San Marco). The staff can arrange city tours and mail handling. May through October, hours are Monday to Saturday from 8am to 8pm for currency exchange and 9am to 5:30pm for all other transactions; November through April, hours are Monday to Friday from 9am to 5:30pm and Saturday from 9am to 12:30pm.

Babysitters   In lieu of a central booking agency, arrangements have to be made individually at various hotels. Obviously, the more advance notice you give, the better your chances of getting an English-speaking sitter.

Business Hours   Regular business hours for offices and shops are generally Monday to Friday from 9am to 1pm and 3:30 to 7 or 7:30pm. July through September, offices may not open in the afternoon until 4 or 4:30pm. Banks in Venice are open Monday to Friday from 8:30am to 1:30 or 2pm, and then 3 to 4pm; they're closed all day Saturday, Sunday, and national holidays.

Consulates   The **U.K. Consulate** is at Dorsoduro 1051, at the foot of the Accademia Bridge (© **041-5227207;** vaporetto: Accademia), and is open Monday to Friday from 10am to noon and 2 to 3pm. The **United States, Canada,** and **Australia** have consulates in Milan, about 3 hours away by train. The U.S. Consulate is at Via Principe Amedeo 2–10, Milan (✆ **02-2903-5141**). The Canadian Consulate is located at Via Vittorio Pisani 19, Milan (✆ **02-67-581**). And the Australian Consulate is at Via Borgogna 2, Milan (✆ **02-290-351**). Call ahead to confirm open hours before making the long trip, as all of these consular offices tend to keep odd hours.

Currency Exchange   There are many banks in Venice where you can exchange money. You might try the **Banco Commerciale Italiana,** Via XXII Marzo, San Marco 2188 (✆ **041-5296811;** vaporetto: San Marco), or **Banco San Marco,** Calle Larga San Marco, San Marco 383 (✆ **041-5293711;** vaporetto: San Marco).

Customs   Upon leaving Italy, citizens of the United States who've been outside the country for 48 hours or more are allowed to bring back $400 worth of merchandise duty-free—that is, if they haven't claimed a similar exemption in the past 30 days. If you make purchases in Italy, it's important to keep your receipts.

Dentist/Doctor   Your best bet is to have your hotel set up an appointment with an English-speaking dentist or doctor. The American Express office and the British Consulate also have lists. Also see "Hospitals," below.

Drugstores   If you need a drugstore in the middle of the night, call ✆ **192** for information about which one is open (pharmacies take turns staying open late). A well-recommended central one is **International Pharmacy,** Via XXII Marzo, San Marco 2067 (✆ **041-5222311;** vaporetto: San Marco).

Electricity   The electricity in Italy varies considerably. It's usually alternating current (AC), varying from 42 to 50 cycles. The voltage can be anywhere from 115 to 220. It's recommended that any visitor carrying electrical appliances obtain a transformer. Check the exact local current at the hotel where you're staying. Plugs have prongs that are round, not flat; therefore, an adapter plug is also needed.

Emergencies   Call ✆ **113** for the police, ✆ **118** for an ambulance, or ✆ **115** to report a fire.

Hospitals   Get in touch with the **Ospedale Civile Santi Giovanni e Paolo,** Campo Santi Giovanni e Paolo in Castello

(☎ 041-785111; vaporetto: San Toma), staffed with English-speaking doctors 24 hours a day.

Laundry/Dry Cleaning   One of the most convenient coin-operated laundromats and dry-cleaning enterprises is **Lavanderia Gabriella,** Calle Fiubera, San Marco 985 (☎ 041-5221758; vaporetto: San Marco), set behind Piazza San Marco. Its washing machines are available daily from 8am to 7pm, and its dry-cleaning facilities Monday to Saturday from 8am to 12:30pm and 3 to 7pm.

Luggage Storage & Lockers   These services are available at the main rail station, **Stazione di Santa Lucia,** at Piazzale Roma (☎ 041-785111). The cost is 2.50€ per package.

Newspapers & Magazines   The *International Herald Tribune* and *USA Today* are sold at most newsstands and in many first-class and deluxe hotels, as are the European editions (in English) of *Time* and *Newsweek*.

Police   See "Emergencies," above.

Post Office   The **main post office** is at Salizzada Fondaco dei Tedeschi, San Marco 5554 (☎ 041-2717111; vaporetto: Rialto), near the Rialto Bridge. It's open Monday to Saturday from 8:15am to 5pm.

Mail delivery in Italy is notoriously bad. Your family and friends back home may receive your postcards in 1 week, or it might take 2 weeks (or even longer). Postcards, aerogrammes, and letters weighing up to 20 grams sent to the United States and Canada cost .70€, to the United Kingdom and Ireland .50€, and to Australia and New Zealand .75€. You can buy stamps at all post offices and at *tabacchi* (tobacco) stores.

Restrooms   These are available at Piazzale Roma and various other places, but aren't as plentiful as they should be. A truly spotless one is at the foot of the Accademia Bridge. Often you'll have to rely on the restrooms in cafes, though you should buy something, perhaps a light coffee, as in theory the toilets are for customers only. Most museums and galleries have public toilets. You can also use the public toilets at the Albergo Diurno, Via Ascensione, just behind Piazza San Marco. Remember, *signori* means men and *signore*, women.

Safety   The curse of Venice is the pickpocket. Violent crime is rare. But because of the overcrowding in vaporetti and even on the small narrow streets, it's easy to pick pockets. Purse snatchers are commonplace as well. They can dart out of nowhere, grab a purse, and disappear in seconds down some narrow dark alley. Keep valuables locked in a safe in your hotel, if one is provided.

Taxes   As a member of the European Union, Italy imposes a **value-added tax** (called IVA in Italy) on most goods and services. The tax that most affects visitors is the one imposed on hotel rates, which ranges from 9% in first- and second-class hotels to 19% in deluxe hotels.

Non-EU (European Union) citizens are entitled to a **refund of the IVA** if they spend more than 150€ at any one store, before tax. To claim your refund, request an invoice from the cashier at the store and take it to the Customs office *(dogana)* at the airport to have it stamped before you leave. *Note:* If you're going to another EU country before flying home, have it stamped at the airport Customs office of the last EU country you'll be in (for example, if you're flying home via Britain, have your Italian invoices stamped in London). Once back home, mail the stamped invoice (keep a photocopy for your records) back to the original vendor within 90 days of the purchase. The vendor will, sooner or later, send you a refund of the tax you paid at the time of your original purchase. Reputable stores view this as a matter of ordinary paperwork and are businesslike about it. Less-honorable stores might lose your dossier. It pays to deal with established vendors on large purchases. You can also request that the refund be credited to the credit card with which you made the purchase; this is usually a faster procedure.

Many shops are now part of the **"Tax Free for Tourists"** network (look for the sticker in the window). Stores participating in this network issue a check along with your invoice at the time of purchase. After you have the invoice stamped at Customs, you can redeem the check for cash directly at the Tax Free booth in the airport (in Rome, it's past Customs; in Milan's airports, the booth is inside the Duty-Free shop) or mail it back in the envelope provided within 60 days.

Telephones   A **local phone call** in Italy costs around .15€. **Public phones** accept coins, precharged phone cards (*scheda* or *carta telefonica*), or both. You can buy a *carta telefonica* at any *tabacchi* in increments of 2.50€, 5€, and 7.50€. To make a call, pick up the receiver and insert .5€ or your card (break off the corner first). Most phones have a digital display that will tell you how much money you've inserted (or how much is left on the card). Dial the number, and don't forget to take the card with you after you hang up.

To **call from one city code to another,** dial the city code, complete with initial zero, then the number. To **dial direct internationally,** dial **00,** then the country code, the area code, and the number. **Country codes** are as follows: the United States and Canada 1, the United Kingdom 44, Ireland 353, Australia 61, and New Zealand 64. Make international calls from a public phone if possible, because hotels almost invariably charge ridiculously inflated rates for direct dial, but bring plenty of *schede* to feed the phone. Direct-dial calls from the United States to Italy are much cheaper, so if possible, arrange for your friends or family to call you at your hotel.

Italy has recently introduced a series of **international phone cards** *(scheda telefonica internazionale)* for calling overseas. They come in increments of 6€, 13€, 25€, and 50€ *unita* (units), and they're usually available at tabacchi and bars. Each unita is worth .10€ of phone time; it costs 5 unita (.60€) per minute to call within Europe or to the United States or Canada and 12 unita (1.50€) per minute to call Australia or New Zealand. You don't insert this card into the phone; merely dial ℂ **1740,** then *2 (star 2) for instructions in English when prompted.

To ring free **national telephone information** (in Italian) in Italy, dial ℂ **12. International information** is available at ℂ **176** but costs .60€ a shot.

To make **collect or calling-card calls,** drop in .10€ or insert your card, dial one of the numbers below, and an American operator will shortly come on to assist you (as Italy has yet to discover the joys of the touch-tone phone, you'll have to wait for the operator to come on). The following calling-card numbers work all over Italy: **AT&T** (ℂ **172-1011**), **MCI** ℂ (**172-1022**), and **Sprint** (ℂ **172-1877**). To make collect calls to a country besides the United States, dial ℂ **170** (free), and practice your Italian counting in order to relay the number to the Italian operator. Tell him or her you want it *a carico del destinatario.*

Don't count on all Italian phones having touch-tone service! You may not be able to access your voice mail or answering machine if you call home from Italy.

Time   In terms of standard time zones, Italy is 6 hours ahead of eastern standard time in the United States. Daylight saving time goes into effect in Italy each year from the end of March to the end of September.

Tipping   This custom is practiced with flair in Italy—many people depend on tips for their livelihoods. In **hotels,** a service charge of 15% to 19% is already added to the bill. In addition, it's customary to tip the chambermaid .50€ per day, and the bellhop or porter 1.50 to 2.50€ for carrying your bags to your room. A concierge expects tips for extra services performed, such as procuring hard-to-find tickets.

In **restaurants and cafes,** 15% is usually added to your bill to cover most charges. If you're not sure whether this has been done, ask *"E incluso il servizio?"* (ay een-*cloo*-soh eel sair-*vee*-tsoh?). An additional tip isn't expected, but it's nice to leave the equivalent of an extra couple of dollars if you're pleased with the service. Checkroom attendants expect .75€, and washroom attendants should get .25 to .35€. Restaurants are required by law to give customers official receipts.

(*Tips*   Calling Italy

To call Italy from the United States, dial the **international prefix, 011;** then Italy's **country code, 39;** then the city code (for Venice, it's **041**), which is now built into every number; then the actual **phone number.**

Note that numbers in Italy range from four to eight digits in length. Even when you're calling within the same city, you must dial that city's area code—including the zero.

3

Getting to Know Venice

For more than 1,000 years, people have flocked to Venice because it is unlike any other city in the world. This chapter will give you information about the city layout, how to get around, and facts that you'll need to know to settle yourself into this unique city.

1 Orientation

VISITOR INFORMATION

Visitor information is available at the **Azienda di Promozione Turistica,** Palazzetto Selva–Giardinetti Reali (Molo S. Marco) (© **041-5298711**). Summer hours are daily from 9:30am to 6:30pm; off-season, Monday to Saturday from 9:30am to 3:30pm. However, these hours aren't that consistent. Ask for a schedule of the month's special events and an updated list of museum and church hours, which can change erratically and often. There's also a tourist office at the train station, **Stazione Venezia–Santa Lucia** (© **041-5298727**).

Anyone between 16 and 29 is eligible for a **"Rolling Venice" pass,** offering discounts in museums, certain restaurants and stores, language courses, some hotels, and even some bars. Valid for 1 year, it costs 2.58€ and can be picked up at a special "Rolling Venice" office set up in the train station during summer.

CITY LAYOUT

Venice lies 4km (2½ miles) from the Italian mainland (connected to Mestre by the Ponte della Libertà) and 2km (1¼ miles) from the open Adriatic. It's an archipelago of 118 islands. Most visitors, however, concern themselves only with **Piazza San Marco** and its vicinity. In fact, the entire city has only one piazza, which is San Marco (all the other squares are *campos*). Venice is divided into six quarters *(sestieri):* **San Marco, Santa Croce, San Polo, Castello, Cannaregio,** and **Dorsoduro.**

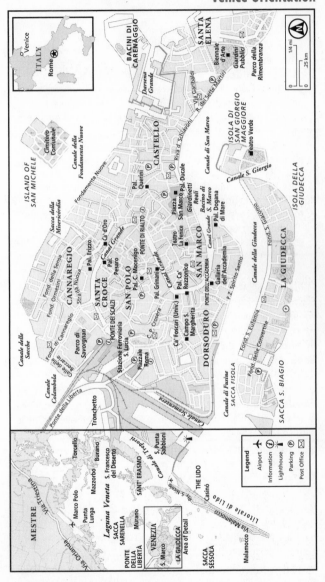

Venice Orientation

ITALY
Venice
Rome

ISLAND OF SAN MICHELE

Cimitero Comunale

BACINI DI CARENAGGIO

SANTA ELENA

Biennale d'Arte

Giardini Pubblici

Parco della Rimembranza

Darsena Grande

1/4 mi

25 km

Canale della Fondamenta Nuove

Sacca della Misericordia

Fondamenta Nuove

CASTELLO

Via Garibaldi

R. dei Sette Martiri

Riva degli Schiavoni

Canale di San Marco

ISOLA DI SAN GIORGIO MAGGIORE

Teatro Verde

Fond. della Sensa

Fond. Ormesini

Ca' d'Oro

Pal. Erizzo

CANNAREGIO

Pal. Querini

Canale S. Giorgio

ISOLA DELLA GIUDECCA

Canal Grande

PONTE DI RIALTO

Pal. Pesaro

Pal. C. Mocenigo

SANTA CROCE

SAN POLO

Piazza San Marco

Pal. Ducale

Giardinetti Reali

SAN MARCO

Bacino di S. Marco

Pal. Dogana di Mare

Teatro La Fenice

Fond. delle Beccarie

Strada Nuova

Fond. di Cannaregio

Parco di Savorgnan

Canale delle Sacche

Pal. Ca' Rezzonico

Pal. Grimani

Canal Grande

Galleria dell'Accademia

PONTE DELL'ACCADEMIA

F.ta S. Spirito Santo

Canale della Giudecca

LA GIUDECCA

Canale delle Converte

Fond. S. Eufemia

Ca' Foscari (Univ.)

DORSODURO

Campo S. Margherita

S.ta Croce

Canale delle Sacche

Calle delle Beccarie

PONTE DEGLI SCALZI

S. Lucia

Piazzale Roma

Stazione Ferroviaria

Canale di Fusina

SACCA FISOLA

SACCA S. BIAGIO

Canale Scomenzera

Canale Colombola

Ponte della Libertà

Tronchetto

Legend

✈ Airport
ℹ Information
🗼 Lighthouse
Ⓟ Parking
✉ Post Office

MESTRE

Via Oranda

Via Trieste

Laguna Veneta

Marco Polo

Punta Lunga

SACCA SARENELLA

Murano

Mazzorbo

Burano

S. Francesco del Deserto

Torcello

SANT'ERASMO

S. Punta Sabbioni

Canale di Treporti

VENEZIA

LA GIUDECCA

S. Marco

Area of Detail

PONTE DELLA LIBERTÀ

SACCA SESSOLA

THE LIDO

Casinò

Riv. S. Nicolò

Litorale di Lido

Via Malamocco

Malamocco

Tips Finding an Address

A maniac must have numbered Venice's buildings at least 6 centuries ago. Before you set out for a specific place, get detailed instructions and have someone mark the place on your map. Don't depend on street numbers; try to locate the nearest cross street. Because old signs and numbers have decayed over time, it's best to look for signs posted outside rather than for a number.

Every building has a street address and a mailing address. For example, a business at Calle delle Botteghe 3150 (3150 Botteghe St.) will have a mailing address of San Marco 3150, since it's in the San Marco sestiere and all buildings in each district are numbered continuously from 1 to 6,000. (To confuse things, several districts have streets of the same name, so it's important to know the sestiere.) In this chapter, we give the street name first, followed by the mailing address.

Many of Venice's so-called streets are actually *rios* (canals), somewhere around 150 in all, spanned by a total of 400 bridges. Venice's version of a main street is the **Grand Canal** (or Canal Grande), which snakes through the city like an inverted "S" and is spanned by three bridges: the white marble **Ponte di Rialto,** the wooden **Ponte Accademia,** and the stone **Ponte degli Scalzi.** The Grand Canal splits Venice into two unequal parts.

South of Dorsoduro, which is south of the Grand Canal, is the **Canale della Giudecca,** a major channel separating Dorsoduro from the large island of La Giudecca. At the point where Canale della Giudecca meets the **Canale di San Marco,** you'll spot the little **Isola di San Giorgio Maggiore,** with a church by Palladio. The most visited islands in the lagoon, aside from the **Lido,** are **Murano, Burano,** and **Torcello.**

If you really want to tour Venice and experience that hidden, romantic trattoria on a nearly forgotten street, don't even think about doing it unless you have a map that details every street and has an index on the back. The best of the lot is the **Falk map** of Venice, sold at many news kiosks and all bookstores.

A broad street running along a canal is a *fondamenta,* a narrower street running along a canal is a *calle,* and a paved road is a *salizzada, ruga,* or *calle larga.* A *rio terrà* is a filled canal channel now used as a walkway, and a *sotoportego,* a passage beneath buildings. When you come to an open-air area, you'll often encounter the word *campo*— that's a reference to the fact that such a place was once grassy, and in days of yore cattle grazed there.

THE NEIGHBORHOODS IN BRIEF

This section will give you some idea of where you may want to stay and where the major attractions are.

SAN MARCO   Welcome to the center of Venice. Napoleon called it "the drawing room of Europe," and it's one crowded drawing room today. It has been the heart of Venetian life for more than a thousand years. **Piazza San Marco** (St. Mark's Square) is dominated by **St. Mark's Basilica.** Just outside the basilica is the **campanile** (bell tower), a reconstruction of the one that collapsed in 1902. Around the corner is the **Palazzo Ducale** (Doge's Palace), with its **Bridge of Sighs.** Piazza San Marco is lined with some of the world's most overpriced cafes, including **Florian's** (opened 1720) and **Quadri** (opened 1775). The most celebrated watering hole, however, is away from the square: **Harry's Bar,** founded by Giuseppe Cipriani but made famous by Hemingway. In and around the square are some of the most convenient hotels in Venice (though not necessarily the best) and an array of expensive tourist shops and trattorie.

CASTELLO   The shape of Venice is often likened to that of a fish. If so, Castello is the tail. The largest and most varied of the six sestieri, Castello is home to many sights, such as the **Arsensale,** and some of the city's plushest hotels, such as the Danieli. One of the neighborhood's most notable attractions is the Gothic **Santa Giovanni e Paolo (Zanipolo),** the Pantheon of the Doges. Cutting through the sestiere is **Campo Santa Maria Formosa,** one of Venice's largest open squares.

The most elegant street is **Riva degli Schiavoni,** which runs along the Grand Canal; it's lined with some of the finest hotels and restaurants and is one of the city's favorite promenades.

CANNAREGIO   This is Venice's gateway, the first of the six sestieri. It lies away from the rail station at the northwest side of Venice and shelters about a third of the population, some 20,000 residents. At its heart is the **Santa Lucia Station** (1955). The area also embraces the old **Jewish Ghetto,** the first one on the continent.

Jews began to move here at the beginning of the 16th century, when they were segregated from the rest of the city. From here, the word *ghetto* later became a generic term used all over the world. Attractions in this area include the **Ca' d'Oro,** the finest example of the Venetian Gothic style; the **Madonna dell'Orto,** a 15th-century church known for its Tintorettos; and **Santa Maria dei Miracoli,** with a Madonna portrait supposedly able to raise the dead. Unless you're coming for one of these attractions, this area doesn't offer much else; its hotels and restaurants aren't the best. Some of the cheapest lodging is found along **Lista di Spagna,** to the left as you exit the train station.

SANTA CROCE   This area generally follows the snakelike curve of the Grand Canal from Piazzale Roma to a point just short of the Ponte di Rialto. It's split into two rather different neighborhoods. The eastern part is in the typically Venetian style and is one of the least crowded parts of Venice, though it has some of the Grand Canal's loveliest palazzi. The western side is more industrialized and isn't very interesting to explore.

SAN POLO   This is the heart of commercial Venice and the smallest of the six sestieri. It's reached by crossing the **Ponte di Rialto** (Rialto Bridge), which spans the Grand Canal. The shopping here is much more reasonable than that around Piazza San Marco. One of the major sights is the **Erberia,** which Casanova wrote about in his 18th-century autobiography. Both wholesale and retail markets still pepper this ancient site. At its center is **San Giacomo di Rialto,** the city's oldest church. The district also encloses the **Scuola Grande di San Rocco,** a repository of the works of Tintoretto. **Campo San Polo** is one of the oldest and widest squares and one of the principal venues for Carnevale. San Polo is also filled with moderately priced hotels and a large number of trattorie, many specializing in seafood. In general, the hotels and restaurants are cheaper here than along San Marco but not as cheap as those around the train station in Cannaregio.

DORSODURO   The least populated of the sestieri, this funky neighborhood is filled with old homes and half-forgotten churches. Dorsoduro is the southernmost section of the historic district, and its major sights are the **Accademia Gallery** and the **Peggy Guggenheim Foundation.** It's less trampled than the areas around the Rialto Bridge and Piazza San Marco. Its most famous church is **La Salute,** whose first stone was laid in 1631. The **Zattere,** a broad quay built after 1516, is one of Venice's favorite promenades. Cafes, trattorie, and pensiones abound in the area.

THE LAGOON ISLANDS

THE LIDO   This slim, sandy island 12km (7½ miles) long and about 1km (half a mile) wide, though reaching 4km (2½ miles) at its broadest point, cradles the Venetian lagoon, offering protection against the Adriatic. The Lido is a chic beach resort and site of the fabled **Venice Film Festival.** It was the setting for many famous books, including Thomas Mann's *Death in Venice* and Evelyn Waugh's *Brideshead Revisited.* Some of the most fashionable and expensive hotels are found along the Lido Promenade. The most famous are the Grand Hotel Excelsior and Grand Hotel des Bains, but there are cheaper places as well. The best way to get around is by bike or tandem, which you can rent at Via Zara and Gran Viale.

TORCELLO   Lying 9km (5½ miles) northeast of Venice, Torcello is called "the mother of Venice," having been settled in the 9th century. It was once the most populous of the islands in the lagoon, but since the 18th century it has been nearly deserted. If you ever hope to find solitude in Venice, you'll find it here. It's visited today chiefly by those wishing to see its **Cattedrale di Torcello,** with its stunning Byzantine mosaics, and to lunch at the Locanda Cipriani restaurant.

BURANO   Perched 9km (5½ miles) northeast of Venice, Burano is the most populous of the lagoon islands. In the 16th century, it produced the finest lace in Europe. Lace is still made here, but it's nothing like the product of centuries past. Inhabited since Roman times, Burano is different from either Torcello or Murano. Forget lavish palaces. The houses are often simple and small and painted in deep blues, strong reds, and striking yellows. The island is still peopled by fishers, and one of the reasons to visit is to dine at one of its trattorie, where, naturally, the specialty is fish.

MURANO   This island, about 1.5km (less than a mile) northeast of Venice, has been famed for its glassmaking since 1291. Today Murano is the most visited island in the lagoon, with tons of guided tours visiting the glassblowing shops. You can also visit a glass museum, the **Museo Vetrario di Murano,** and see two of the island's notable churches, **San Pietro Martire** and **Sante Maria e Donato.** You'll likely be on the island for lunch, and there are a number of moderately priced trattorie.

2 Getting Around

Since you can't hail a taxi, at least not on land, get ready to walk and walk and walk. Of course, you can break up your walks with vaporetto or boat rides, which are great respites from dealing with the packed (and we mean *packed*) streets in summer.

However, note that in autumn, the high tide *(acqua alta)* is a real menace. The squares often flood, beginning with Piazza San Marco, one of the city's lowest points. Many visitors and locals wear knee-high boots to navigate their way. In fact, some hotels maintain a storage room full of boots in all sizes for their guests.

With packed streets, more than 400 bridges, and difficult-to-board vaporetti, Venice isn't too user-friendly for those with disabilities. Nevertheless, some improvements have been made. The tourist office distributes a free map called *Veneziapertutti* ("Venice for All"), illustrating what part of Venice is accessible by the use of different color-coded references; it also outlines a list of accessible churches, monuments, gardens, public offices, hotels, and lavatories with facilities for the handicapped.

Time and again while exploring, you'll think you know where you're going, only to wind up on a dead-end street or at the side of a canal with no bridge to get to the other side. Just remind yourself that Venice's physical complexity is an integral part of its charm—getting lost is part of the fun.

Fortunately, around the city are yellow signs whose arrows direct you toward one of five major landmarks: FERROVIA (the train station), PIAZZALE ROMA, the RIALTO (Bridge), SAN MARCO (Piazza), and the ACCADEMIA (Bridge). You'll often find these signs grouped together, their arrows pointing off in different directions.

BY PUBLIC TRANSPORTATION

Much to the chagrin of the once-ubiquitous gondoliers, Venice's **vaporetti** (motorboat buses) provide inexpensive and frequent, if not always fast, transportation in this canal city. The service is operated by **ACTV** (Azienda del Consorzio Trasporti Veneziano), Calle Fisero, San Marco 1810 (© **041-5287886**). An *accelerato* is a vessel that makes every stop; a *diretto* makes only express stops. The average fare is 3.10€. Note that in summer the vaporetti are often fiercely crowded. Pick up a map of the system at the tourist office. They run daily, with frequent service from 7am to midnight, then hourly from midnight to 7am.

Visitors to Venice can buy a 10-ticket carnet costing 25€, which must be validated before use and shown together with the matrix (the last ticket of the booklet).

The Grand Canal is long and snakelike and can be crossed via only three bridges, including the one at Rialto. If there's no bridge in sight, the trick in getting across is to use one of the *traghetti* gondolas strategically placed at key points. Look for them at the end of any passage called "Calle del Traghetto." Under government control, the fare is only .50€.

BY MOTOR LAUNCH (WATER TAXI)

Motor launches *(taxi acquei)* cost more than public vaporetti, but you won't be hassled as much when you arrive with your luggage if you hire one of the many private ones. You may or may not have the cabin of one of these sleek vessels to yourself, since the captains fill their boats with as many passengers as the law allows before taking off. Your porter's uncanny radar will guide you to one of the inconspicuous piers where a water taxi waits.

The price of a transit by water taxi from Piazzale Roma (the road/rail terminus) to Piazza San Marco is 60€ for up to four passengers and 6€ more for each additional person. The captains adroitly deliver you, with luggage, to the canal-side entrance of your hotel or on one of the smaller waterways within a short walking distance of your destination. You can also call for a water taxi; try the **Cooperativa San Marco** at © 041-5222303.

BY CAR

Obviously you won't need a car in Venice, but you might want one when you leave, to head off to nearby cities like Padua. Most of the car-rental agencies lie near the rail station in the traffic-clogged Piazzale Roma (meaning also that you can return a rental car here as you arrive in Venice). You'll get the best rate if you reserve before leaving home.

Hertz is at Piazzale Roma 496E (© **800/654-3131** in the United States, or 041-5284091; www.hertz.com). November through March, it's open Monday to Friday from 8am to 12:30pm and 3 to 5:30pm, Saturday from 8am to 1pm; April hours are Monday to Friday from 8am to 6pm, Saturday from 8am to 1pm; May through October, hours are Monday to Friday from 8am to 6pm, Saturday from 8am to 1pm.

(Tips) Useful Terms for Finding Your Way Around the City

You'll have to get used to a lot of unfamiliar street designations in Venice. Even the Italians (non-Venetian ones) look befuddled when trying to decipher street names and signs (if you can even find any of the latter). Venice's colorful thousand-year history as a once-powerful maritime republic has everything to do with its local dialect, which absorbed nuances and vocabulary from the East and from the flourishing communities of foreign merchants who for centuries lived and traded in Venice. The following should give you the basics.

Ca' This abbreviated form of the word *casa* is used for the noble palazzi, once private residences and now museums, lining the Grand Canal: Ca' d'Oro, Ca' Pesaro, and Ca' Rezzonico. There was only one palazzo: the Palazzo Ducale, the former doge's residence. However, as time went on, some great houses gradually began to be called *palazzi,* so today you'll encounter the Palazzo Grassi and the Palazzo Labia. The term *piano nobile* refers to the second or third floor of a palazzo where the principal rooms are located.

Calle Taken from the Spanish, this is the most commonplace word for "street," known as *via* or *strada* elsewhere in Italy. There are numerous variations. *Ruga,* from the French

Europcar (associated with National in the United States) is at Piazzale Roma 496H (© **800/328-4567** or 041-5238616). May through October, it's open Monday to Friday from 8:30am to 1pm and 2 to 6:30pm, Saturday and Sunday from 8:30am to 12:30pm; November through April, hours are Monday to Friday from 8:30am to noon and 2 to 6:30pm, Saturday from 8:30am to noon.

word *rue,* once meant a street flanked with stores, a designation no longer valid. A *ramo* is the branch or offshoot of a street and is often used interchangeably with calle. *Salizzada* once meant a paved street, implying that all other less important streets were just dirt alleyways. A *sotoportego* is a covered passageway.

Campo   Elsewhere in Italy it's *piazza.* In Venice, the only piazza is Piazza San Marco (and its two bordering *piazzette*); all other squares are *campi* or the diminutive, *campielli.* Translated as "field" or "meadow," these were once small unpaved grazing spots for the odd chicken or cow. Almost every one of Venice's campi carries the name of the church that dominates it (or once did).

Canale   There are three wide principal canals: the Canal Grande, the Canale della Giudecca, and the Canale di Cannaregio. Each of the other 160 smaller canals is called a *rio.* A *rio terrà* is a filled-in canal, wide and straight, now used as a street.

Fondamenta   Referring to the foundations of the houses lining a canal, this is a walkway along the side of a rio. Promenades along the Grand Canal near Piazza San Marco and the Rialto are called *riva.*

Avis is at Piazzale Roma 496G (© **800/331-2112** in the United States, or 041-5225825; www.avis.com). November through March, it's open Monday to Friday from 8:30am to 12:30pm and 2:30 to 6pm, and Saturday from 8:30am to 12:30pm; April through October, hours are Monday to Friday from 8am to 6pm, Saturday to Sunday from 8am to 12:30pm.

4

Where to Stay

Venice has some of the most expensive hotels in the world, but we've also found some wonderful lesser-known, moderately priced places, often on hard-to-find narrow streets. However, Venice has never been known as an inexpensive destination.

Because of the age and lack of uniformity of Venice's hotels, they offer widely varying rooms. For example, it's entirely possible to stay in a hotel generally considered "expensive" while paying only a "moderate" rate—if you'll settle for a less desirable room. Many "inexpensive" hotels and boarding houses have two or three rooms in the "expensive" category. Usually these are more spacious and open onto a view. Also, if an elevator is essential for you, always inquire in advance when booking a room, because they don't always exist in old buildings.

The cheapest way to visit Venice is to book into a *locanda* (small inn), which is rated below the *pensione* (boarding house) in official Italian hotel lingo. Standards are highly variable in these places, many of which are dank, dusty, and dark. The rooms even in many second- or first-class hotels are often cramped, because space has always been a problem in Venice. In this "City of Light," most of the rooms in any category are dark, so be duly warned. Those with lots of light and opening onto the Grand Canal carry a hefty price tag.

The most difficult times to find rooms are during the February Carnevale, around Easter, and from June through September. Because of the tight hotel situation, it's advisable to make reservations as far in advance as possible (months in advance for summer, and even a year in advance for Carnevale). After those peak times, you can virtually have your pick of rooms. Most hotels, if you ask at the reception desk, will grant you a 10% to 15% discount in winter (Nov 1–Mar 15). But getting this discount may require a little negotiation. A few hotels close in January if there's no prospect of business.

Should you arrive without a reservation, go to one of the **AVA (Hotel Association) reservations booths** at the train station, the municipal parking garage at Piazzale Roma, the airport, or the information point on the mainland where the highway comes to an end. The main office is at Piazzale Roma (℡ **041-5228640**). To get a room, you'll have to pay a deposit that's then rebated on your hotel bill. Depending on the hotel classification, deposits are 11€ to 46€ per person. All hotel booths are open daily from 9am to 8 or 9pm.

See "The Neighborhoods in Brief" in chapter 3 to get an idea of where you might want to base yourself, whether it be in less touristy San Polo or Dorsoduro or in and around Piazza San Marco (where hotels tend to be expensive, but you're in the heart of the action).

1 Near Piazza San Marco

VERY EXPENSIVE

Gritti Palace 🏰🏰🏰   The Gritti, in a stately Grand Canal setting, is the renovated palazzo of 15th-century doge Andrea Gritti. Even after its takeover by ITT Sheraton, it's still a bit starchy and has a museum aura (some of the furnishings are roped off), but for sheer glamour and history, only the Cipriani (p. 61) tops it. (Stay at the Cipriani for quiet, isolation, and more recreational facilities, but stay here for a completely central location and service that's just as good.) Guests here are more pampered than those at the Danieli, the Gritti's closest rival in the heart of Venice, but expect to pay a great deal more at the Gritti for that extra notch in service. This was Hemingway's "home in Venice," and it has drawn some of the world's greatest theatrical, literary, political, and royal figures.

The variety of guest rooms seems almost limitless, from elaborate suites to small singles. But throughout, the elegance is evident. The most spacious rooms face the campo, but we prefer the big corner doubles (second and third floors) with balconies overlooking the canal. Elegant linen and hypoallergenic pillows grace the antique beds, and thoughtful extras include thermostats, bottled water, and two-line phones. Most of the bathrooms are sumptuous, sheathed in red Verona marble and amply stocked. For a splurge, ask for Hemingway's old suite or the Doge Suite, once occupied by author W. Somerset Maugham.

Campo Santa Maria del Giglio, San Marco 2467, 30124 Venezia. ℡ **800/325-3535** in the U.S., 416/947-4864 in Canada, or 041-794611. Fax 041-5200942. www.luxury collection.com/grittipalace. 93 units. 705€–995€ double; from 1,640€ suite. Rates include breakfast. AE, DC, MC, V. Vaporetto: Santa Maria del Giglio. **Amenities:** Elegant restaurant and bar; 24-hr. concierge and butler service; private boat launches and sightseeing tours; salon; 24-hr. room service; babysitting; laundry/dry cleaning. *In room:* A/C, TV, minibar, hair dryer, safe.

Venice Accommodations

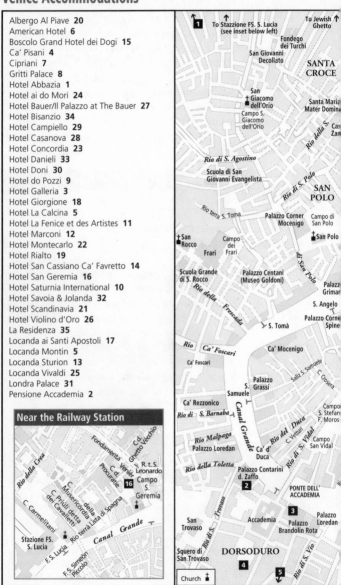

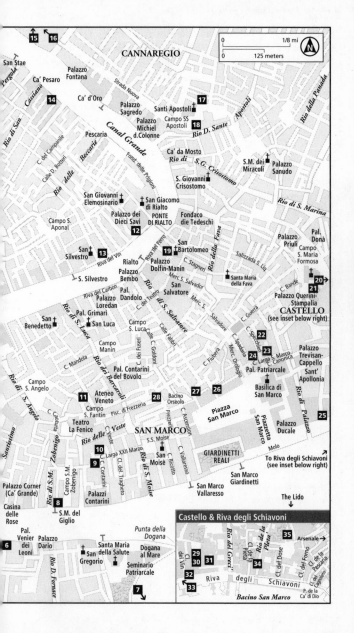

Hotel Bauer/Il Palazzo at the Bauer 🉀   This deluxe hotel, known since 1880 as the zGrand Hotel d'Italie Bauer Grunwald but now as simply the Hotel Bauer, is better than ever, although it can never obtain the pedigree of the Danieli and the Gritti. Long a favorite of prime ministers, royalty, and jet-setters, it's the combination of an ornate 13th-century palazzo facing the Grand Canal, a massive Stalinesque concrete wing that was "an architectural scandal" when it opened in the 1960s, and the new Bauer Palace, or "Il Palazzo," a VIP wing. Il Palazzo was coaxed out of an 18th-century residence with a stunning Gothic facade. Even the more modest accommodations are fitted with baroque furniture, walk-in closets, and marble floors in the bathrooms. The suites are totally sumptuous, almost "explosively" Venetian with their bacchanalian marble tubs, fireplaces, and Murano chandeliers, with balconies overlooking tourists in gondolas. The guest rooms are decorated in classic European style, with both French and Venetian pieces. No other luxury hotel has such a stunning location—just steps from Piazza San Marco.

Campo San Moisè, San Marco 1459, 30124 Venezia. (C) **041-5207022.** Fax 041-5207557. www.bauervenezia.com. 190 units. Hotel Bauer: 260€–500€ double; 600€–950€ suite. Il Palazzo: 415€–685€ double; from 930€ suite. AE, DC, MC, V. Vaporetto: San Marco. **Amenities:** 2 restaurants; bar; golf course; tennis courts; fitness center; sauna; watersports; concierge; business center; salon; room service; babysitting; laundry/dry cleaning. *In room:* A/C, TV, minibar, hair dryer, safe.

EXPENSIVE

Hotel Casanova 🉀   This former home is a few short blocks from Piazza San Marco. Although the name Casanova sounds romantic, the hotel doesn't have a lot of character; it does, however, contain a collection of church art and benches from old monasteries. For the most part, the modernized guest rooms are unremarkable, but they're well maintained. The accommodations vary considerably in size; some are quite small. The most intriguing units are on the top floor, with exposed brick walls and sloping beamed ceilings.

Frezzeria, San Marco 1284, 30124 Venezia. (C) **041-5206855.** Fax 041-5206413. www.side7.it/casanova/. 49 units. 150€–256€ double; 187€–292€ triple. Rates include breakfast. AE, DC, MC, V. Vaporetto: Calle Vallaresso. **Amenities:** Room service; babysitting; laundry/dry cleaning. *In room:* A/C, TV, minibar, hair dryer, safe.

Hotel Concordia 🉀   The Concordia, in a russet-colored building with stone-trimmed windows, is the only hotel with rooms overlooking St. Mark's Square (only a few do, and they command a high price). A series of gold-plated marble steps takes you to the lobby, where you'll find a comfortable bar area, good service, and elevators to whisk you to the labyrinthine halls. The (quite small) guest rooms are decorated in a Venetian antique style, with small Murano chandeliers, coordinated fabrics, hand-painted furnishings, and marble bathrooms.

Calle Larga, San Marco 367, 30124 Venezia. (✆ **041-5206866**. Fax 041-5206775. 57 units (some with shower only). 300€–400€ double; 400€–500€ suite. Rates include buffet breakfast. AE, DC, MC, V. Vaporetto: San Marco. **Amenities:** Restaurant; bar; room service; babysitting; laundry/dry cleaning. *In room:* A/C, TV, minibar, hair dryer, safe.

Hotel Saturnia International ★★

Far superior to the Scandinavia (see below), this is one of Venice's most successful adaptations of a 14th-century palazzo. You're surrounded by richly embellished beauty: a grand hall with a wooden staircase, iron chandeliers, fine paintings, and beamed ceilings. The individually styled guest rooms are generally spacious and furnished with chandeliers, Venetian antiques, tapestry rugs, gilt mirrors, and carved ceilings. A few on the top floor have small balconies; others overlook the garden in back.

Calle Larga XXII Marzo, San Marco 2398, 30124 Venezia. (✆ **041-5208377**. Fax 041-5207131. www.hotelsaturnia.it. 95 units (a few with tub or shower only). 216€–396€ double. Rates include breakfast. AE, DC, MC, V. Vaporetto: San Marco. **Amenities:** Restaurant; lounge; room service; babysitting; laundry/dry cleaning. *In room:* A/C, TV, minibar, hair dryer, safe.

Hotel Scandinavia ★

This hotel isn't actually in San Marco (it's in neighboring Castello, just off a colorful square), but it has a convenient location not far from Piazza San Marco. The public rooms are rococo, filled with copies of 18th-century Italian chairs and Venetian-glass chandeliers. The guest rooms are of a decent size and are decorated in the Venetian style, but modern comforts have been added. The bathrooms are a bit cramped. The lobby lounge overlooks the campo. Breakfast is the only meal served, but the hotel staff will direct you to several good dining spots within a short walk of the entrance.

Campo Santa Maria Formosa, Castello 5240, 30122 Venezia. (✆ **041-5223507**. Fax 041-523523. www.scandinaviahotel.com. 34 units (some with shower only). High season 300€ double; low season 150€ double. Rates include breakfast. AE, DC, MC, V. Vaporetto: San Zaccaria or Rialto. **Amenities:** Bar; room service; babysitting; laundry. *In room:* A/C, TV, minibar, hair dryer, safe.

Hotel Violino d'Oro ★

The 18th-century Palazzo Barozzi is now a restored three-story hotel. The midsize guest rooms are handsomely furnished, with well-kept bathrooms. Two rooms and the junior suite open onto private terraces. Ms. Cristina and her family run the hotel with style and grace.

Campiello Barozzi, San Marco 2091, 30124 Venezia. © **041-2770841.** Fax 041-2771001. www.violinodoro.com. 26 units. 214€–275€ double. Rates include breakfast. AE, DC, MC, V. Vaporetto: San Marco. **Amenities:** Breakfast room; bar; babysitting; laundry. *In room:* A/C, TV, minibar, hair dryer.

MODERATE

Hotel do Pozzi ↷ A short stroll from Piazza San Marco, this small place feels more like a country tavern than a hotel. Its original structure is 200 years old, and it opens onto a paved courtyard with potted greenery. The sitting and dining rooms are furnished with antiques (and near-antiques) intermixed with utilitarian modern decor. Half the guest rooms open onto the street and half onto a view of an inner garden where breakfast is served in summer. Some have Venetian styling with antique reproductions; others are in a more contemporary and more sterile vein. A major refurbishment has given a fresh touch to the bathrooms.

Corte do Pozzi, San Marco 2373, 30124 Venezia. © **041-5207855.** Fax 041-5229413. www.hoteldopozzi.it. 35 units (some with shower only). 125€–196€ double. Rates include breakfast. AE, DC, MC, V. Vaporetto: Santa Maria del Giglio. **Amenities:** Dining room; bar; babysitting; laundry/dry cleaning. *In room:* A/C, TV, minibar, hair dryer.

Hotel La Fenice et des Artistes *(Overrated)* For decades one of the most famous hotels of Venice, this landmark is now in sad decline, although it still has its fans and one of the most desirable of all Venetian locations. Maintenance could be better, and the staff has grown complacent. This hotel offers widely varying accommodations in two connected buildings, each at least 100 years old. One is rather romantic, though timeworn, with an impressive staircase leading to the ornate rooms (one building even has its own small garden and terraces). Your satin-lined room might have an inlaid desk and a wardrobe painted in the Venetian manner to match a baroque bed frame. The main building, site of the reception desk, is the more desirable, furnished in a more typically Venetian style, with nicely padded walls and art reproductions, gilt mirrors, Murano chandeliers, and spacious old bathrooms.

Campiello de la Fenice, San Marco 1936, 30124 Venezia. © **041-5232333.** Fax 041-5203721. www.fenicehotels.it. 69 units. 135€–218€ double; 200€–295€ suite. Rates include breakfast. AE, DC, MC, V. Vaporetto: San Marco. **Amenities:** Restaurant; bar; room service; babysitting; laundry/dry cleaning. *In room:* A/C, TV, hair dryer, safe.

Hotel Montecarlo This hotel, which hides behind a 17th-century facade just 2 minutes from Piazza San Marco, was vastly renovated and improved in 2001. The upper halls are lined with paintings by Venetian artists. The guest rooms are decorated with Venetian-style furniture and Venetian-glass chandeliers. Some are quite dark, the curse of many Venetian hotels. All have well-kept bathrooms.

Calle dei Specchieri, San Marco 463, 30124 Venezia. © **041-5207144.** Fax 041-5207789. www.venicehotelmontecarlo.com. 48 units. 104€ standard double; 400€ deluxe double. Rates include buffet breakfast. AE, DC, MC, V. Vaporetto: San Marco. **Amenities:** Restaurant; bar; room service; babysitting; laundry. *In room:* A/C, TV, hair dryer, safe.

INEXPENSIVE

Hotel ai do Mori 🛏 *(Value)* This 1450s town house lies about 10 paces from tourist central. You'll have to balance your need for space with your desire for a view (and your willingness to climb stairs because there's no elevator): The lower-level rooms are larger but don't have views; the third- and fourth-floor rooms are cramped but have sweeping views over the basilica's domes. The building is frequently upgraded by owner Antonella Bernardi. The furniture in the guest rooms is simple and modern, bathrooms are clean, and most of the street noise is muffled by double-paned windows. No meals are served, but there are dozens of cafes in the neighborhood.

Calle Larga San Marco, San Marco 658, 30124 Venezia. © **041-5204817.** Fax 041-5205328. www.hotelaidomori.com. 11 units, 9 with private bathroom (showers only). 50€ double without bathroom; 130€ double with bathroom. MC, V. Vaporetto: San Marco. **Amenities:** Lounge. *In room:* A/C, TV, hair dryer, safe.

2 In Castello/On Riva degli Schiavoni

Several of the hotels in this section are also very close to Piazza San Marco.

VERY EXPENSIVE

Hotel Danieli 🛏🛏🛏 The Cipriani is more exclusive and isolated, almost like a spa, and the Gritti coddles its guests a bit more, but the Danieli is clearly number three among the fabulous palazzi hotels of Venice. Comparisons between the Danieli and the Gritti are inevitable. The Danieli broods, as the Gritti sparkles. The Danieli is more baronial, and the Gritti is more like home (that is, if your home is a palazzo). The Danieli sprawls, whereas the Gritti is intimate. The Danieli's rates are also a good deal lower than those of either of its two rivals, making it a better value (if upwards of 500€ a night can ever be considered a good value).

The Danieli was built as a grand showcase by Doge Dandolo in the 14th century and in 1822 was transformed into a "hotel for kings." In a spectacular Grand Canal location, it has sheltered not only kings but also princes, cardinals, ambassadors, and such literary figures as George Sand and Charles Dickens. The atmosphere is luxurious; even the balconies opening off the main lounge are illuminated by stained-glass skylights. The guest rooms range widely in price, dimension, decor, and vistas (those opening onto the lagoon cost a lot more but are also susceptible to the noise of Riva degli Schiavoni). Alfred de Musset and Ms. Sand made love in room no. 10, the most requested accommodation. You're housed in one of three buildings: a modern structure (least desirable), a 19th-century building, or the 14th-century Venetian-Gothic Palazzo Dandolo (most desirable). On the downside, although the palazzo rooms are the most romantic, they also are the smallest.

Riva degli Schiavoni, Castello 4196, 30122 Venezia. ℂ **800/325-3535** in the U.S. and Canada, or 041-5226480. Fax 041-2961100. www.hoteldanieli.it. 233 units. 565€–845€ double; 2,200€–3,000€ suite. AE, DC, MC, V. Vaporetto: San Zaccaria. **Amenities:** Elegant restaurant; lounge; bar; concierge; room service; babysitting; laundry/dry cleaning. *In room:* A/C, TV, minibar, hair dryer, safe.

Londra Palace ⭐⭐   It's no Danieli, but the Londra is a gabled manor on the lagoon, a few yards from Piazza San Marco. The hotel's most famous guest was arguably Tchaikovsky, who wrote his *Fourth Symphony* in room no. 108 in December 1877; he also composed several other works here. The cozy reading room is reminiscent of an English club, boasting leaded windows and paneled walls with framed blowups of some of Tchaikovsky's sheet music. The guest rooms are luxurious, often with lacquered Venetian furniture. Romantics ask for one of the two Regency-style attic rooms with beamed ceilings. The courtyard rooms are quieter and cheaper, opening onto rooftop views instead of the Grand Canal. The best units are those on the fifth floor, with beamed ceilings and private terraces. Bathrooms come with deluxe toiletries and robes; many also have whirlpool tubs.

Riva degli Schiavoni, Castello 4171, 30122 Venezia. ℂ **041-5200533.** Fax 041-5225032. www.hotelondra.it. 53 units. 270€–470€ double; 475€–770€ junior suite. Rates include breakfast. AE, DC, MC, V. Vaporetto: San Zaccaria. **Amenities:** Restaurant; bar; concierge; room service; babysitting; laundry. *In room:* A/C, TV, minibar, hair dryer, safe.

EXPENSIVE

Hotel Bisanzio ♠   A few steps from Piazza San Marco, this hotel in the former home of sculptor Alessandro Vittoria offers good service. It has an elevator and terraces, plus a little bar and a mooring for gondolas and motorboats. The lounge opens onto a traditional courtyard. The guest rooms are generally quiet, each in a Venetian antique style. The most requested rooms are the eight opening onto private balconies.

Calle della Pietà, Riva degli Schiavoni 3651, 30122 Venezia. ℂ **041-5203100.** Fax 041-5204114. www.bisanzio.com. 50 units (half with shower only). 140€– 330€ double. Rates include breakfast. AE, DC, MC, V. Vaporetto: San Zaccaria. **Amenities:** Breakfast room; bar; room service; babysitting; laundry/dry cleaning. *In room:* A/C, TV, minibar, hair dryer.

Locanda Vivaldi ♠ *Finds*   Here is a rare chance to immerse yourself in a cliché of Venetian charm. The house of the composer Antonio Vivaldi (1678–1741) has been converted into a hotel. The most original and influential Italian composer of his day, Vivaldi was *maestro de' concerti* in Venice from 1716 to 1738, during which time he lived at this house. In keeping with the spirit of the maestro, the Locanda has been decorated with baroque ornamentation. Bedrooms are comfortably lush, evoking a time gone by but with modern conveniences such as tiled bathrooms, each with a shower/box sauna and Jacuzzi. Standard doubles have a view of the Grand Canal, and superior double units offer a lagoon view and also contain a hydromassage tub. Anchor here and you'll be right in the heart of Venice.

Riva degli Schiavoni 4152, 30122 Venezia. ℂ **041-2770477.** Fax 041-2770489. www.locandavivaldi.it. 22 units (some with shower only). 170€–440€ double; 340€–565€ suite. Rates include buffet breakfast. AE, DC, MC, V. Vaporetto: San Zaccaria. **Amenities:** Bar; room service; laundry/dry cleaning. *In room:* A/C, TV, minibar, safe.

MODERATE

Hotel Campiello   This pink-fronted Venetian town house dates from the 1400s, but today you'll find cost-conscious Venetian-style accommodations. This government-rated two-star hotel is better than its rating implies because of a spectacular location and Renaissance touches such as marble mosaic floors and carefully polished hardwoods. The only room with a separate entrance is a ground-floor hideaway that, fortunately, has been flooded by high tides only once in the past century. The guest rooms are cozy, with tidy bathrooms.

Campiello del Vin, Castello 4647, 30122 Venezia. ℂ 041-5205764. Fax 041-5205798. www.hcampiello.it. 17 units (showers only). 80€–170€ double, 120€–210€ triple. Rates include breakfast. AE, DC, MC, V. Closed Jan. Vaporetto: San Zaccaria. **Amenities:** Bar; babysitting. *In room:* A/C, TV, hair dryer, safe.

Hotel Savoia & Jolanda ⟨R⟩   The Savoia & Jolanda occupies a prize position on Venice's premier boulevard, with a lagoon as its front yard. Although its exterior reflects old Venice, the interior is somewhat spiritless; the staff, however, makes life comfortable. Most of the modern guest rooms have a view of the boats and the Lido; they contain desks and armchairs. All the rooms were last renovated in 1999. Some units are large enough to contain three or four beds.

Riva degli Schiavoni, Castello 4187, 30122 Venezia. ℂ 041-5206644. Fax 041-5207494. www.hotelsavoiajolanda.com. 75 units (some with shower only). 200€–300€ double; 320€–599€ suite. Rates include buffet breakfast. AE, DC, MC, V. Vaporetto: San Zaccaria. **Amenities:** Restaurant; lounge; room service; babysitting; laundry. *In room:* A/C, TV, minibar, hair dryer, safe.

La Residenza ⟨RR⟩   In a 14th-century building that looks a lot like a miniature Doge's Palace, this little hotel is on a residential square where children play soccer and older people feed the pigeons. You'll pass through a stone vestibule lined with ancient Roman columns before ringing another doorbell at the bottom of a flight of stairs. First an iron gate and then a door will open into an enormous salon filled with antiques, 300-year-old paintings, and some of the most marvelously preserved walls in Venice. The guest rooms are far less opulent, with contemporary pieces and small bathrooms, but beds are comfortable. The choice rooms are usually booked far in advance, especially for Carnevale.

Campo Bandiera e Moro, Castello 3608, 30122 Venezia. ℂ 041-5285315. Fax 041-5238859. 15 units (showers only). 105€–145€ double. Rates include breakfast. MC, V. Vaporetto: Arsenale. **Amenities:** Lounge. *In room:* A/C, TV, minibar, hair dryer, safe.

INEXPENSIVE

Albergo Al Piave ⟨Value⟩   For Venice, this centrally located hotel is a real bargain, and the Puppin family welcomes you with style. Although the hotel is rated only one star by the government, its level of comfort is excellent, and its decor and ambience are inviting. Even some guests who could afford to pay more select the Piave for its cozy warmth. The small but comfortable guest rooms come with clean bathrooms. A visit here is relaxed and enjoyable.

Ruga Giuffa, Castello 4838–4840, 30122 Venezia. (*C*) **041-5285174**. Fax 041-5238512. www.hotelalpiave.com. 15 units (showers only). 115€–145€ double; 160€–205€ suite for 3. Rates include continental breakfast. AE, DC, MC, V. Vaporetto: San Zaccaria. **Amenities:** Lounge. *In room:* A/C, TV, minibar, hair dryer, safe.

Hotel Doni   The Doni sits about a 3-minute walk from St. Mark's. Most of its very basic guest rooms overlook either a garden with a tall fig tree or a little canal where four or five gondolas are usually tied up. Simplicity and cleanliness prevail, especially in the down-to-earth rooms. The beds, often brass, are a little worn but still comfortable, and the plumbing is antiquated but still working fine.

Calle de Vin, Castello 4656, 30122 Venezia. (*C*) and fax **041-5224267**. 13 units, 3 with private bathroom. 80€ double without bathroom; 105€ double with bathroom. Rates include breakfast. No credit cards. Vaporetto: San Zaccaria. **Amenities:** Breakfast room; lounge. *In room:* No phone.

3 Near the Ponte di Rialto

The epicenter of this neighborhood is the bustling activity of the Rialto Market itself. This area is a mixed bag, with plenty of decaying apartment houses alongside tourist sights. There are some fine shops and restaurants, but also some of the worst tourist traps in Venice. Our recommendations will steer you clear of these.

MODERATE

Hotel Marconi   This old relic is still going strong. The Marconi, less than 15m (50 ft.) from the Rialto Bridge, was built in 1500, when Venice was at the height of its supremacy. The drawing-room furnishings would be appropriate for visiting archbishops, and the Maschietto family operates everything efficiently. Only four of the lovely old guest rooms open onto the Grand Canal, and these are the most eagerly sought. The rooms vary from small to medium, each with a comfortable bed, and the small bathrooms are tiled. Breakfast is served in a room with Gothic chairs, but in fair weather the sidewalk tables facing the Grand Canal are preferred by many.

Riva del Vin, San Polo 729, 30125 Venezia. (*C*) **041-5222068**. Fax 041-5229700. www.hotelmarconi.it. 26 units. 68€–310€ double, 100€–403€ triple. Rates include buffet breakfast. AE, DC, MC, V. Vaporetto: Rialto. **Amenities:** Dining room; bar; room service; babysitting; laundry/dry cleaning. *In room:* A/C, TV, minibar, hair dryer, safe.

Hotel Rialto   The Rialto opens right onto the San Marco side of the Grand Canal at the foot of the Ponte di Rialto, the famous bridge flanked with shops. Its guest rooms combine modern or Venetian furniture with ornate Venetian ceilings and wall decorations. The hotel has been considerably improved in recent years, with its furnishings upgraded and made more inviting. All rooms have well-kept bathrooms. The most desirable and expensive doubles overlook the canal.

Riva del Ferro, San Marco 5149, 30124 Venezia. (C) 041-5209166. Fax 041-5238958. www.rialtohotel.com. 79 units (half with showers only). 155€–217€ double; 207€–387€ junior suite. Rates include buffet breakfast. AE, DC, MC, V. Vaporetto: Rialto. **Amenities:** Dining room; bar; room service; babysitting; laundry/dry cleaning. *In room:* A/C, TV, minibar, hair dryer, safe.

Locanda Sturion *(Finds)*   You may recognize the facade of this building from a painting by Carpaccio hanging in the Galleria dell'Accademia. In the early 1200s, the Venetian doges commissioned this site as a place where foreign merchants could stay for the night. After long stints as a private residence, the Sturion caters to visitors once again. A private entrance leads up four steep flights of marble steps, past apartments, to a labyrinth of cozy, clean, but not overly large guest rooms. Most have views over the terra-cotta rooftops of this congested neighborhood; two open onto Grand Canal views. The intimate breakfast room is homey—almost like a parlor, with red brocaded walls, a Venetian chandelier, and a trio of big windows overlooking the canal.

Calle del Sturion, San Polo 679, 30125 Venezia. (C) 041-5236243. Fax 041-5228378. www.locandasturion.com. 11 units. 90€–200€ double; 250€ triple. Rates include continental breakfast. AE, MC, V. Vaporetto: Rialto. **Amenities:** Lounge; room service; babysitting; laundry. *In room:* A/C, TV, minibar, hair dryer, safe.

4 In Cannaregio

This is one of our favorite sections of Venice because it affords you a chance to see some of the local life. Otherwise, you'd think that nobody lived in Venice except tourists. Nearly a third of the shrinking population of Venice calls Cannaregio home.

EXPENSIVE

Boscolo Grand Hotel dei Dogi *(Finds)*   Once an embassy and later a convent, this is one of the hotel secrets of Venice, definitely a hidden gem. On the northern tier of Venice, Dei Dogi looks across the lagoon to the mainland. As you sit in the beautiful little garden of rose bushes, you will think that you've arrived at a Venetian Shangri-La. Acquired by the Boscolo chain in 1998, the hotel lies just a short stroll down the canal from the Church of Madonna dell'Orto, where Tintoretto lies buried. Bedrooms are elegantly decorated in a palatial Venetian style, with gilt and polish. The bathrooms still retain their old-fashioned personality, pouring out either scalding hot or lethally cold water at their own unpredictable pace. Some 18th-century frescoes often decorate the walls of the bedrooms, as do antique mirrors, swag draperies, and doors intricately inlaid with veneer.

Fondamenta Madonna dell'Orto 3500, 30121 Venezia. ⓒ **041-2208111.** Fax 041-722278. www.boscolohotels.com. 68 units. 284€–465€ double; 775€–1,500€ suite. AE, DC, MC, V. Vaporetto: Madonna dell'Orto. **Amenities:** Restaurant; bar; room service; babysitting; laundry/dry cleaning. *In room:* A/C, TV, minibar, hair dryer, safe.

Locanda ai Santi Apostoli ⓐ *(Kids* If you can't afford the Gritti but you still fantasize about living in a palazzo overlooking the Grand Canal, near the Rialto, here's your chance. This inn isn't cheap, but it's a lot less expensive than the palaces nearby. The hotel is on the top floor of a 15th-century building, and the guest rooms, though simple, are roomy and decorated in pastels, and they often contain antiques. Naturally, the two rooms opening onto the canal are the most requested. The bathrooms are small but tidy. Extra beds can often be set up in the rooms to accommodate children. This is one of three 14th- or 15th-century Venetian palaces still owned by the family that built it.

Strada Nuova, Cannaregio 4391, 30131 Venezia. ⓒ **041-5212612.** Fax 041-5212611. www.veneziaweb.com/santiapostoli. 11 units (showers only). 180€–223€ double; 387€ double with Grand Canal view; 390€ suite. Rates include breakfast. AE, DC, MC, V. Vaporetto: Ca d'Oro. **Amenities:** Breakfast room; lounge; babysitting; laundry/dry cleaning. *In room:* A/C, TV, minibar, hair dryer.

MODERATE

Hotel Giorgione ⓐ Here's a modern hotel with traditional Venetian decor. The lounges and public rooms boast fine furnishings and decorative accessories, and the comfortable and stylish guest rooms are designed to coddle guests. Each accommodation comes with an excellent bed and a tiled bathroom. The hotel also has a typical Venetian garden. It's rated second class by the government, but the Giorgione maintains higher standards than many first-class places.

Campo SS. Apostoli, Cannaregio 4587, 30131 Venezia. ℰ **041-5225810.** Fax 041-5239092. www.hotelgiorgione.it. 71 units (some with shower only). 130€–230€ double; 200€–330€ suite. Rates include buffet breakfast. AE, DC, MC, V. Vaporetto: Ca' d'Oro. **Amenities:** Bar; room service; babysitting; laundry. *In room:* A/C, TV, minibar, hair dryer, safe.

Hotel San Geremia *(Value)* For years, the small Geremia was a government-rated one-star hotel that many guests considered worthy of two-star status. In 1997, the government raised it to two stars, justifying an increase in rates. Neither grand nor well located, the Geremia still fills up every night because it offers value for the money. Located in a modernized early 1900s setting, this hotel is a 5-minute walk from the rail station. Inside, you'll find well-maintained pale-green guest rooms. They're often small, but each comes with a good bed. There's no elevator, but no one can deny that the price is appealing.

Campo San Geremia, Cannaregio 290A, 30121 Venezia. ℰ **041-716245.** Fax 041-5242342. 20 units, 14 with private bathroom (showers only). 90€ double without bathroom; 145€ double with bathroom. Rates include breakfast. Discounts of 20% in winter. AE, MC, V. Vaporetto: Ferrovia. **Amenities:** Breakfast room; lounge. *In room:* TV, minibar, hair dryer, safe.

INEXPENSIVE

Hotel Abbazia The benefit of staying here is that there's no need to transfer onto any vaporetto—you can walk from the rail station, about 10 minutes away. This hotel was built in 1889 as a monastery for barefooted Carmelite monks, who established a verdant garden in what's now the courtyard; it's planted with subtropical plants that thrive, sheltered as they are from the cold Adriatic winds. You'll find a highly accommodating staff and comfortable but very plain guest rooms with well-kept bathrooms. Twenty-five rooms overlook the courtyard, ensuring quiet in an otherwise noisy neighborhood.

Calle Priuli ai Cavaletti, Cannaregio 68, 30121 Venezia. ℰ **041-717333.** Fax 041-717949. www.abbaziahotel.com. 39 units (some with shower only). 100€–170€ double. Rates include buffet breakfast. AE, DC, MC, V. Vaporetto: Ferrovia. **Amenities:** Breakfast room; bar; room service; laundry. *In room:* A/C, TV, minibar, hair dryer, safe.

5 In Santa Croce

The eastern part of Santa Croce is rarely visited by most tourists, but it represents a slice of authentic Venetian life. Although Santa Croce sprawls all the way to Piazzale Roma, its heart is the Campo San Giacomo dell'Orio.

MODERATE

Hotel San Cassiano Ca' Favretto 🐦   The hotel's gondola pier affords views of the lacy Ca' d'Oro, perhaps Venice's most beautiful building. The hotel is a 14th-century palace (it contained the studio of 19th-c. painter Giacomo Favretto), and the owner has worked closely to preserve the original details, such as a 6m (20-ft.) beamed ceiling in the entrance. Fifteen of the conservatively decorated guest rooms overlook one of two canals, and many are filled with antiques or high-quality reproductions. Generally the housekeeping is excellent. The bathrooms are small but exceedingly well maintained.

Calle della Rosa, Santa Croce 2232, 30135 Venezia. ☎ **041-5241768.** Fax 041-721033. www.sancassiano.it. 35 units. 200€–310€ double. Rates include breakfast. AE, DC, MC, V. Vaporetto: San Stae. **Amenities:** Dining room; bar; room service; babysitting. *In room:* A/C, TV, minibar, hair dryer, safe.

6 In Dorsoduro

On the opposite side of the Accademia Bridge from San Marco, Dorsoduro is one of our favorite neighborhoods of Venice, with a real flavor of the city and a dash of funky chic. Accommodations are limited but rather special and full of character.

EXPENSIVE

American Hotel 🐦 *(Value*   There's nothing American about this ocher building across the Grand Canal from the most heavily touristed areas of Venice. The modest lobby is filled with murals, warm colors, and antiques. The guest rooms are comfortably furnished in a Venetian style, but they vary in size; some of the smaller ones are a bit cramped. Each contains a small bathroom. Many rooms with their own private terrace face the canal. On the second floor is a beautiful terrace where guests can relax over drinks. The staff is attentive and helpful.

Campo San Vio, Accademia 628, 30123 Venezia. ☎ **041-5204733.** Fax 041-5204048. www.hotelamerican.com. 29 units. 130€–268€ double; 150€–310€ triple. Rates include buffet breakfast. AE, MC, V. Vaporetto: Accademia. **Amenities:** Breakfast room; bar; room service; babysitting; laundry/dry cleaning. *In room:* A/C, TV, minibar, hair dryer, safe.

Ca' Pisani 🐦🐦 *(Finds*   This is a new boutique hotel for Venice located near the Accademia gallery. Its style evokes the 1930s and 1940s, but the setting is a former Venetian nobleman's residence from the end of the 16th century. Accommodations come in a wide variety of styles and sizes, ranging from standard doubles to spacious suites. The style is unusual for Venice in that it concentrates on the avant-garde trends that blossomed "between the wars." The lobby, for example, recalls the forms of Futurism with a wealth of marble and walnut wood. The walls in the bedrooms evoke the graphics of Mondrian. We prefer the two studios with loft sleeping areas. The bedrooms are equipped with modern technology such as room darkening by electric curtains and remote-control door openings. The bathrooms are under "starlight," creating the effect of small shining stars. A roof terrace solarium opens onto the rooftops of Venice. On-site is a wine-and-cheese bar whose name, La Rivista, comes from an original flower design in 1925 by Fortunato Depero, the Futuristic painter.

Dorsoduro 979A, 30123 Benezia. ℭ **041-2401411.** Fax 041-2771061. www.capisan ihotel.it. 29 units. 204€–285€ double; 279€–381€ suite. Rates include breakfast. AE, DC, MC, V. Vaporetto: Accademia. **Amenities:** Restaurant; bar; access to next-door gym; sauna; room service; babysitting; laundry/dry cleaning. *In room:* A/C, TV, minibar, hair dryer, safe.

MODERATE

Hotel La Calcina   Recently renovated (and not a moment too soon), La Calcina lies in a secluded and less-trampled district that used to be the English enclave before the area developed a broader base of tourism. John Ruskin, who wrote *The Stones of Venice*, stayed here in 1877, and he charted the ground for his latter-day compatriots. This pensione is absolutely spotless, and the furnishings are well chosen but hardly elaborate. The guest rooms are cozy and comfortable, each with a compact tiled bathroom.

Zattere al Gesuati, Dorsoduro 780, 30123 Venezia. ℭ **041-5206466.** Fax 041-5227045. www.lacalcina.com. 29 units (showers only). 93€–176€ double. Rates include buffet breakfast. AE, DC, MC, V. Vaporetto: Zattere. **Amenities:** Restaurant; bar; room service; babysitting; laundry/dry cleaning. *In room:* A/C, hair dryer, safe.

Pensione Accademia 🐀🐀 *Value*   The Accademia is the most patrician of the pensioni, in a villa whose garden is bounded by the junction of two canals. The interior features Gothic-style paneling, Venetian chandeliers, and Victorian-era furniture, and the upstairs sitting room is flanked by two large windows. This place has long been a favorite of the *Room with a View* crowd of Brits and scholars; it's often booked months in advance. The guest rooms are airy and bright, decorated in part with 19th-century furniture.

Fondamenta Bollani, Dorsoduro 1058, 30123 Venezia. ℭ **041-5237846.** Fax 041-5239152. www.pensioneaccademia.it. 27 units (showers only). 124€–266€ double. Rates include breakfast. AE, DC, MC, V. Vaporetto: Accademia. **Amenities:** Bar; room service; babysitting; laundry/dry cleaning. *In room:* A/C, TV, minibar, hair dryer, safe.

INEXPENSIVE

Hotel Galleria If you've dreamed of opening your windows to find the Grand Canal before you, step through this 17th-century palazzo's leaded-glass doors. But reserve way in advance—these are the cheapest rooms on the canal and possibly the most charming. Six guest rooms varying in size overlook the canal, and the others have partial views that include the Accademia Bridge. The bathrooms are small but were redone in 1998.

Dorsoduro 878A (at the foot of the Accademia Bridge), 30123 Venezia. ℂ 041-5232489. Fax 041-5204172. www.hotelgalleria.it. 10 units, 6 with private bathroom (showers only). 88€–93€ double without bathroom; 104€–135€ double with bathroom. Rates include continental breakfast. AE, DC, MC, V. Vaporetto: Accademia. **Amenities:** Breakfast room; lounge; babysitting. *In room:* Hair dryer.

Locanda Montin ℛ *(Finds)* The Montin is an old-fashioned Venetian inn whose adjoining restaurant is one of the area's most loved. The guest rooms are cozy and quaint. Only a few units have private bathrooms, and in-room extras are scarce aside from a phone. Most guests have to share the small corridor bathrooms, which are barely adequate in number, especially if the house is full. The inn is a bit difficult to locate (it's marked by only a small carriage lamp etched with the name), but is worth the search.

Fondamenta di Borgo, Dorsoduro 1147, 31000 Venezia. ℂ 041-5227151. Fax 041-5200255. 11 units, 5 with bathroom. 105€ double without bathroom; 130€ double with bathroom. Rates include breakfast. AE, DC, MC, V. Vaporetto: Accademia. **Amenities:** Restaurant; bar; laundry/dry cleaning.

7 On Isola della Giudecca

Even though this is traditionally a blue-collar neighborhood, it contains one of the grandest pockets of posh in northeast Italy, the Cipriani. If you can afford to stay here you'll be isolated, but just across the water from Piazza San Marco.

VERY EXPENSIVE

Cipriani ℛℛℛ For old-world Venetian splendor, check into the Gritti or Danieli. But for chic, contemporary surroundings, flawless service, and refinement at every turn, the Cipriani is in a class by itself—as long as you can swing its jaw-dropping prices, some of the highest hotel rates in Europe.

Set in a 16th-century cloister on the isolated island of Giudecca (reached by private hotel launch from St. Mark's Square), this pleasure palace was opened in 1958 by Giuseppe Cipriani, the founder of Harry's Bar. The guest rooms range in design from tasteful contemporary to grand antique, but all have splendid views and are sumptuous. We prefer the corner rooms, the most spacious and most elaborately decorated. The bathrooms are large, with phones, deep tubs, robes, and deluxe toiletries.

The Cipriani is the only hotel on Giudecca. The location is either calm, quiet, and exclusive, or inconvenient for exploring the rest of the city, depending on how you look at it. Service is the best in Venice, with two employees for every room. The staff can arrange for tee times at golf courses about 40 minutes away by boat.

Isola della Giudecca 10, 30133 Venezia. ℂ **800/992-5055** in the U.S., or 041-5207744. Fax 041-5207745. www.orient-expresshotels.com. 110 units. 767€– 1,177€ double; from 1,998€ suite. Rates include breakfast. AE, DC, MC, V. Closed Nov–Mar. Vaporetto: Zitele. **Amenities:** 2 superb and very expensive restaurants; 3 bars (including a piano bar); Olympic-size swimming pool; Venice's only tennis court; fitness center; Turkish bath and sauna; private boat shuttle; room service; massage; babysitting; laundry/dry cleaning. *In room:* A/C, TV, minibar, hair dryer, safe.

8 On the Lido

If you visit when the weather is nice, you can have a beach holiday on the Lido with time out for sightseeing in the heart of Venice.

VERY EXPENSIVE

Hotel des Bains 𝄞𝄞   This is the best old-world spa hotel along this fabled strip of Adriatic sand. This hotel was built in the grand era of European resort hotels, but long ago lost its supremacy on the Lido to the Excelsior (see below). It has its own wooded park and beach with individual cabanas. Thomas Mann stayed here several times before making it the setting for *Death in Venice,* and later it was used as a set for the film. The renovated interior exudes the flavor of the leisurely life of the Belle Epoque. The guest rooms are large, each elegantly furnished with rich fabrics, Oriental rugs, antiques, and paneled walls.

Lungomare Marconi 17, 30126 Lido di Venezia. ℂ **800/325-3535** in the U.S. and Canada, or 041-5265921. Fax 041-5260113. www.sheraton.com. 191 units. 422€– 620€ double; from 1,160€ suite. Rates include breakfast. AE, DC, MC, V. Closed Nov–Mar. Vaporetto: Lido, then bus A, B, or C. **Amenities:** Restaurant; bar; pool; 2 tennis courts; fitness center; sauna; private boat shuttle; room service; babysitting; laundry/dry cleaning. *In room:* A/C, TV, minibar, hair dryer, safe.

Westin Excelsior 𝄞𝄞𝄞   This luxe palace caters to the most pampered beach crowd in Europe. When the Excelsior was built, it was the world's biggest resort hotel, and its presence helped make the Lido fashionable. Today it offers the most luxury on the Lido, although it doesn't have the antique character of the Hotel des Bains (see above). Its guest rooms range in style and amenities, but all have walk-in closets. The good-size bathrooms boast deluxe toiletries and deep tubs. Most of the social life takes place around the angular pool or on the flowered terraces leading up to the cabanas on the sandy beach.

Lungomare Marconi 41, 30126 Venezia Lido. (C) 800/325-3535 in the U.S. and Canada, or 041-5260201. Fax 041-5267276. www.westin.com. 196 units. 422€–707€ double; from 1,160€ suite. Rates include breakfast. AE, DC, MC, V. Parking 20€. Closed Nov–Mar 15. Vaporetto: Lido, then bus A, B, or C. **Amenities:** 3 restaurants; 2 bars; pool; 6 tennis courts; fitness center; sauna; boat rental; private boat shuttle; room service; babysitting; laundry/dry cleaning. *In room:* A/C, TV, minibar, hair dryer, safe.

EXPENSIVE

Hotel Quattro Fontane ★   The Quattro Fontane is one of the most charming hotels on the Lido. The trouble is, a lot of people know that, so it's likely to be booked. This former summer home of a 19th-century Venetian family is most popular with the British, who seem to appreciate the homey atmosphere, the garden, the helpful staff, and the rooms with superior luxuries, not to mention the good food served at tables set under shade trees. Many of the guest rooms are furnished with antiques, and all have tile or terrazzo floors and excellent beds.

Via Quattro Fontane 16, 30126 Lido di Venezia. (C) 041-5260227. Fax 041-5260726. www.quattrofontane.com. 60 units. 248€–320€ double. Rates include buffet breakfast. AE, DC, MC, V. Closed Nov–Apr 4. Vaporetto: Lido, then bus A, B, or C. **Amenities:** Restaurant; bar; tennis court; room service; babysitting; laundry/dry cleaning. *In room:* A/C, TV, minibar, hair dryer, safe.

MODERATE

Hotel Belvedere *Kids*   The modernized Belvedere has been a family favorite since 1857. Right across from the vaporetto stop, the hotel is open year-round, which is unusual for the Lido, and offers simply furnished guest rooms, each with a good bed and tiled bathroom. As an added courtesy, the Belvedere offers guests free entrance to the Casino Municipale; in summer, guests can use the hotel's cabanas on the Lido.

Piazzale Santa Maria Elisabetta 4, 30126 Lido di Venezia. (C) 041-5260115. Fax 041-5261486. www.belvedere-venezia.com. 30 units (showers only). 115€–155€ double, 290€ suite. Rates include breakfast. AE, DC, MC, V. Vaporetto: Lido. **Amenities:** Restaurant; bar; room service; babysitting; laundry. *In room:* A/C, TV, hair dryer, safe.

Hotel Helvetia   This 19th-century building, on a side street near the lagoon side of the island, is an easy walk from the vaporetto stop. The quieter guest rooms face away from the street, and rooms in the older wing have Belle Epoque high ceilings and attractively comfortable furniture. The newer wing has a more conservative style. About half of the rooms have recently been renovated. Breakfast is served, weather permitting, in a flagstone-covered wall garden behind the hotel.

Gran Viale 4, 30126 Lido di Venezia. ℂ **041-5260105.** Fax 041-5268903. www. hotelhelvetia.com. 60 units. 150€–200€ double. Rates include breakfast. AE, DC, MC, V. Closed Nov–Mar. Vaporetto: Lido. **Amenities:** Breakfast room; bar; room service; babysitting; laundry. *In room:* TV, hair dryer.

5

Where to Dine

Even though Venice doesn't grow much of its own produce, it's surrounded by a rich agricultural district and plentiful vineyards, and specializes in fresh seafood. Venice's restaurants are among the most expensive in Italy, but we've found some wonderful moderately priced trattorie.

Some restaurants still offer a *menu turistico* (tourist menu) at a set price. It includes soup (nearly always minestrone) or pasta, followed by a meat dish with vegetables, topped off by dessert (fresh fruit or cheese), plus a quarter liter of wine or mineral water, bread, cover charge, and service (you'll still be expected to tip). Some restaurants serve a fixed-price meal called a *menu a presso fisso,* which rarely includes the cost of your wine but does include taxes and service.

If you want only a plate of spaghetti or something light, you can patronize any number of fast-food cafeterias (also look for *rôsticcerias* or *tavola caldas*). You don't pay a cover charge and can order as much or as little as you wish. Pizzerias are another good option for light meals or snacks. Many bars or cafe-bars also offer both hot and cold food throughout the day. If you're lunching light in the heat, ask for *panini,* rolls stuffed with meat. *Tramezzini* are white-bread sandwiches with the crust trimmed.

1 Near Piazza San Marco

VERY EXPENSIVE

Harry's Bar ★★★ VENETIAN   Harry's Bar serves the best food in Venice, though your tab will be painful. Harry, by the way, is an Italian named Arrigo, son of the late Commendatore Cipriani. Like his father, Arrigo is an entrepreneur extraordinaire known for his fine cuisine. His bar is a big draw for martini-thirsty Americans, but Hemingway and Hotchner always ordered bloody marys in their day. The most famous drink, which was originally concocted here, is the Bellini Prosecco and white-peach juice, wonderful when created properly, though we've had a watered-down horror here in the off-season (a real disappointment at 11€). You can have your choice

Venice Dining

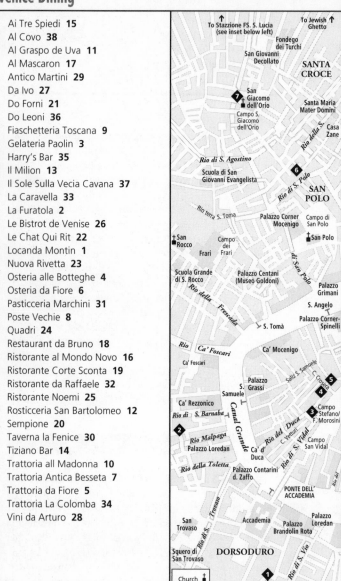

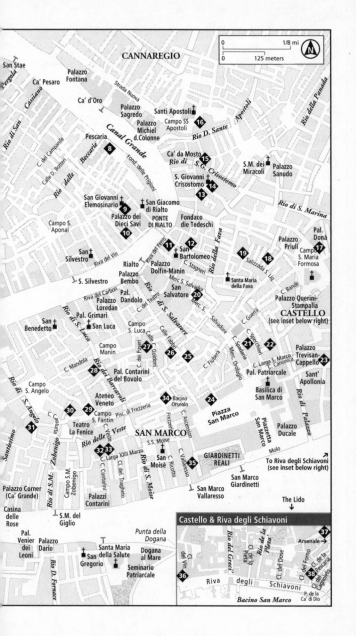

of dining in the bar downstairs or the room with a view upstairs. We recommend the Venetian fish soup, followed by the scampi thermidor with rice pilaf or the seafood ravioli. The food is relatively simple but absolutely fresh.

Calle Vallaresso, San Marco 1323. ✆ **041-5285777.** Reservations required. Main courses 50€–100€. AE, DC, MC, V. Apr–Oct daily 10:30am–1am; Nov–Mar daily 10:30am–11pm. Vaporetto: San Marco.

EXPENSIVE

Antico Martini 🐒🐒🐒 VENETIAN/INTERNATIONAL   Antico Martini elevates Venetian cuisine to its highest level (though we still give Harry's a slight edge). Elaborate chandeliers glitter and gilt-framed oil paintings adorn the paneled walls. The courtyard is splendid in summer. An excellent beginning is the *risotto di frutti di mare* ("fruits of the sea") in a creamy Venetian style with plenty of fresh seafood. For a main dish, try the *fegato alla veneziana,* tender liver fried with onions and served with polenta, a yellow cornmeal mush. The chefs are better at regional dishes than at international ones. The restaurant has one of the city's best wine lists, featuring more than 350 choices. The yellow Tocai is an interesting local wine and especially good with fish dishes.

Campo San Fantin, San Marco 1983. ✆ **041-5224121.** Reservations required. Main courses 24€–64€; fixed-price menus 46€–51€ 4-course, 79€ 6-course. AE, DC, MC, V. Thurs–Mon noon–2:30pm; Wed–Mon 7–11:30pm. Vaporetto: San Marco or Santa Maria del Giglio.

La Caravella 🐒🐒 VENETIAN/INTERNATIONAL   La Caravella has an overblown nautical atmosphere and a leather-bound menu that may make you think you're in a tourist trap. But you're not. The restaurant contains four dining rooms and a courtyard that's open in summer. The decor is rustically elegant, with frescoed ceilings, flowers, and wrought-iron lighting fixtures. You might begin with an antipasti *misto de pesce* (assortment of fish) with olive oil and lemon juice, or prawns with avocado. Star specialties are *granceola* (Adriatic sea crab on carpaccio) and chateaubriand for two. The best item to order, however, is one of the poached-fish options, such as bass, priced according to weight and served with a tempting sauce. The ice cream in champagne is a soothing finish.

In the Hotel Saturnia International, Calle Larga XXII Marzo, San Marco 2397. ✆ **041-5208901.** Reservations required. Main courses 30€–40€; fixed-price lunch 45€. AE, DC, MC, V. Daily noon–3pm and 7pm–midnight. Vaporetto: San Marco.

Tips   Fish Tips

Venice's restaurants specialize in the choicest seafood from the Adriatic—but beware that the fish dishes are *very* expensive. On most menus, the price of fresh grilled fish *(pesce alla griglia)* commonly refers to the *etto* (per 100g) and so is a fraction of the real cost. Have the waiter estimate it before you order to avoid a shock when your bill comes.

The fish merchants at the Mercato Rialto (Venice's main open-air market) take Monday off, which explains why so many restaurants are closed on Monday. Those that are open on Monday are selling Saturday's goods—beware.

Quadri 𝕽𝕽𝕽 INTERNATIONAL   One of Europe's most famous restaurants, the Quadri is even better known as a cafe (p. 167); its elegant premises open onto Piazza San Marco, where a full orchestra often adds to the magic. Many diners come just for the view and are often surprised by the high-quality cuisine and impeccable service (and the whopping tab). Harry's Bar and the Antico Martini serve better food, though the skills of Quadri's chef are considerable. He's likely to tempt you with dishes like scallops with saffron, salt codfish with polenta, marinated swordfish, and sea bass with crab sauce. Dessert specialties are "baked" ice cream and lemon mousse with fresh strawberry sauce.

Piazza San Marco, San Marco 120–124. ℭ **041-5289299.** Reservations required. Main courses 33€–43€. AE, DC, MC, V. Tues–Sun noon–2:30pm and 7– 10:30pm. Vaporetto: San Marco.

MODERATE

Da Ivo 𝕽 TUSCAN/VENETIAN   Da Ivo has a faithful crowd. The rustic atmosphere is cozy and relaxing, your well-set table bathed in candlelight. Florentines head here for fine Tuscan cookery, but regional Venetian dishes are also served. In season, game, prepared according to ancient traditions, is cooked over an open charcoal grill. One cold December day our hearts were warmed by homemade *tagliatelle* (flat noodles) topped with slivers of *tartufi bianchi,* the unforgettable pungent white truffle from Piedmont. Dishes change according to the season and the availability of ingredients, but are likely to include swordfish, anglerfish, or cuttlefish in its own ink.

Calle dei Fuseri, San Marco 1809. ☎ 041-5285004. Reservations required. Main courses 30€–40€. AE, DC, MC, V. Mon–Sat noon–2:30pm and 7pm–midnight. Closed Jan 6–31. Vaporetto: San Marco.

Do Forni ✹ VENETIAN

Centuries ago, this was where bread was baked for monasteries, but today it's the busiest restaurant in Venice, even when the rest of the city slumbers under a wintertime Adriatic fog. It's divided into two sections, separated by a narrow alley. The locals prefer the front part, which is decorated in Orient Express style. The larger section in back is like a country tavern, with ceiling beams and original paintings. The English menu (with at least 80 dishes, prepared by 14 cooks) is entitled "Food for the Gods" and lists specialties like spider crab in its own shell, risotto primavera, linguine with rabbit, and sea bass in parchment.

Calle dei Specchieri, San Marco 457. ☎ 041-5232148. Reservations recommended. Main courses 20€–26€. AE, DC, MC, V. Daily noon–3pm and 7pm–midnight. Vaporetto: San Marco.

Ristorante Noemi VENETIAN

The decor of this simple place includes a multicolored marble floor in abstract patterns and swag curtains covering big glass windows. The foundations date from the 14th century, and the restaurant opened in 1927, named after the matriarch of the family that continues to own it. Specialties, many bordering on *nuova cucina,* include thin black spaghetti with cuttlefish in its own sauce, salmon crepes with cheese, and fillet of sole Casanova, with a velouté of white wine, shrimp, and mushrooms. For dessert, try the special lemon sorbet, made with sparkling wine and fresh mint.

Calle dei Fabbri, San Marco 912. ☎ 041-5225238. Reservations recommended. Main courses 17€–25€. AE, DC, MC, V. Tues–Sun 11:30am–midnight. Closed Dec 15–Jan 15. Vaporetto: San Marco.

Ristorante da Raffaele ✹ ITALIAN/VENETIAN

The Raffaele has long been a favorite canal-side restaurant. It's often overrun with tourists, but the veteran kitchen staff handles the onslaught well. The restaurant offers the kind of charm and atmosphere unique to Venice, with its huge inner sanctum and high-beamed ceiling, 17thto 19th-century pistols and sabers, wrought-iron chandeliers, a massive fireplace, and hundreds of copper pots. The food is excellent, beginning with a choice of tasty antipasti or well-prepared pastas. Seafood specialties include scampi, squid, and deep-fried fish. The grilled meats are wonderful. Finish with a tempting dessert.

Calle Larga XXII Marzo (Fondamenta delle Ostreghe), San Marco 2347. ☎ 041-5232317. Reservations recommended Sat–Sun. Main courses 12€–24€. AE, DC, MC, V. Fri–Wed noon–3pm and 7–10:30pm. Closed Dec 10 through Jan. Vaporetto: San Marco or Santa Maria del Giglio.

Taverna la Fenice ☆☆ ITALIAN/VENETIAN Opened in 1907, when Venetians were flocking in record numbers to hear the bel canto performances in nearby La Fenice opera house (which burned down a few years ago), this taverna is one of Venice's most romantic dining spots. The interior is suitably elegant, but the preferred spot in fine weather is outdoors beneath a canopy. The service is smooth and efficient. The most appetizing beginning is the selection of seafood antipasti. The fish is fresh from the Mediterranean. You might enjoy the *risotto con scampi e arugula,* *tagliatelle* with cream sauce and exotic mushrooms, John Dory fillets with butter and lemon, turbot roasted with potatoes and tomato sauce, scampi with tomatoes and rice, or *carpaccio alla Fenice.*

Campiello de la Fenice, San Marco 1939. ☎ 041-5223856. Reservations required. Main courses 14€–40€. AE, DC, MC, V. Mon–Sat noon–3pm and 7–11pm. Vaporetto: San Marco.

Trattoria La Colomba ☆ VENETIAN/INTERNATIONAL This is one of Venice's most distinctive trattorie, its history going back at least a century. Modern paintings adorn the walls; they change periodically and are usually for sale. Menu items are likely to include at least five daily specials based on Venice's time-honored cuisine, as well as *risotto di funghi del Montello* (risotto with mushrooms from the local hills of Montello) and *baccalà alla vicentina* (milk-simmered dry cod seasoned with onions, anchovies, and cinnamon and served with polenta). The fruits and vegetables used are for the most part grown on the lagoon islands.

Piscina Frezzeria, San Marco 1665. ☎ 041-5221175. Reservations recommended. Main courses 23€–40€. AE, DC, MC, V. Daily noon–3pm and 7–11pm. Closed Wed Nov–Apr. Vaporetto: San Marco or Rialto.

Vini da Arturo ☆ *Finds* VENETIAN Vini da Arturo attracts many devoted regulars to its seven tables, including an artsy crowd. You get delectable local cooking, not just the standard clichés (and not seafood, which may be unique for a Venetian restaurant). Instead of ordering plain pasta, try the tantalizing *spaghetti alla Gorgonzola.* The beef is also good, especially when prepared with a cream sauce flavored with mustard and pepper. The salads are made with fresh ingredients, often in unusual combinations; particularly interesting is the pappardelle radicchio.

Calle degli Assassini, San Marco 3656. ℂ **041-5286974.** Reservations recommended. Main courses 21€–31€. No credit cards. Mon–Sat noon–2:30pm and 7–10:30pm. Closed Aug. Vaporetto: San Marco or Rialto.

INEXPENSIVE

Le Bistrot de Venise ⭐ VENETIAN   A classic Venetian cuisine, based on time-tested recipes handed down from generations, is served at this well-attended cafe-brasserie, which is also the site of occasional live music and poetry readings. It is counter-cultural hip, and attracts a lively crowd, often young and often local, until late at night. Many of the recipes are from the 16th century, and until the revival of this bistro were relatively forgotten by Venetian chefs. A soup, for example, is made with rice flour, pomegranates, chicken, and slivered almonds. Ever had baked eel in bay leaf with a rose pepper sauce, or a prawn and Treviso red chicory tartlet in a pumpkin sauce? One of the best dishes is a sausage made of fish and "fruits of the sea" (various shellfish) served with a garlic-laced green herb sauce. We're especially fond of their pheasant, and their baked sturgeon with grapes and prunes in a sour sauce. One of the most delectable items on the menu is wild duck stuffed with orange and red wine. Most dishes except for fresh fish are priced at the lower end of the scale.

Calle dei Fabbri, San Marco 4685. ℂ **041-5236651.** Main courses 13€–20€. MC, V. Daily noon–3pm and 7pm–1am. Vaporetto: Rialto.

Le Chat Qui Rit *Value* VENETIAN/PIZZA   This self-service cafeteria/pizzeria offers food prepared "just like mama made." It's very popular because of its low prices. Dishes might include cuttlefish simmered in stock and served on a bed of yellow polenta, or various fried fish. You can also order a steak grilled very simply, flavored with oil, salt, and pepper or a little garlic and herbs. Main-dish platters are served rather quickly after you order them.

Calle Frezzeria, San Marco 1131. ℂ **041-5229086.** Main courses 7€–9€; pizzas 6€–7€. No credit cards. Nov–Mar Sun–Fri 11am–9:30pm; Apr–Oct daily 11am–9:30pm. Vaporetto: San Marco.

Osteria alle Botteghe VENETIAN/ITALIAN   Once you've located the bigger-than-life Campo Santo Stefano, you'll find this osteria a great choice for a light snack or an elaborate meal. Stand-up hors d'oeuvres *(cicchetti)* and fresh sandwiches can be enjoyed at the bar or the window-side counter; more serious diners can choose from pasta dishes or *tavola calda* (a buffet of prepared dishes like eggplant parmigiana, lasagna, and fresh cooked vegetables in

Something Sweet

If you're in the mood for some tasty gelato, head to the **Gelateria Paolin**, Campo Stefano Morosini (℃ 041-5225576), which offers 20 flavors. It has stood on the corner of this busy square since the 1930s, making it Venice's oldest ice-cream parlor. You can order your ice cream to go or eat it at one of the sidewalk tables (it costs more if you eat it at a table). April through October, it's open daily from 10am to midnight; November through March, hours are daily from 10am to 8:30pm.

One of the city's finest pastry shops is the **Pasticceria Marchini**, Ponte San Maurizio, San Marco 676 (℃ 041-5229109), whose cakes, muffins, and pastries are the stuff of childhood memories for many locals. The high-calorie output of the busy kitchens is displayed behind glass cases and sold by the piece for eating at the bar (there are few tables) or by the kilogram for take-out. The pastries include traditional versions of *torte del Doge,* made from almonds and pine nuts; *zaleti,* made from a mix of corn-meal and eggs; and *bigna,* akin to zabaglione, concocted from chocolate and cream. It's open daily from 8:30am to 8:30pm.

season, reheated when you order) and repair to tables in the back. Vegetarians will be happy with the vegetable lasagna. Classic dishes include a tender Venetian liver with polenta.

Calle delle Botteghe, San Marco 3454. ℃ **041-5228181.** Main courses 6.20€–10€. AE, DC, MC, V. Mon–Sat 11am–4pm and 7–10pm. Vaporetto: Accademia or Sant'Angelo.

Sempione VENETIAN   The Sempione has done an admirable job of feeding locals and visitors for almost 90 years. Set adjacent to a canal in a 15th-century building near Piazza San Marco, it contains three dining rooms done in a soothingly traditional style, a well-trained staff, and a kitchen focusing on traditional cuisine. Examples are grilled fish, spaghetti with crabmeat, risotto with fish, fish soup, and delectable Venetian calf's liver that hasn't been significantly changed since the restaurant was founded. Try for a table by the window so you can watch the gondolas glide by.

Ponte Beretteri, San Marco 578. © **041-5226022**. Reservations recommended. Main courses 8€–17€. AE, DC, MC, V. Wed–Mon 11:30am–3pm and 6:30–10pm. Closed Thurs Nov–Dec. Vaporetto: Rialto.

Trattoria da Fiore *(Value* VENETIAN/ITALIAN   Don't confuse this trattoria with the well-known and very expensive Osteria da Fiore. You might not eat better here, but you'll be a lot happier when your bill arrives. Start with the house specialty, *penne alla Fiore* (prepared with olive oil, garlic, and seven in-season vegetables), and you may be happy to call it a night. Or skip right to another popular specialty, *fritto misto,* comprising more than a dozen varieties of fresh fish and seafood. The *zuppa di pesce,* a delicious bouillabaisse-like soup, is stocked with mussels, crab, clams, shrimp, and chunks of fresh tuna. This is a great place for an afternoon snack or light lunch at the Bar Fiore next door (10:30am–10:30pm).

Calle delle Botteghe, San Marco 3461. © **041-5235310**. Reservations suggested. Pasta dishes 8€–20€; main courses 15€–35€. AE, DC, V. Wed–Mon noon–3pm and 7–10pm. Vaporetto: Accademia.

2 In Castello

EXPENSIVE

Do Leoni *ⓡⓡ* VENETIAN/INTERNATIONAL   For years, this restaurant was known by the French version of its name, Les Deux Lions. In the elegant Londra Palace, it offers a panoramic view of a 19th-century equestrian statue ringed with heroic women taming (you guessed it) lions. The restaurant is filled with scarlet and gold, a motif of lions patterned into the carpeting, and reproductions of English furniture. Lunches are brief buffet-style affairs, where diners serve themselves from a large choice of hot and cold Italian and international food. The appealing candlelit dinners are more formal, emphasizing Venetian cuisine. The chef's undeniable skill is reflected in such dishes as chilled fish terrine, baked salmon in champagne sauce, and baby rooster with green-pepper sauce. If the weather permits, you can dine out on the piazza overlooking the lions and their masters.

In the Londra Palace, Riva degli Schiavoni, Castello 4171. © **041-5200533**. Reservations required. Main courses 25€–50€. Guests of the Londra Palace receive 20% off (excludes fixed-price menu). AE, DC, MC, V. Restaurant, daily noon–3pm and 7:30–11pm; bar, daily 10am–1am. Vaporetto: San Zaccaria.

MODERATE

Al Covo VENETIAN/SEAFOOD   Al Covo has a special charm, due to its atmospheric setting, sophisticated service, and the fine cooking of Cesare Benelli and his Texas-born wife, Diane. What's their preferred dish? They respond, "That's like asking us, 'Which of your children do you prefer?'" Look for a reinvention of a medieval version of fish soup; potato gnocchi flavored with go (local white-fish); seafood ravioli; linguine blended with zucchini and fresh peas; and delicious *fritto misto* with scampi, squid, a bewildering array of fish, and deep-fried vegetables like zucchini flowers. Al Covo prides itself on not having any freezers, guaranteeing that all food is fresh every day. Note that this place is near Piazza San Marco, not near Rialto, as you might think when you see a square on your map with a similar name.

Campiello della Pescaria, Castello 3968. ✆ **041-5223812.** Reservations recommended for dinner. Main courses 9€–25€; fixed-price lunch 35€. No credit cards. Fri–Tues 12:45–2:15pm and 7:45–10pm. Vaporetto: Arsenale.

Al Mascaron VENETIAN   Crowd into one of the three loud, boisterous dining rooms here, where you'll probably be directed to sit next to a stranger at a long trestle table. The waiters will come by and slam down copious portions of fresh-cooked local specialties: deep-fried calamari, spaghetti with lobster, monkfish in a salt crust, pastas, savory risottos, and Venetian-style calf's liver (which locals prefer rather pink), plus the best seafood of the day made into salads. There's also a convivial bar, where locals drop in to spread the gossip of the day, play cards, and order vino and snacks.

Calle Lunga Santa Maria Formosa, Castello 5225. ✆ **041-5225995.** Reservations recommended. Main courses 13€–22€. No credit cards. Mon–Sat noon–3pm and 7:30–11pm. Vaporetto: Rialto or San Marco.

Nuova Rivetta *Value* SEAFOOD   Nuova Rivetta is an old-fashioned trattoria where you get good food at a good price. The most popular dish is *frittura di pesce,* a mixed fish fry that includes squid or various other "sea creatures" from the day's market. Other specialties are gnocchi stuffed with spider crab, pasticcio of fish (a main course), and spaghetti flavored with squid ink. The most typical wine is sparkling Prosecco, whose bouquet is refreshing and fruity with a slightly sharp flavor; for centuries it has been one of the most celebrated wines of the Veneto.

Campo San Filippo, Castello 4625. ⓒ 041-5287302. Reservations required. Main courses 7.75€–14€. AE, MC, V. Tues–Sun 10am–10pm. Closed July 23–Aug 20. Vaporetto: San Zaccaria.

Restaurant da Bruno VENETIAN   On a narrow street about halfway between the Rialto Bridge and Piazza San Marco, this "country taverna" grills its meats on an open-hearth fire. You get your antipasti at the counter and watch your prosciutto being prepared—paper-thin slices of spicy ham wrapped around bread-sticks *(grissini)*. In season, Bruno does some of Venice's finest game dishes; if featured, try its *capriolo* (roebuck) or its *fagiano* (pheasant). A typical Venetian dish prepared well here is *zuppa di pesce* (fish soup). Other specialties are beef filet with pepper sauce, scampi and calamari, veal scaloppini with wild mushrooms, and squid with polenta.

Calle del Paradiso, Castello 5731. ⓒ **041-5221480.** Main courses 8€–15€; fixed-price menu 14€. AE, DC, MC, V. Daily noon–3pm and 7–11pm. Vaporetto: San Marco or Rialto.

Ristorante Corte Sconta SEAFOOD   The Corte Sconta is behind a narrow storefront you'd ignore if you didn't know about this place. This modest restaurant boasts a multicolored marble floor, plain wooden tables, and not much of an attempt at decoration. It has become well known, however, as a gathering place for artists, writers, and filmmakers. As the depiction of the satyr chasing the mermaid above the entrance implies, it's a fish restaurant, serving a variety of grilled creatures (much of the "catch" is largely unknown in North America). The fresh fish is flawlessly fresh; the gamberi, for example, is placed live on the grill. A great start is marinated salmon with arugula and pomegranate seeds in olive oil. If you don't like fish, a tender beef fillet is available. The big bar is popular with locals.

Calle del Pestrin, Castello 3886. ⓒ **041-5227024.** Reservations required. Main courses 15€–30€; fixed-price menus 55€–60€. MC, V. Tues–Sat 12:30–2:30pm and 7:30–9:30pm. Closed Jan 7–Feb 7 and July 15–Aug 15. Vaporetto: Arsenale.

3 Near the Ponte di Rialto
EXPENSIVE

Al Graspo de Uva ⓡ SEAFOOD/VENETIAN   "The Bunch of Grapes" is a great place for a special meal. Decorated in old taverna style, it offers several air-conditioned dining rooms. One has a beamed ceiling, hung with garlic and copper bric-a-brac. Among Venice's best fish restaurants, it's hosted biggies like Liz Taylor,

Jeanne Moreau, and Giorgio de Chirico. You can help yourself to all the hors d'oeuvres you want (the menu tells you it's "self-service mammoth"). Next try the *gran fritto dell'Adriatico,* a mixed treat of deep-fried fish. The desserts are also good, especially the peach Melba.

Calle Bombaseri, San Marco 5094. © 041-5200150. Reservations required. Main courses 28€–35€. AE, DC, MC, V. Tues–Sun noon–3pm and 7–11pm. Closed Aug 5–20. Vaporetto: Rialto.

MODERATE

Fiaschetteria Toscana ⚔ *Value* VENETIAN There may be some rough points in the service at this hip restaurant (the staff is frantic), but lots of local foodies come here to celebrate special occasions or to soak in the see-and-be-seen ambiance. The dining rooms are on two levels; the upstairs level is somewhat more claustrophobic. In the evening, the downstairs is especially appealing with its romantic candlelit ambiance. Menu items include *frittura della Serenissima* (mixed platter of fried seafood with vegetables), veal scallops with lemon-Marsala sauce and mushrooms, ravioli stuffed with whitefish and herbs, and several kinds of Tuscan-style beefsteak.

Campo San Giovanni Crisostomo, Cannaregio 5719. © 041-5285281. Reservation required. Main courses 14€–30€. AE, DC, MC, V. Wed–Mon 12:30–2:30pm; Wed–Sun 7:30–10:30pm. Vaporetto: Rialto.

Il Milion VENETIAN With a tradition extending back more than 300 years and a location near the rear of San Giovanni Crisostomo, this restaurant is named after the book written by Marco Polo, *Il Milion,* describing his travels. In fact, it occupies a town house once owned by members of the explorer's family. The bar, incidentally, is a favorite with some of the gondoliers. The menu items read like a who's who of well-recognized Venetian platters, each fresh and well prepared. Examples are veal kidneys, calf's liver with fried onions, grilled sardines, spaghetti with clams, risotto with squid ink, and assorted fried fish. The staff is charming and friendly.

Corte Prima al Milion, Cannaregio 5841. © 041-5229302. Reservations recommended. Main courses 10€–20€. AE, MC, V. Thurs–Tues noon–3pm and 6:30–11pm. Closed Aug. Vaporetto: Rialto.

Il Sole Sulla Vecia Cavana ⚔ *Finds* SEAFOOD This restaurant is off the tourist circuit and well worth the trek through the winding streets. A *cavana* is a place where gondolas are parked, a sort of liquid garage, and the site of this restaurant was such a place in the

Middle Ages. When you enter, you'll be greeted by brick arches, stone columns, terra-cotta floors, framed modern paintings, and a photo of 19th-century fishermen relaxing after a day's work. The menu specializes in seafood, like a mixed grill from the Adriatic, fried scampi, fresh sole, squid, three types of risotto (each with seafood), and a spicy *zuppa di pesce*. *Antipasti di pesce Cavana* is an assortment of just about every sea creature. The food is authentic and seems prepared for the Venetian palate—not necessarily for the visitor's.

Rio Terrà SS. Apostoli, Cannaregio 4624. ⓒ **041-5287106.** Main courses 16€– 22€; fixed-price menu 20€. AE, DC, MC, V. Tues–Sun noon–3pm and 6:30– 10:30pm. Vaporetto: Ca' d'Oro.

Poste Vecie 🎄 SEAFOOD   This charming restaurant is near the Rialto fish market and connected to the rest of the city by a small, privately owned bridge. It opened in the early 1500s as a post office, and the kitchen used to serve food to fortify the mail carriers. Today it's the oldest restaurant in Venice, with a pair of intimate rooms (both graced with paneling, murals, and 16th-century mantelpieces) and a courtyard. Menu items include fresh fish from the nearby markets; a salad of shellfish and exotic mushrooms; tagliolini fla-vored with squid ink, crabmeat, and fish sauce; and the pièce de résistance, *seppie* (cuttlefish) *à la veneziana* with polenta. If you don't like fish, calf's liver or veal shank with ham and cheese are also well prepared. The desserts come rolling to your table on a trolley and are usually delicious.

Pescheria Rialto, San Polo 1608. ⓒ **041-721822.** Reservations recommended. Main courses 12€–24€. AE, DC, MC, V. Wed–Mon noon–3:30pm and 7–10:30pm. Vaporetto: Rialto.

Ristorante al Mondo Novo VENETIAN/SEAFOOD   In a Renaissance building, with a dining room outfitted in a regional style, this restaurant offers professional service and a kindly staff. Plus, it stays open later than many of its nearby competitors. Menu items include a selection of seafood, prepared fried or charcoal grilled. Other items are *maccheroni alla verdura* (with fresh vegeta-bles and greens), an antipasti of fresh fish, and beef fillets with pepper sauce and rissole potatoes. Locals who frequent the place always order the fresh fish, because the owner is a wholesaler in the Rialto fish market.

Salizzada di San Lio, Castello 5409. ⓒ **041-5200698.** Reservations recommended. Main courses 18€–31€. AE, DC, MC, V. Daily 11:30am–11pm. Vaporetto: Rialto or San Marco.

Rosticceria San Bartolomeo VENETIAN/ITALIAN This *rosticceria* is Venice's most popular fast-food place and has long been a blessing for cost-conscious travelers. Downstairs is a *tavola calda* ("hot table") where you can eat standing up, but upstairs is a restaurant with waiter service. Typical dishes are *baccalà alla vicentina* (codfish simmered in herbs and milk), deep-fried mozzarella (which the Italians call *in carrozza*), and *seppie con polenta* (squid in its own ink sauce, served with polenta). Everything is accompanied by typical Veneto wine.

Calle della Bissa, San Marco 5424. ✆ **041-5223569.** Main courses 10€–25€. AE, DC, MC, V. Tues–Sun 9am–9pm (Easter–Nov 14 and for Carnevale open daily). Vaporetto: Rialto.

Trattoria alla Madonna VENETIAN No, this place has nothing to do with *that* Madonna. It opened in 1954 in a 300-year-old building and is one of Venice's most characteristic trattorie, specializing in traditional Venetian recipes and grilled fresh fish. A good beginning might be the *antipasto frutti di mare.* Pastas, polentas, risottos, meats (including *fegato alla veneziana,* liver with onions), and many kinds of irreproachably fresh fish are widely available. Many creatures of the sea are displayed in a refrigerated case near the entrance.

Calle della Madonna, San Polo 594. ✆ 041-5223824. Reservations recommended but not always accepted. Main courses 12€–20€. AE, MC, V. Thurs–Tues noon–3pm and 7:15–10pm. Closed Dec 24 through Jan and Aug 4–17. Vaporetto: Rialto.

INEXPENSIVE

Ai Tre Spiedi *Value* VENETIAN Venetians bring their visiting friends here to make a good impression without breaking the bank, and then swear them to secrecy. Rarely will you find as pleasant a setting and as appetizing a meal as in this casually elegant trattoria with exposed beam ceilings and some of the most reasonably priced fresh-fish dining that will keep meat-eaters happy as well. If you order à la carte, ask the English-speaking waiters to estimate the cost of your fish entree, since it'll typically appear priced by the *etto* (100g).

Salizzada San Cazian, Cannaregio 5906. ✆ 041-5208035. Main courses 9.50€–13€. AE, MC, V. Tues–Sat noon–2:30pm and 7–9:30pm, Sun 12:30–3:30pm. Vaporetto: Rialto.

Tiziano Bar SANDWICHES/PASTA/PIZZA The Tiziano Bar is a *tavola calda* ("hot table"). There's no waiter service; you eat standing at a counter or sitting on one of the high stools. The place is known in Venice for selling pizza by the yard. From noon to 3pm, it serves hot pastas such as rigatoni and cannelloni. But throughout the day you can order sandwiches or perhaps a plate of mozzarella.

Salizzada San Crisostomo, Cannaregio 5747, in front of the Sanctuary. © 041-5235544. Main courses 7€–9.50€. No credit cards. Daily 7:30am–10:30pm. Vaporetto: Rialto.

4 In Santa Croce

MODERATE

Trattoria Antica Besseta *Finds* VENETIAN   If you manage to find this place (go with a good map), you'll be rewarded with true Venetian cuisine at its most unpretentious. Head for Campo San Giacomo dell'Orio; then negotiate your way across infrequently visited piazzas and winding alleys. Push through saloon doors into a bar area filled with modern art. The dining room is hung with paintings and illuminated with wagon-wheel chandeliers. Nereo Volpe, his wife Mariuccia, and one of their sons are the guiding force, the chefs, the buyers, and even the "talking menus." The food depends on what looked good in the market that morning, so the menu could include roast chicken, fried scampi, *fritto misto*, spaghetti in sardine sauce, various roasts, and a selection from the day's catch. The Volpe family produces two kinds of their own wine, a pinot blanc and a cabernet.

Campo SS. de Ca' Zusto, Santa Croce 1395. © 041-721687. Reservations required. Main courses 13€–25€. AE, MC, V. Thurs–Mon noon–2:30pm and 7–10:30pm. Vaporetto: Riva di Biasio.

5 In San Polo

EXPENSIVE

Osteria da Fiore *Finds* SEAFOOD   The breath of the Adriatic seems to blow through this place, though how the wind finds this little restaurant tucked away in a labyrinth is a mystery. An imaginative fare is served, depending on the availability of fresh fish and produce. If you have a love of maritime foods, you'll find everything from scampi (a sweet Adriatic prawn, cooked in as many ways as there are chefs) to granzeola, a type of spider crab. In days gone by, we've sampled fried calamari (cuttlefish), risotto with scampi, tagliata with rosemary, masenette (tiny green crabs you eat shell and all), and canoce (mantis shrimp). For your wine, we suggest Prosecco, with a distinctive golden-yellow color and a bouquet that's refreshing and fruity. The proprietors extend a hearty welcome to match their fare.

Calle del Scaleter, San Polo 2202. ☎ **041-721308**. Reservations required. Main courses 34€–43€. AE, DC, MC, V. Tues–Sat 12:30–2:30pm and 8–10:30pm. Closed 3 weeks in Aug and Dec 25–Jan 14. Vaporetto: San Tomà.

6 In Dorsoduro

MODERATE

La Furatola SEAFOOD   La Furatola is very much a neighborhood hangout, but it has captured the imagination of local foodies. It occupies a 300-year-old building, along a narrow flagstone-paved street that you'll need a good map and a lot of patience to find. Perhaps you'll have lunch here after a visit to San Rocco, a short distance away. In the simple dining room, the specialty is fish brought to your table in a wicker basket so you can judge its size and freshness by its bright eyes and red gills. A display of seafood antipasti is set out near the entrance. A standout is the baby octopus boiled and eaten with a drop of red-wine vinegar. Eel comes with a medley of mixed fried fish, including baby cuttlefish, prawns, and squid rings.

Calle Lunga San Barnaba, Dorsoduro 2870A. ☎ **041-5208594**. Reservations required. Main courses 20€–25€. AE, DC, MC, V. Fri–Sun 12:30–3pm; Fri–Mon 7:30–10:30pm. Closed Aug and Jan. Vaporetto: Ca' Rezzonico.

Locanda Montin ☆ INTERNATIONAL/ITALIAN   The Montin opened after World War II, and has hosted Ezra Pound, Jackson Pollock, Mark Rothko, and the artist friends of the late Peggy Guggenheim. It's owned and run by the Carretins, who have covered the walls with paintings donated by or bought from their many friends and guests. The arbor-covered garden courtyard is filled with regulars, many of whom allow their favorite waiter to select most of the items for their meal. The frequently changing menu includes a variety of salads, grilled meats, and fish caught in the Adriatic. Desserts might include *semifreddo di fragoline,* a tempting chilled liqueur-soaked cake, capped with whipped cream and wild strawberries.

Fondamenta di Borgo, Dorsoduro 1147. ☎ **041-5227151**. Reservations recommended. Main courses 14€–20€. AE, DC, MC, V. Thurs–Tues 12:30–2:30pm; Thurs–Mon 7:30–9:30pm. Closed 10 days in mid-Aug and 20 days in Jan. Vaporetto: Accademia.

7 On Isola della Giudecca

VERY EXPENSIVE

Ristorante Cipriani ☆☆☆ ITALIAN   The grandest of the hotel restaurants, the Cipriani offers a sublime but relatively simple cuisine, with the freshest of ingredients used by one of the best-trained staffs along the Adriatic. This isn't the place to bring the kids—in fact, children under 6 aren't allowed (a babysitter can be arranged). You can dine in the formal room with Murano chandeliers and Fortuny curtains when the weather is nippy, or on the extensive terrace overlooking the lagoon. Freshly made pasta is a specialty, and it's among the finest we've ever sampled. Try the *taglierini verdi* with noodles and ham au gratin. Chef's specialties include mixed fried scampi and squid with tender vegetables and sautéed veal fillets with spring artichokes. Come here in October for the last Bellinis of the white-peach season and the first white truffles of the season served in champagne risotto.

In the Hotel Cipriani, Isola della Giudecca 10. ℂ 041-5207744. Reservations required. Main courses 38€–43€. AE, DC, MC, V. Daily 12:30–3pm and 8–10:30pm. Closed Nov–Mar. Vaporetto: Zitelle.

EXPENSIVE

Harry's Dolci 𝒜 INTERNATIONAL/ITALIAN   The people at the famed Harry's Bar (see listing earlier in this chapter) have established their latest enclave far from the maddening crowds of Piazza San Marco on this little-visited island. From the quay-side windows of this chic place, you can watch seagoing vessels, from yachts to lagoon barges. White napery and uniformed waiters grace a modern room, where no one minds if you order only coffee and ice cream or perhaps a selection from the large pastry menu (the zabaglione cake is divine). Popular items are carpaccio Cipriani, chicken salad, club sandwiches, gnocchi, and house-style cannelloni. The dishes are deliberately kept simple, but each is well prepared.

Fondamenta San Biago 773, Isola della Giudecca. ℂ 041-5208337. Reservations recommended, especially Sat–Sun. Main courses 28€–31€; fixed-price menu 50€. AE, MC, V. Wed–Mon noon–3pm and 7–10:30pm. Closed Nov 1–Mar 30. Vaporetto: Santa Eufemia.

8 On the Lido

MODERATE

Favorita SEAFOOD   Occupying two rustic dining rooms and a garden, Favorita has thrived here since the 1920s, operated by the Pradel family, now in their third generation of ownership. Their years of experience contribute to flavorful, impeccably prepared seafood and shellfish, many of them grilled. Try the *trenette* (spaghetti-like pasta) with baby squid and eggplant, potato-based gnocchi with crabs from the Venetian lagoon, or grilled versions of virtually every fish in the Adriatic, including eel, sea bass, turbot, and sole.

Via Francesco Duodo 33, Lido di Venezia. ✆ **041-5261626**. Main courses 13€–20€. AE, DC, MC, V. Tues–Sun 12:30–2:30pm and 7:30–10:30pm. Vaporetto: Lido di Venezia.

Ristorante Belvedere VENETIAN   Outside the big hotels, the best food on the Lido is served at the Belvedere, across from the vaporetto stop. It attracts a lot of locals, who come here knowing they can get some of the best fish along the Adriatic. Tables are placed outside, and there's a glass-enclosed portion for windy days. The main dining room is attractive, with cane-backed bentwood chairs and big windows. In back, reached through a separate entrance, is a busy cafe. Main dishes include the chef's special sea bass, grilled dorade (or sole), and fried scampi. You might begin with the special fish antipasti or *spaghetti en papillote* (cooked in parchment).

Piazzale Santa Maria Elisabetta 4, Lido di Venezia. ✆ **041-5260115**. Reservations recommended. Main courses 8.30€–16€. AE, DC, MC, V. Tues–Sun noon–2:30pm and 7–9:30pm. Closed Nov 4 to Easter. Vaporetto: Lido.

9 The Lagoon Islands of Murano, Burano & Torcello

ON MURANO

Ai Vetrai VENETIAN   Ai Vetrai entertains and nourishes its guests in a large room not far from the Canale dei Vetrai. If you're looking for fish prepared in the local style, with arguably the widest selection on Murano, this is it. Most varieties of crustaceans and gilled creatures are available on the spot. However, if you phone ahead and order food for a large party, as the Venetians sometimes do, the owners will prepare what they call "a noble fish." You might begin with spaghetti in green clam sauce and follow with *griglia misto di pesce,* a dish that combines all the seafood of the Adriatic or other types of grilled or baked fish accented with vegetables.

Fondamenta Manin 29. ✆ **041-739293**. Reservations recommended. Main courses 8€–15€. AE, DC, MC, V. Daily 9am–7pm. Closed Jan. Vaporetto: 41.

ON BURANO

Ostaria ai Pescatori SEAFOOD   This restaurant opened 200 years ago in a building that was antique even then. Today, Paolo Torcellan and his wife are the gracious owners, serving a cuisine prepared with gusto by his stalwart mother, Iolanda, who is in her seventies. The place has gained a reputation as the preserver of a type of simple restaurant unique to Burano. Patrons often take the vaporetto from other sections of Venice (the restaurant lies close to the boat landing) to eat at the plain wooden tables set up indoors or on the small square in front. Specialties feature all the staples of the Venetian seaside diet, like fish soup, *risotto di pesce*, pasta seafarer style, *tagliolini* in squid ink, and a wide range of crustaceans, plus grilled, fried, and baked fish. Dishes prepared with local game are also available, but you must request them two or three days in advance. Your meal might include a bottle of fruity wine from the region.

Piazza Baldassare Galuppi 371. ✆ **041-730650.** Reservations recommended. Main courses 13€–20€. AE, DC, MC, V. Thurs–Tues noon–3pm and 6–9:30pm. Closed Jan. Vaporetto: Line 12 or 52.

Trattoria de Romano VENETIAN   If you're on the island at mealtime, you may want to join a long line of people who enjoy this rather simple-looking spot around the corner from the lace school. It was founded in 1920 by the Nono family, whose grandchildren continue to manage it today. You can enjoy a superb dinner here, perhaps *fritto misto di pesce,* a mixed fish fry from the Adriatic with savory bits of mullet, squid, and shrimp, or risotto *nero de seppia* (flavored with squid ink).

Via Baldassare Galuppi 221, Burano. ✆ **041-730030.** Reservations recommended. Main courses 13€–18€. AE, MC, V. Wed–Mon noon–3pm and 7–9pm. Closed Dec 15–Jan 31. Vaporetto: 12 or 52.

ON TORCELLO
Locanda Cipriani 𝆎𝆎 VENETIAN   This place is operated by the same folks behind the Hotel Cipriani and Harry's Bar (actually by the very cosmopolitan Bonifacio Brass, nephew of Harry Cipriani). This artfully simple locanda is deliberately rustic, light-years removed from the family's grander venues. Menu items are uncompromisingly classic, with deep roots in family tradition. A good example is *filleto di San Pietro alla Carlina* (fillet of John Dory in the style of Carla, a late and much-revered matriarch, who made the dish for decades using tomatoes and capers). Also look for carpaccio Cipriani, *risotto alla Torcellano* (with fresh vegetables and herbs from the family's garden), fish soup, *tagliolini verdi gratinati* (pasta with ham and a creamy cheese sauce), and a traditional roster of veal, liver, fish, and beef dishes.

Piazza San Fosca 29, Torcello. ✆ **041-730150.** Reservations recommended. Main courses 20€–26€. AE, DC, MC, V. Wed–Mon noon–3pm; Fri–Sat 7–10pm. Closed Jan 15–Feb 15. Vaporetto: Line 12 and 14.

Exploring Venice

Centuries ago, in an effort to flee barbarians, Venetians left dry dock and drifted out to a flotilla of "uninhabitable" islands in the lagoon. Survival was difficult enough, but no Venetian has ever settled for mere survival. The remote ancestors of the present inhabitants created the world's most beautiful city. To your children's children, however, Venice may be nothing more than a legend. It's sinking at a rate of about 2½ inches per decade. Estimates are that if no action is taken soon, one-third of the city's art will deteriorate hopelessly within the next decade or so. Clearly, Venice is in peril. One recent headline proclaimed, "The Enemy's at the Gates."

But for however long Venice lasts, decaying or not, it will be one of the highlights of your trip through Italy. It lacks the speeding cars and roaring Vespas of Rome; instead, you make your way through the city either by boat or on foot. The situation would be ideal if it weren't for the hordes of tourists that descend every year, overwhelming the squares and making the streets almost impossible to navigate. In the sultry summer heat of the Adriatic, the canals become a smelly stew. Steamy and overcrowded July and August are the worst times to visit; May, June, September, and October are much better.

Although Venice is one of the world's most enchanting cities, you do pay a price, literally and figuratively, for all this beauty. Venice is virtually selling its past to the world, even more so than Florence, and anybody who has been here leaves complaining about the outrageous prices, which can be double what they are elsewhere in the country. Since the 19th century, Venice has thrived on its visitors, but these high prices have forced out many locals. They've fled across the lagoon to dreary Mestre, an industrial complex launched to help boost the regional economy.

Today the city is trying belatedly to undo the damage its watery environs and tourist-based economy have wrought. In 1993, after a 30-year hiatus, the canals were again dredged in an attempt to reduce water loss and reduce the stench brought in with the low tides. In an effort to curb residential migration to Mestre, state subsidies are now being offered to the citizens of Venice as an incentive to not only stay but also to renovate their crumbling properties.

Despite all its problems and relatively modest plans (so far) for saving itself, Venice still endures. But for how long? That is the question.

In the pages ahead, we'll explore the city's great art and architecture. But, unlike Florence, Venice rewards its guests with treasures even if they never duck inside a museum or church. Take some time just to stroll and let yourself get lost in this gorgeous city.

1 St. Mark's Square (Piazza San Marco)

Piazza San Marco 🐾🐾🐾 was the heart of Venice in the heyday of its glory as a seafaring republic. If you have only 1 day for Venice, you need not leave the square, because some of the city's major attractions, like St. Mark's Basilica and the Doge's Palace, are centered here or nearby.

The traffic-free square, frequented by visitors and pigeons and sometimes even by Venetians, is a source of bewilderment and interest. If you rise at dawn, you can almost have the piazza to yourself, and as you watch the sun come up, the sheen of gold mosaics glistens with a mystical beauty. At around 9am, the overstuffed pigeons are fed by the city (if you're caught under the whir, you'll think you're witnessing a remake of Hitchcock's *The Birds*). At mid-afternoon the tourists reign supreme, and it's not surprising in July to witness a scuffle over a camera angle. At sunset, when the two Moors in the Clock Tower strike the end of another day, lonely sailors begin a usually frustrated search for those hot spots that characterized the Venice of yore. Deeper into the evening, the strollers parade by or stop for an espresso at the Caffè Florian and sip while listening to the orchestra play.

Thanks to Napoleon, the square was unified architecturally. The emperor added the Fabbrica Nuova facing the basilica, thus bridging the Old and New Procuratie on either side. Flanked with medieval-looking palaces, the Sansovino Library, elegant shops, and colonnades, the square is now finished—unlike Piazza della Signoria in Florence.

If Piazza San Marco is Europe's drawing room, then the piazza's satellite, **Piazzetta San Marco** 🐾, is Europe's antechamber. Hedged in by the Doge's Palace, Sansovino Library, and a side of St. Mark's, the tiny square faces the Grand Canal. Two tall granite columns grace the square. One is surmounted by a winged lion, representing

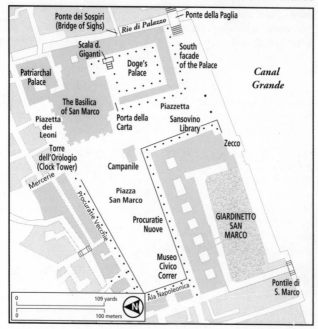

St. Mark. The other is topped by a statue of a man taming a dragon, supposedly the dethroned patron saint Theodore. Both columns came from the East in the 12th century.

During Venice's heyday, dozens of victims either lost their heads or were strung up here, many of them first being subjected to torture that would've made the Marquis de Sade flinch. One, for example, had his teeth hammered in, his eyes gouged out, and his hands cut off before being strung up. Venetian justice became notorious throughout Europe. If you stand with your back to the canal, looking toward the south facade of St. Mark's, you'll see the so-called *Virgin and Child of the Poor Baker,* a mosaic honoring Pietro Fasiol (also Faziol), a young man unjustly sentenced to death on a charge of murder.

To the left of the entrance to the Doge's Palace are four porphyry figures, whom, for want of a better description, the Venetians called "Moors." These puce-colored fellows are huddled close together, as if afraid. Considering the decapitations and tortures that have occurred on the piazzetta, it's no wonder.

Venice Attractions

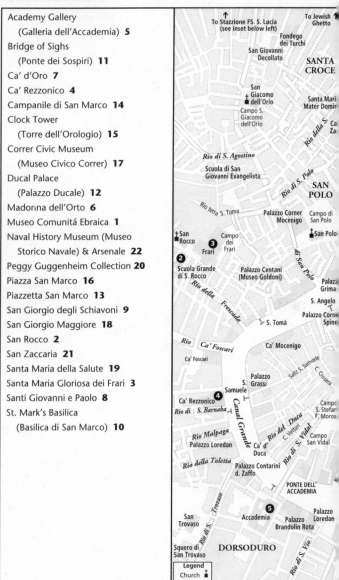

CANNAREGIO

Ca' Pesaro
Palazzo
Fontana
Ca' d'Oro ⑦
Palazzo
Sagredo
Palazzo
Michiel
d.Colonne
Santi Apostoli
Campo SS
Apostoli
Strada Nuova
Rio della Panada
Pescaria
Canal Grande
Rio D. Sante
Rio di
S.G. Crisostomo
Apostoli
Rio delle Beccarie
Fond. delle Prigioni
Ca' da Mosto
S. Giovanni
Crisostomo
S.M. dei
Miracoli
Palazzo
Sanudo ⑧
C. del Campanile
Calle D. Botteri
Rio delle
San Giovanni
Elemosinario
San Giacomo
di Rialto
PONTE
DI RIALTO
Fondaco
die Tedeschi
Rio di S. Marina
Palazzo dei
Dieci Savi
Campo S.
Aponal
San
Silvestro
Rio del Vin
Palazzo
Bembo
San
Bartolomeo
Palazzo
Dolfin-Manin
Rialto
C. Stagneri
Salizzada S. Liq.
Palazzo
Priuli
Pal.
Donà
Campo
S. Maria
Formosa
Rio della Fava
S. Silvestro
Riva del Carbon
Pal.
Dandolo
San
Salvatore
Merc S. Salvador
Merc S.
Santa Maria
della Fava
C. Bande
Palazzo Querini-
Stampalia
Palazzo
Loredan
Pal. Grimari
San
Benedetto
Rio di S. Luca
San Luca
Campo
S. Luca
Calle Cavalli
Salvadore
C. Guerra
CASTELLO
(see inset below right)
Rio di S. Salvatore
Campo
Manin
C. dei Fuseri
C. dei Goldoni
C. della Mandola
Rio dei Barcaroli
Pal. Contarini
del Bovolo
C. Fiubera
C. Specchieri
Merc. Orologio
C. Spadaria
C. Larga S. Marco
C. Canonica
Palazzo
Trevisan-
Cappello ⑨
Sant'
Apollonia
Ateneo
Veneto
Campo
S. Angelo
Campo
S. Fantin
Pisc. di Frezzeria
Bacino
Orseolo
Frezzeria
⑰
Piazza
San Marco
⑯
⑮
Pal. Patriarcale
⑩
Basilica di
San Marco
Rio di Palazzo
⑪
Teatro
La Fenice
Rio delle Veste
SAN MARCO
Ascension
⑭
⑫
Piazzetta
San Marco
Palazzo
Ducale
C. Mandola
C. Larga XXII Marzo
S.S. Moise
C. Vallaresso
⑬
Campo S.M.
Zobenigo
C. del Traghetto
C. Contarini
San
Moisè
C. Ricotto
GIARDINETTI
REALI
Molo
To Riva degli Schiavoni
(see inset below right)
Rio di S.M.
Zobenigo
Rio di S. Moise
San Marco
Vallaresso
San Marco
Giardinetti ⑱
The Lido
Palazzi
Contarini
S.M. del
Giglio
Punta della
Dogana
Castello & Riva degli Schiavoni
Pal.
enier
Leoni
⑳
Palazzo
Dario
Santa Maria
della Salute
San
Gregorio
Dogana
al Mare
Seminario
Patriarcale
⑲
Rio D. Fornier
Rio di S. Gregorio
㉑
Riva
Rio del Greci
Rio della Pietà
degli
Schiavoni
Cl. del Dose
Cl. del Forno
Cl. del Forno
Cl. della Pescaria
Cl. della Cappollera
P. de la
Ca' di Dio
Riva de la Ca' di Dio
Cp. de
l'Arsenale
Arsenale
Cl. dei Forni
㉒
P. de l'Arsenal
Bacino San Marco

0   1/8 mi
0   125 meters

89

A St. Mark's Warning

A dress code for men and women prohibiting shorts, bare arms and shoulders, and skirts above the knee is strictly enforced at all times in the basilica. You *will* be turned away. In addition, you must remain silent and cannot take photographs.

St. Mark's Basilica (Basilica di San Marco) ⋆⋆⋆ Dominating Piazza San Marco is the Church of Gold (Chiesa d'Oro), one of the world's greatest and most richly embellished churches, its cavernous candlelit interior gilded with mosaics added over some 7 centuries. The basilica is a conglomeration of styles, though it's particularly indebted to Byzantium. In fact, it looks as if it was moved intact from Istanbul. Like Venice, St. Mark's is adorned with booty from every corner of the city's once far-flung mercantile empire: capitals from Sicily, columns from Alexandria, porphyry from Syria, and sculpture from old Constantinople.

The basilica is capped by a dome that, like a spider plant, sends off shoots, in this case a quartet of smaller-scale bulbed cupolas. Spanning the facade is a loggia, surmounted by replicas of the four famous St. Mark's horses, the *Triumphal Quadriga*. The facade's rich marble slabs and mosaics depict scenes from the lives of Christ and St. Mark. One of the mosaics re-creates the entry of the evangelist's body into Venice—according to legend, St. Mark's body, hidden in a pork barrel, was smuggled out of Alexandria in A.D. 828 and shipped to Venice. The evangelist dethroned Theodore, the Greek saint who up until then had been the patron of the city that had outgrown him.

In the **atrium** are six cupolas with mosaics illustrating scenes from the Old Testament, including the story of the Tower of Babel. The interior of the basilica, once the private chapel and pantheon of the doges, is a stunning wonderland of marbles, alabaster, porphyry, and pillars. You'll walk in awe across the undulating multicolored ocean floor, patterned with mosaics.

To the right is the **baptistry**, dominated by the Sansovino-inspired baptismal font, upon which John the Baptist is ready to pour water. If you look back at the aperture over the entry, you can see a mosaic of the dance of Salome in front of Herod and his court. Salome, wearing a star-studded russet-red dress and three white fox tails, is dancing under a platter holding John the Baptist's head. Her glassy face is that of a Madonna, not an enchantress.

After touring the baptistry, proceed up the right nave to the doorway to the oft-looted **treasury** *(tesoro)* ⊕. Here you'll find the inevitable skulls and bones of some ecclesiastical authorities under glass, plus goblets, chalices, and Gothic candelabra. The entrance to the **presbytery** is nearby. In it, on the high altar, the alleged sarcophagus of St. Mark rests under a green marble blanket and is held by four Corinthian alabaster columns. Behind the altar is the rarest treasure at St. Mark's: the **Pala d'Oro** ⊕⊕⊕, a Byzantine-style golden altar screen measuring 10 feet by 4 feet. It's set with 300 emeralds, 300 sapphires, 400 garnets, 90 amethysts, and 1,300 pearls, plus rubies and topazes accompanying 157 enameled rondels and panels. Second in importance is the 10th-century *Madonna di Nicopeia,* a bejeweled icon taken from Constantinople and exhibited in its own chapel to the left of the high altar.

On leaving the basilica, head up the stairs in the atrium to the **Marciano Museum** and the **Loggia dei Cavalli.** The star of the museum is the world-famous *Triumphal Quadriga* ⊕⊕⊕, four horses looted from Constantinople by Venetian crusaders during the sack of that city in 1204. These horses once surmounted the basilica but were removed because of pollution damage and subsequently restored. This is the only *quadriga* (a quartet of horses yoked together) to have survived from the classical era. It's believed to have been cast in the 4th century. Napoleon once carted these much-traveled horses off to Paris for the Arc de Triomphe du Carrousel, but they were returned to Venice in 1815. The museum, with its mosaics and tapestries, is especially interesting, but also be sure to walk out onto the loggia for a view of Piazza San Marco.

Piazza San Marco. ℂ **041-5225205.** Basilica, free; treasury, 2€; presbytery, 1.50€; Marciano Museum, 1.50€. Basilica and presbytery Apr–Sept Mon–Sat 9:30am–5:30pm, Sun 2–5:30pm; Oct–Mar Mon–Sat 10am–4:30pm, Sun 2–4:30pm. Treasury Mon–Sat 9:30am–5pm, Sun 2–5pm. Marciano Museum Apr–Sept Mon–Sat 10am–5:30pm, Sun 2–4:30pm; Oct–Mar Mon–Sat 10am–4:45pm, Sun 2–4:30pm. Vaporetto: San Marco.

Impressions

Venice is like eating an entire box of chocolate liqueurs at one go.

—Truman Capote

Campanile di San Marco 𝒜𝒜   One summer night in 1902, the bell tower of St. Mark's, suffering from years of rheumatism in the damp Venetian climate, gave out a warning sound that sent the fashionable coffee drinkers in the piazza below scurrying for their lives. But the campanile gracefully waited until the next morning, July 14, before tumbling into the piazza. The Venetians rebuilt their belfry, and it's now safe to climb to the top. Unlike Italy's other bell towers, where you have to brave narrow, steep spiral staircases to reach the top, this one has an elevator so that you can get a pigeon's-eye view. It's a particularly good vantage point for viewing the cupolas of the basilica.

Piazza San Marco. 🕿 041-5224064. Admission 6€. Oct–Feb daily 9:30am–4pm; Mar–June daily 9am–7pm; July–Sept daily 9am–9pm. Closed Jan 7–31. Vaporetto: San Marco.

Clock Tower (Torre dell'Orologio)   The two Moors striking the bell atop this Renaissance clock tower, soaring over the Old Procuratie, are one of the most characteristic Venetian scenes. The clock under the winged lion not only tells the time but also is a boon to the astrologer: It matches the signs of the zodiac with the position of the sun. If the movement of the Moors striking the hour seems slow in today's fast-paced world, remember how many centuries the poor wretches have been at their task without time off. The "Moors" originally represented two European shepherds, but after having been reproduced in bronze, they've grown darker with the passing of time. As a consequence, they came to be called "Moors" by the Venetians.

The base of the tower has always been a favorite *punto di incontro* (meeting point) for Venetians and is the entrance to the ancient **Mercerie** (from the word for merchandise), the principal souklike retail street of both high-end boutiques and trinket shops that zigzags its way to the Rialto Bridge.

The clock tower was closed for years, despite original plans to reopen it in time for the 500-year anniversary of its construction in 1996. The clock mechanism has been getting a cleaning up by Piaget, the sponsor of its elaborate renovation. It didn't make a revised timetable (to ring in the Jubilee Year 2000), and the latest estimate is that it will be completed in summer of 2004. Visits to the top will resume upon the tower's reopening. The cost of admission was tentatively slated to be 3€; hours were planned to be daily from 9:45am to 4pm.

Piazza San Marco. 🕿 041-5224951. Vaporetto: San Marco.

Ducal Palace & Bridge of Sighs (Palazzo Ducale & Ponte dei Sospiri) ★★★   You enter the Palace of the Doges through the magnificent 15th-century **Porta della Carta** ★★ at the piazzetta. This Venetian Gothic palazzo gleams in the tremulous light somewhat like a frosty birthday cake in pinkish-red marble and white Istrian stone. Italy's grandest civic structure, it dates to 1309, though a 1577 fire destroyed much of the original building. That fire made ashes of many of the palace's masterpieces and almost spelled doom for the building itself, because the new architectural fervor of the post-Renaissance was in the air. However, sanity prevailed. Many of the greatest Venetian painters of the 16th century contributed to the restored palace, replacing the canvases or frescoes of the old masters.

If you enter from the piazzetta, past the four porphyry Moors, you'll be in the splendid Renaissance courtyard, one of the most recent additions to a palace that has benefited from the work of many architects with widely varying tastes. To get to the upper loggia, you can take the **Giants' Stairway (Scala dei Giganti),** so called because of the two Sansovino statues of mythological figures.

If you want to understand something of this magnificent palace, the fascinating history of the 1,000-year-old maritime republic, and the intrigue of the government that ruled it, search out the infrared **audioguide** at the entrance, costing 4.50€. Unless you can tag along with an English-language tour group, you may otherwise miss out on the importance of much of what you're seeing.

After climbing the Sansovino stairway, you'll enter some get-acquainted rooms. Proceed to the **Sala di Antecollegio,** housing the palace's greatest works, notably Veronese's *Rape of Europa,* to the far left on the right wall. Tintoretto is well represented with his *Three Graces* and *Bacchus and Ariadne.* Some critics consider the latter his supreme achievement. The ceiling in the adjoining **Sala del Collegio** bears allegorical paintings by Veronese. As you proceed to the right, you'll enter the **Sala del Senato o Pregadi,** with its allegorical painting by Tintoretto in the ceiling's center.

It was in the **Sala del Consiglio dei Dieci,** with its gloomy paintings, that the dreaded Council of Ten (often called the Terrible Ten, for good reason) used to assemble to decide who was in need of decapitation. In the antechamber, bills of accusation were dropped in the lion's mouth.

The excitement continues downstairs. You can wander through the once-private apartments of the doges to the grand **Maggior Consiglio,** with Veronese's allegorical *Triumph of Venice* on the ceiling. The most outstanding feature, however, is over the Grand

Council chamber: Tintoretto's *Paradise,* said to be the world's largest oil painting. Paradise seems to have an overpopulation problem, perhaps reflecting Tintoretto's too-optimistic point of view (he was in his seventies when he began this monumental work and died 6 years later). The second grandiose hall, which you enter from the grand chamber, is the **Sala dello Scrutinio,** with paintings telling of Venice's past glories.

Reentering the Maggior Consiglio, follow the arrows on their trail across the **Bridge of Sighs (Ponte dei Sospiri)** ☾☾, linking the Doge's Palace with the Palazzo delle Prigioni. Here you'll see the cell blocks that once lodged the prisoners who felt the quick justice of the Terrible Ten. The changing roster of the Terrible Ten was a series of state inquisitors appointed by the city of Venice to dispense justice to the citizens. This often meant torture on the rack even for what could be viewed as a minor infraction. The reputation of the Terrible Ten for the ferocity of their sentences became infamous in Europe. The "sighs" in the bridge's name stem from the sad laments of the numerous victims forced across it to face certain torture and possible death. The cells are somber remnants of the horror of medieval justice.

If you're really intrigued by the palace, you may want to check out the **Secret Trails of the Palazzo Ducale (Itinerari Segreti del Palazzo Ducale).** These 12.50€ guided tours, given by appointment only, are so popular they've recently been introduced in English; tours start daily at 9:50am, 10:30am, and 11:30am (you must reserve in advance at the ticket-buyers' entrance or by calling **041-5209070**). You'll peek into otherwise restricted quarters and hidden passageways of this enormous palace, such as the doge's private chambers and the torture chambers where prisoners were interrogated. The tour is offered in Italian daily at 10am and noon.

Piazzetta San Marco. ☎ **041-5224951.** Admission 9.50€. (Includes admission to Civic Museum, reviewed below.) Mar–Oct daily 9am–5:30pm; Nov–Feb daily 9am–5pm. Vaporetto: San Marco.

2 The Grand Canal (Canal Grande) ☆☆☆

Peoria may have its Main Street, Paris its Champs-Elysées, New York City its Fifth Avenue—but Venice, for uniqueness, tops them all with its **Canal Grande.** Lined with palazzi (many in the Venetian Gothic style), this great road of water is filled with vaporetti, motorboats, and gondolas. The boat moorings are like peppermint sticks. The canal begins at Piazzetta San Marco on one side and Longhena's La Salute

Tips   Venice by Gondola

You and your gondolier have two major agreements to reach: the price and the length of the ride. If you aren't careful, you're likely to be taken on both counts. It's a common sight to see a gondolier huffing and puffing to take his passengers on a "quickie," often reducing an hour to 15 minutes.

The "official" rate is 62€ per hour, but we've never known anyone to honor it. The actual fare depends on how well you stand up to the gondolier, *beginning* at 100€ for up to 50 minutes. Most gondoliers will ask at least double the "official" rate and reduce your trip to 30 to 40 minutes or even less. Prices go up after 8pm. In fairness to them, we must say their job is hard and has been overly romanticized: They row boatloads of tourists across hot, smelly canals with such endearments screamed at them as, "No sing! No pay!" And these fellows have to make plenty of lire while the sun shines, because their work ends when the first cold winds blow in from the Adriatic.

A word to the wise: Try to schedule your gondola ride at high tide. Otherwise you'll have an eye-level view of scum and gunk on the sides of the canals, exposed at low tide.

Two major stations where you can hire gondolas are **Piazza San Marco** (© 041-5200685) and **Ponte di Rialto** (© 041-5224904).

church opposite. At midpoint it's spanned by the Rialto Bridge. Eventually, the canal winds its serpentine course to the rail station.

Some of the most impressive buildings along the Grand Canal have been converted into galleries and museums. Others have been turned into cooperative apartments, but often the lower floors are now deserted. (Venetian housewives aren't as incurably romantic as foreign visitors. A practical lot, these women can be seen stringing up their laundry to dry in front of thousands of tourists.)

The best way to see the Grand Canal is to board **vaporetto no. 1** (push and shove until you secure a seat at the front of the vessel). Settle yourself in and prepare yourself for a view that can thrill even the most experienced world traveler.

3 Museums & Galleries

Academy Galleries (Gallerie dell'Accademia) ☞☞☞   The pomp and circumstance, the glory that was Venice, lives on in this remarkable collection of paintings spanning the 13th to 18th centuries. The hallmark of the Venetian school is color and more color. From Giorgione to Veronese, from Titian to Tintoretto, with a Carpaccio cycle thrown in, the Accademia has samples of its most famous sons—often their best work. Here we've highlighted only some of the most-renowned masterpieces for the first-timer in a rush.

You'll first see works by such 14th-century artists as Paolo and Lorenzo Veneziano, who bridged the gap from Byzantine art to Gothic (see the latter's *Annunciation*). Next, you'll view Giovanni Bellini's *Madonna and Saint* (poor Sebastian, not another arrow) and Carpaccio's fascinating yet gruesome work of mass crucifixion. As you move on, head for the painting on the easel by the window, attributed to the great Venetian artist Giorgione. On this canvas he depicted the Madonna and Child, along with the mystic St. Catherine of Siena and John the Baptist (a neat trick for Catherine, who seems to have perfected transmigration to join the cast of characters).

Two of the most important works with secular themes are Mantegna's armored *St. George,* with the slain dragon at his feet, and Hans Memling's 15th-century portrait of a young man. A most unusual *Madonna and Child* is by Cosmé Tura, the master of Ferrara, who could always be counted on to give a new twist to an old subject.

The Madonnas and bambini of **Giovanni Bellini** ☞☞, an expert in harmonious color blending, are the focus of another room. None but the major artists could stand the test of a salon filled with the same subject, but under Bellini's brush each Virgin achieves her individual spirituality. **Giorgione's** *Tempest* ☞☞☞, displayed here, is the single most famous painting at the Accademia. It depicts a baby suckling from the breast of its mother, while a man with a staff looks on. What might've emerged as a simple pastoral scene by a lesser artist comes forth as rare and exceptional beauty. Summer lightning pierces the sky, but the tempest seems to be in the background, far away from the foreground figures, who are unaware of the approaching danger.

You can see the masterpiece of Lorenzo Lotto, a melancholy portrait of a young man, before coming to a room dominated by **Paolo Veronese's** *The Banquet in the House of Levi* ☞☞. This is really a "Last Supper" but was considered a sacrilege in its day, so Veronese

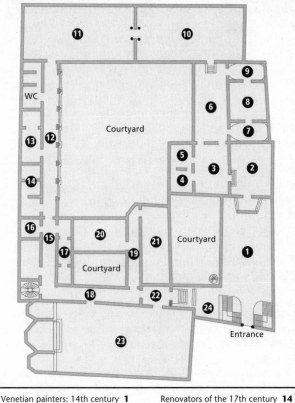

Venetian painters: 14th century **1**

Giovanni Bellini and
Cima da Conegliano **2**

Late 15th century to
early 16th century **3**

Italian painters: 15th century **4**

Giovanni Bellini and Giorgione **5**

16th century **6**

Lorenzo Lotto and Salvodo **7**

Palma the Elder **8**

16th-century schools of painting **9**

Titian, Veronese, and Tintoretto **10**

Veronese, Tintoretto, and Tiepolo **11**

18th-century landscape painters **12**

Tintoretto and Bassano **13**

Renovators of the 17th century **14**

Minor painters of the
18th century **15**

Giambattista Piazzetta **16**

Longhi, Canaletto, Carriera,
and Guardi **17**

18th-century painters and
engravers **18**

15th-century painters **19**

Gentile Bellini and Vittorio
Carpaccio **20**

Vittorio Carpaccio **21**

Bookshop **22**

Venetian painters: 15th century **23**

Albergo Room and Titian **24**

was forced to change its name and pretend it was a secular work. (Impish Veronese caught the hot fire of the Inquisition by including dogs, a cat, midgets, Huns, and drunken revelers in the mammoth canvas.) Four large paintings by Tintoretto, noted for their swirling action and powerful drama, depict scenes from the life of St. Mark. Finally, painted in his declining years (some have suggested in his 99th year, before he died from the plague) is **Titian's majestic *Pietà*.**

After an unimpressive long walk, search out Canaletto's *Porticato.* Yet another room is heightened by **Gentile Bellini's stunning portrait of St. Mark's Square** 🅡, back in the days (1496) when the houses glistened with gold in the sun. All the works in this salon are intriguing, especially the re-creation of the Ponte de Rialto and a covered wood bridge by Carpaccio.

Also displayed is the cycle of narrative paintings that Vittore Carpaccio did of St. Ursula for the Scuola of Santa Orsola. The most famous is no. 578, showing Ursula asleep on her elongated bed, with a dog nestled on the floor nearby, as the angels come for a visitation. Finally, on the way out, look for Titian's ***Presentation of the Virgin,*** a fitting farewell to this galaxy of great Venetian art.

Campo della Carità, Dorsoduro. ℭ **041-5222247.** Admission 6.50€. Mon 8am–2pm; Tues–Sun 8am–7:15pm. Vaporetto: Accademia.

Correr Civic Museum (Museo Civico Correr) 🅡🅡

This museum traces the development of Venetian painting from the 14th to 16th centuries. On the second floor are the red-and-maroon robes once worn by the doges, plus some fabulous street lanterns and an illustrated copy of *Marco Polo in Tartaria.* You can see Cosmè Tura's *Pietà* 🅡🅡, a miniature of renown from the genius in the Ferrara School. This is one of his more gruesome works, depicting a bony, gnarled Christ sprawled on the lap of the Madonna. Farther on, search out Schiavone's *Madonna and Child* (no. 545), our candidate for ugliest bambino ever depicted on canvas (no wonder his mother looks askance).

One of the most important rooms boasts three masterpieces: a *Pietà* by **Antonello da Messina,** a *Crucifixion* by **Flemish Hugo van der Goes,** and a *Madonna and Child* by **Dieric Bouts,** who depicted the baby suckling at his mother's breast in a sensual manner. The star attraction of the Correr is the **Bellini salon,** which includes works by founding padre Jacopo and his son, Gentile. But the real master of the household was the other son, Giovanni, the major painter of the 15th-century Venetian school (look for his *Crucifixion* and compare it with his father's treatment of the same subject). A small but celebrated portrait of St. Anthony of Padua by Alvise Vivarini is here, plus works by Bartolomeo Montagna. The most important work is **Vittore Carpaccio's *Two Venetian Ladies*** 𝒸𝒸, though their true gender is a subject of much debate. In Venice they're popularly known as "The Courtesans." A lesser work, *St. Peter,* depicting the saint with the daggers piercing him, hangs in the same room.

The entrance is under the arcades of Ala Napoleonica at the western end of the square.

In the Procuratie Nuove, Piazza San Marco. © 041-5225625. Admission (including admission to Ducal Palace, reviewed above) 9.50€. Mar–Oct daily 9am–7pm; Nov–Feb daily 9am–5pm. Vaporetto: San Marco.

Ca' d'Oro 𝒸𝒸𝒸

The only problem with the use of this building as an art museum is the fact that the Ca' d'Oro is so opulent, its architecture and decor compete with the works contained within. It was built in the early 1400s, and its name translates as "House of Gold," though the gilding that once covered its facade eroded away long ago, leaving softly textured pink and white stone carved into lacy Gothic patterns. Historians compare its majesty to that of the Ducal Palace. The building was meticulously restored in the early 20th century by philanthropist Baron Franchetti, who attached it to a smaller nearby palazzo (Ca' Duodo), today part of the Ca' d'Oro complex. The interconnected buildings contain the baron's valuable private collection of paintings, sculpture, and furniture, all donated to the Italian government during World War I.

You enter into a stunning courtyard, 50 yards from the vaporetto stop. The courtyard has a multicolored patterned marble floor and is filled with statuary. Proceed upstairs to the lavishly appointed palazzo. One of the gallery's major paintings is Titian's voluptuous *Venus.* She coyly covers one breast, but what about the other?

In a special niche reserved for the masterpiece of the Franchetti collection is Andrea Mantegna's icy-cold ***St. Sebastian*** 𝒸, the central figure of which is riddled with what must be a record number of arrows. You'll also find works by Carpaccio. If you walk onto the loggia, you'll have one of the grandest views of the Grand Canal, a panorama that inspired even Lord Byron—when he could take his eyes off the ladies.

For a delightful break, step out onto the palazzo's loggia, overlooking the Grand Canal, for a view up and down the aquatic waterway and across to the Pescheria (fish market), a timeless vignette of an unchanged city.

Cannaregio 3931–3932. ℂ **041-5238790.** Admission 3€. Mon 8:15am–2pm; Tues–Sun 8:15am–7:15pm. Closed Jan 1, May 1, and Dec 25. Vaporetto: Ca' d'Oro.

Ca' Rezzonico 🐼🐼 This 17th- and 18th-century palace along the Grand Canal is where Robert Browning set up his bachelor headquarters and eventually died in 1889. Pope Clement XIII also stayed here. It's a virtual treasure house, known for its baroque paintings and furniture. First you enter the **Grand Ballroom** with its allegorical ceiling, and then you proceed through lavishly embellished rooms with Venetian chandeliers, brocaded walls, portraits of patricians, tapestries, gilded furnishings, and touches of chinoiserie. Eventually you come to the **Throne Room,** with its allegorical ceilings by Giovanni Battista Tiepolo.

On the first floor you can walk out onto a **balcony** for a view of the Grand Canal as the aristocratic tenants of the 18th century saw it. Another group of rooms follows, including the library. In these salons, look for a bizarre collection of paintings: One, for example, depicts half-clothed women beating up a defenseless naked man (one Amazon is about to stick a pitchfork into his neck, another to crown him with a violin). In the adjoining room, another woman is hammering a spike through a man's skull.

Upstairs is a survey of 18th-century Venetian art. As you enter the main room from downstairs, head for the **first salon** on your right (facing the canal), which contains the best works, paintings from the brush of Pietro Longhi. His most famous work, *The Lady and the Hairdresser* 🐼🐼, is in this salon. Others depict the life of the idle Venetian rich. On the rest of the floor are bedchambers, a chapel, and salons, some with badly damaged frescoes, including a romp of satyrs.

Fondamenta Rezzonico, Dorsoduro 3136. ℂ **041-2410100.** Admission 6.50€. Oct–Apr Sat–Thurs 10am–5pm; May–Sept daily 10am–5pm. Vaporetto: Ca' Rezzonico.

Peggy Guggenheim Collection (Collezione Peggy Guggenheim) 🐼🐼🐼 This is one of the most comprehensive and brilliant modern-art collections in the Western world and reveals both the foresight and the critical judgment of its founder. The collection is housed in an unfinished palazzo, the former Venetian home of Peggy Guggenheim, who died in 1979. In the tradition of her family, Peggy Guggenheim was a lifelong patron of contemporary painters and sculptors. In the 1940s, she founded the avant-garde Art of This Century Gallery in New York, impressing critics not only with the high quality of the artists she sponsored but also with her methods of displaying them.

As her private collection increased, she decided to find a larger showcase and selected Venice. While the Solomon R. Guggenheim Museum was going up in New York City according to Frank Lloyd Wright's specifications, she was creating her own gallery here. You can wander through and enjoy art in an informal and relaxed way.

Max Ernst was one of Peggy Guggenheim's early favorites (she even married him), as was Jackson Pollock (she provided a farm-house where he could develop his technique). Displayed here are works not only by Pollock and Ernst but also by Picasso (see his 1911 cubist *The Poet*), Duchamp, Chagall, Mondrian, Brancusi, Delvaux, and Dalí, plus a garden of modern sculpture with Giacometti works (some of which he struggled to complete while resisting the amorous intentions of Marlene Dietrich). Temporary modern-art shows may be presented during winter. Since Peggy Guggenheim's death, the collection has been administered by the Solomon R. Guggenheim Foundation, which also operates New York's Guggenheim Museum. In the new wing are a museum shop and a cafe, overlooking the sculpture garden.

In the Palazzo Venier dei Leoni, Calle Venier dei Leoni, Dorsoduro 701. ℭ 041-5206288. Admission 8€ adults, 4€ students/children. Free for children under 9. Wed–Mon 10am–6pm. Vaporetto: Accademia.

Naval History Museum (Museo Storico Navale) & Arsenale 𝒜

The Naval History Museum is filled with cannons, ships' models, and fragments of old vessels dating to the days when Venice was supreme in the Adriatic. The prize exhibit is a gilded model of the *Bucintoro,* the great ship of the doge that surely would've made Cleopatra's barge look like an oil tanker. In addition, you'll find models of historic and modern fighting ships, local fish-ing and rowing craft, and a collection of 24 Chinese junks, as well as a number of maritime *ex voto* (offerings left at shrines) from churches of Naples.

If you walk along the canal as it branches off from the museum, you'll arrive at the Ships' Pavilion, where historic vessels are displayed (about 270 yd. from the museum and before the wooden bridge). Proceeding along the canal, you'll soon reach the Arsenale (Campo dell'Arsenale) guarded by stone lions, Neptune with a trident, and other assorted ferocities. You'll spot it readily enough because of its two towers flanking the canal. In its day, the Arsenale turned out gal-ley after galley at speeds usually associated with wartime production.

Campo San Biasio, Castello 2148. ℭ 041-5200276. Admission 1.55€. Mon–Sat 9am–1:30pm. Closed holidays. Vaporetto: Arsenale.

Moments Carnevale

Venetians take to the piazzas and streets for the pre-Lenten holiday of **Carnevale.** The festival traditionally marked the unbridled celebration that preceded Lent, the period of penitence and abstinence prior to Easter. It lasts about 5 to 10 days today (and culminates in the Friday to Tuesday before Ash Wednesday).

In the 18th-century heyday of Carnevale, well-heeled revelers came from all over Europe to take part in the festivities. Masks became ubiquitous, affording anonymity and pardoning 1,000 sins. They permitted the fishmonger to attend the ball and dance with the baroness. The doges condemned the festival and the popes denounced it, but nothing could dampen the Venetian Carnevale spirit until Napoleon arrived in 1797 and put an end to the festivities.

Resuscitated in 1980 by local tourism powers to fill the empty winter months, Carnevale is calmer now, though just barely. In the 1980s it attracted an onslaught of what seemed to be the entire student population of Europe, backpackers who slept in the piazzas and the train station. Politicians and city officials adopted a middle-of-the-road policy that helped establish Carnevale's image as neither a backpackers' free-for-all outdoor party nor a continuation of the exclusive private balls in the Grand Canal palazzi available only to a very few.

Each year the festival opens with a series of lavish balls and private parties, most of which aren't open to the public. But the candlelit **Doge's Ball (Ballo del Doge)** is a dazzling exception, traditionally held the Saturday before Shrove Tuesday in the 15th-century Palazzo Pisani Moretta on the Grand Canal. Historic costumes are a must, and you can rent them. Of course, this ball isn't exactly cheap—expect to spend at least 150€ per person—but it's the extravagant experience of a lifetime. If you're interested in finding out more and arranging for a costume rental, contact Antonia Sautter at the Ballo del Doge at © **041-5233851** (fax 041-5287543).

Even if you don't attend a ball, there's still plenty of fun in the streets. You'll find a patchwork of musical and cultural events, many of them free of charge, that appeal to all tastes, nationalities, ages, and budgets. At any given moment, musical events are staged in any of the city's dozens of piazzas—from reggae to zydeco to jazz to chamber music—and special art exhibits are mounted at numerous museums and galleries. The recent involvement of international corporate sponsors has met with a mixed reception, but it seems to be the wave of the future.

Carnevale is not for those who dislike crowds. The crowds are what it's all about. All of life becomes a stage, and everyone is on it. Whether you spend months creating an elaborate costume, or grab one from the countless stands set up around town, Carnevale is about giving in to the spontaneity of the magic and surprise around every corner, the mystery behind every mask. It's a chance to relive the glory days of the 1700s, when Venetian life was at its most extravagant, which is why masks and costumes place an emphasis on the historical. Groups travel in coordinated get-ups that range from a contemporary passel of Fellini-esque clowns to the court of the Sun King in all its wigged-out glory. You might see the Three Musketeers riding the vaporetto and your waiter may be dressed as a nun. The places to be seen in costume are the cafes lining Piazza San Marco. Don't expect to be seated at a full-view window seat unless your costume is straight off the stage of the local opera house. The merrymakers carry on until Shrove Tuesday, when the bells of San Francesco della Vigna toll at midnight. But before they do, the grand finale involves fireworks over the lagoon.

The city is the quintessential set, the perfect venue; Hollywood could not create a more evocative location. This is a celebration of history, art, theater, and drama. Venice and Carnevale were made for each other.

4 Churches & Guild Houses

Much of the great art of Venice lies in its churches and *scuole* (guild houses or fraternities). Most of the guild members were drawn from the rising bourgeoisie. The guilds were said to fulfill both the material and the spiritual needs of their (male) members, who often engaged in charitable works in honor of the saint for whom their scuole were named. Many of Venice's greatest artists, including Tintoretto, were commissioned to decorate these guild houses. Some created masterpieces you can still see today. Narrative canvases that depicted the lives of the saints were called *teleri*.

San Rocco ✫✫✫   Of all Venice's scuole, none is as richly embellished as this one, filled with epic canvases by Tintoretto. Born Jacopo Robusti in 1518, he became known for paintings of mystical spirituality and phantasmagoric light effects. He won a competition to decorate this darkly illuminated early-16th-century building, and began painting in 1564. The work stretched on until his powers as an artist waned; he died in 1594. The paintings sweep across the upper and lower halls, mesmerizing you with a kind of passion play. In the grand hallway, they depict New Testament scenes, devoted largely to episodes in the life of Mary (the ***Flight into Egypt*** is among the best). In the top gallery are works illustrating scenes from the Old and New Testaments, the most renowned being those devoted to the life of Christ. In a separate room is Tintoretto's masterpiece: his mammoth ***Crucifixion.*** In it he showed his dramatic scope and sense of grandeur as an artist, creating a deeply felt scene that fills you with the horror of systematic execution, thus transcending its original subject matter. (***Movie trivia:*** Watch Woody Allen try to pick up Julia Roberts in *Everyone Says I Love You* while she studies the Tintorettos in San Rocco—if you can get past the idea of the lovely Ms. Roberts as an art historian.)

Campo San Rocco, San Polo. ✆ 041-5234864. Admission 5.50€ adults, 1.50€ children. Mar 28–Nov 2 daily 9am–5:30pm; Nov 3–30 and Mar 1–27 daily 10am–4pm; Dec–Feb Mon–Fri 10am–1pm, Sat–Sun 10am–4pm. Closed Easter and Dec 25–Jan 1. Vaporetto: San Tomà. Ticket office closes 30 min. before last entrance.

San Giorgio degli Schiavoni ✫✫   At the St. Antonino Bridge (Fondamenta dei Furlani) is the second important guild house to visit. Between 1502 and 1509, Vittore Carpaccio painted a pictorial cycle here of exceptional merit and interest. His works of **St. George and the Dragon** are our favorite art in all Venice and certainly the most delightful. For example, in one frame St. George charges the dragon on a field littered with half-eaten bodies and skulls.

Tips A Note on Museum Hours

As throughout Italy, visiting hours in Venice's museums are often subject to major variations. Many visitors who have budgeted only 2 or 3 days for Venice often express disappointment when, for some unknown reason, a major attraction closes abruptly. When you arrive, check with the tourist office for a list of the latest open hours.

Gruesome? Not at all. Any moment you expect the director to call "Cut!" The pictures relating to St. Jerome are appealing but don't compete with St. George and his ferocious dragon.

Calle dei Furlani, Castello. ℂ 041-5228828. Admission 2€. Nov–Mar Tues–Sun 10am–12:30pm, Tues–Sat 3–6pm; Apr–Oct Tues–Sun 9:30am–12:30pm, Tues–Sat 3:30–6:30pm. Vaporetto: San Zaccaria. Last entrance 20 min. before closing.

Santa Maria Gloriosa dei Frari 🕱🕱   Known simply as the Frari, this Venetian Gothic church is only a short walk from the San Rocco and is filled with great art. The best work is Titian's *Assumption* over the main altar—a masterpiece of soaring beauty depicting the ascension of the Madonna on a cloud puffed up by floating cherubs. In her robe, and especially in the robe of one of the gaping saints below, "Titian red" dazzles as never before.

On the first altar to the right as you enter is Titian's second major work here: *Madonna Enthroned,* painted for the Pesaro family in 1526. Although lacking the power and drama of the *Assumption,* it nevertheless is brilliant in its use of color and light effects. But Titian surely would turn redder than his Madonna's robes if he could see the latter-day neoclassical tomb built for him on the opposite wall. The kindest word for it: large.

Facing the tomb is a memorial to Canova, the Italian sculptor who led the revival of classicism. To return to more enduring art, head to the sacristy for a 1488 Giovanni Bellini triptych on wood; the Madonna is cool and serene, one of Bellini's finest portraits of the Virgin. Also see the almost primitive-looking wood carving by Donatello of St. John the Baptist.

Campo dei Frari, San Polo. ℂ 041-5222637. Admission 2€; free Sun. Mon–Sat 9am–6pm, Sun 1–6pm. Vaporetto: San Tomà.

Madonna dell'Orto 🕱   At this church, a good reason to walk to this remote northern district, you can pay your final respects to **Tintoretto.** The brick structure with a Gothic front is famed not only because of its paintings by that artist but also because the great master is buried in the chapel to the right of the main altar. At the high altar are his *Last Judgment* (on the right) and *Sacrifice of the Golden Calf* (left), monumental paintings curving at the top like a Gothic arch. Over the doorway to the right of the altar is Tintoretto's superb portrayal of the presentation of Mary as a little girl at the temple. The composition is unusual in that Mary isn't the focal point; rather, a pointing woman bystander dominates the scene.

The first chapel to the right of the main altar contains a masterly work by Cima de Conegliano, showing the presentation of a sacrificial lamb to the saints (the plasticity of St. John's body evokes Michelangelo). In the first chapel on the left, as you enter, notice the large photo of Giovanni Bellini's *Madonna and Child.* The original, which was noteworthy for its depiction of the eyes and mouths of the mother and child, was stolen as part of a 1994 theft, and pending the possibility of its hoped-for return, the photograph was installed in its place. In the apse, flanking an *Annunciation,* the work of Palma Giovane, is the *Vision of the Cross to St. Peter,* by Tintoretto, and the *Beheading of St. Paul,* also by Tintoretto.

Campo dell'Orto, Cannaregio 3512. ✆ **041-719933**. Admission 2€. Mon–Sat 10am–5pm, Sun 1–6pm. Vaporetto: Madonna dell'Orto.

San Zaccaria ⭐⭐
Behind St. Mark's is this Gothic church with a Renaissance facade, filled with works of art, notably Giovanni Bellini's restored *Madonna Enthroned,* painted with saints (second altar to the left). Many have found this to be one of Bellini's finest Madonnas, and it does have beautifully subdued coloring, though it appears rather static. Many worthwhile works lie in the main body of the church, but for a view of even more of them, apply to the sacristan for entrance to the church's museum, housed in an area once reserved exclusively for nuns. Here you'll find works by Tintoretto, Titian, Il Vecchio, Anthony Van Dyck, and Bassano. The paintings aren't labeled, but the sacristan will point out the names of the artists. In the Sisters' Choir are five armchairs in which the Venetian doges of yore sat. And if you save the best for last, you can see the faded **frescoes of Andrea del Castagno** in the shrine honoring San Tarasio.

Campo San Zaccaria, Castello. ✆ **041-5221257**. Admission 1.50€ to museum; church free. Mon–Sat 10am–noon; daily 4–6pm. Vaporetto: San Zaccaria.

San Giorgio Maggiore ⭐
This church, on the little island of San Giorgio Maggiore, was designed by the great Renaissance architect **Palladio**—perhaps as a consolation prize, since he wasn't

chosen to rebuild the burned-out Doge's Palace. The logical rhythm of the Vicenza architect is played here on a grand scale. But inside it's almost too stark; Palladio wasn't much on gilded adornment. The chief art hangs on the main altar: two epic paintings by Tintoretto, the *Fall of Manna* to the left and the far more successful *Last Supper* to the right. It's interesting to compare Tintoretto's *Cena* with that of Veronese at the Accademia. Afterward you may want to take the elevator (for 1.50€) to the top of the belfry for a view of the greenery of the island itself, the lagoon, and the Doge's Palace across the way. It's unforgettable.

Isola San Giorgio Maggiore, across from Piazzetta San Marco. ℭ 041-5227827. Free admission. Apr–Oct daily 9:30am–12:30pm and 2:30–6pm; Nov–Mar daily 10am–12:30pm and 2:30–4:30pm. Closed for Mass on Sun and feast days 10:45am–noon. Vaporetto: Take the Giudecca-bound vaporetto on Riva degli Schiavoni and get off at the first stop, right in the courtyard of the church.

Santa Maria della Salute 🏛🏛

Like the proud landmark it is, La Salute, the pinnacle of the baroque movement in Venice, stands at the mouth of the Grand Canal overlooking Piazzetta San Marco and opening onto Campo della Salute. One of Venice's most historic churches, it was built by Longhena in the 17th century (work began in 1631) as an offering to the Virgin for delivering the city from the plague. Longhena, almost unknown when he got the commission, dedicated half a century to working on this church and died 5 years before the long-lasting job was completed. Surmounted by a great cupola, the octagonal basilica makes for an interesting visit: It houses a small art gallery in its sacristy (tip the custodian), which includes a marriage feast of Cana by Tintoretto, allegorical paintings on the ceiling by Titian, a mounted St. Mark, and poor St. Sebastian with his inevitable arrow.

Campo della Salute, Dorsoduro. ℭ 041-5237951. Free admission (but offering is expected); sacristy 2€. Mar–Nov daily 9am–noon and 3–6pm (to 5:30pm Dec–Feb). Vaporetto: Salute.

Santi Giovanni e Paolo 🏛🏛

This great Gothic church (a.k.a. Zanipolo) houses the **tombs** of many doges. It was built during the 13th and 14th centuries and contains works by many of the most noted Venetian painters. As you enter (right aisle), you'll find a retable by Giovanni Bellini (which includes a St. Sebastian filled with arrows). In the Rosary Chapel are Veronese ceilings depicting New Testament scenes, including *The Assumption of the Madonna*. To the right of the church is one of the world's best-known **equestrian statues,** that of Bartolomeo Colleoni, sculpted in the 15th century by Andrea del Verrochio. The bronze has long been acclaimed as his masterpiece, though it was completed by another artist. The horse is far more beautiful than the armored military hero, who looks as if he had just stumbled onto a three-headed crocodile.

To the left of the pantheon is the **Scuola di San Marco,** with a stunning Renaissance facade (it's now run as a civic hospital). The church requests that Sunday visits be of a religious nature, rather than for sightseeing.

Campo SS. Giovanni e Paolo, Castello 6363. ℂ 041-5235913. Free admission. Daily 9am–12:30pm and 3–7:15pm. Vaporetto: Rialto or Fondamenta Nuove.

5 The Lido 𝒜𝒜

The white sands of the Lido have drawn artists and literary types for centuries, and today they still draw a bikini-clad crowd that includes the occasional celeb. The Lido is a resort area complete with deluxe hotels, a casino, and stratospheric prices.

The Lido is past its heyday. A chic crowd still checks into the Excelsior Palace and the Hotel des Bains, but the beach strip is overrun with tourists and opens onto polluted waters. (For swimming, guests use their hotel pools, though they still stroll along the Lido sands and enjoy the views.)

Even if you aren't planning to stay in this area, you should still come over and explore for an afternoon. There's no denying the appeal of a beach so close to one of the world's most romantic cities. The strips of beachfront in front of the big hotels on the Lido are technically considered private, and the public is discouraged from using the facilities. But because you can use the beachfront on either side of their property, no one seems to really care about shooing nonguests away.

If you don't want to tread on the beachfront property of the rarefied hotels (which have huts lining the beach like those of some tropical paradise), you can try the **Lungomare G. d'Annunzio (Public Bathing Beach)** at the end of the Gran Viale (Piazzale Ettore Sorger), a long stroll from the vaporetto stop. You can book cabins *(camerini)* and enjoy the sand. Rates change seasonally.

To reach the Lido, take vaporetto no. 1, 6, 52, or 82 (the ride takes about 15 min.). The boat departs from a landing stage near the Doge's Palace.

6 The Ghetto 𝒜𝒜

The Ghetto of Venice, called the **Ghetto Nuovo** 𝒜, was instituted in 1516 by the Venetian Republic in the Cannaregio district. It's considered to be the first ghetto in the world and also the best kept. The word *geto* comes from the Venetian dialect and means "foundry" (originally there were two iron foundries here where metals were fused). At one time, Venetian Jews were confined to a walled area and obliged to wear red or yellow marks sewn onto their clothing and distinctive-looking hats. The walls that once enclosed and confined the ghetto were torn down long ago, but much remains of the past.

There are five synagogues in Venice, each built during the 16th century and each representing a radically different aesthetic and cultural difference among the groups of Jews who built them. The oldest is the **German Synagogue (Sinagoghe Grande Tedesca),** restored after the end of World War II with funds from Germany. Others are the **Spanish Synagogue (Sinagoghe Spagnola,** the oldest continuously functioning synagogue in Europe), the **Italian Synagogue (Sinagoghe Italiana),** the **Levantine-Oriental Synagogue (Sinagoghe Levantina,** aka the **Turkish Synagogue),** and the **Canton Synagogue (Sinagoghe del Canton).**

The best way to visit the synagogues is to take one of the guided tours departing from the **Museo Comunità Ebraica,** Campo di Ghetto Nuovo 2902B (© **041-715359).** It contains a small but worthy collection of artifacts pertaining to the Jewish community of Venice and costs 8€ for adults. From June through September, the museum is open Sunday to Friday from 10am to 7pm (Oct–May to 5pm). However, the museum is by no means the focal point of your experience: More worthwhile are the **walking tours** that begin and end here, costing 10€, with free entrance to the museum. The 50-minute tours incorporate a brisk commentary and a stroll through the neighborhood, including visits to the interiors of three of the five synagogues (the ones you visit depend on various factors). From June through September, the tours depart hourly Sunday to Friday from 10:30am to 5:30pm (Oct–May to 3:30pm).

7 Organized Tours

Tours through the streets and canals of Venice are distinctly different from tours through other cities of Italy because of the complete absence of traffic. You can always wander at will through the labyrinth of streets, but many visitors opt for a guided tour to at least familiarize themselves with the city's geography.

American Express, Calle San Moisè, San Marco 1471 (© **041-5200844),** which operates from a historic building a few steps from

St. Mark's Square, offers an array of guided city tours. It's open for tours and travel arrangements Monday to Friday from 9am to 5:30pm and Saturday from 9am to 12:30pm. Call ahead to ask about the current schedule and to make reservations. The offerings include a daily 2-hour guided tour of the city for 24€, an Evening Serenade Tour that's accompanied by the sound of singing musicians in gondolas for 31€, and a tour of the islands of the Venetian lagoon for 29€.

8 The Lagoon Islands of Murano, Burano & Torcello

If you're exploring these islands for the day and are looking for a good lunch spot, see chapter 5, "Where to Dine," which offers a listing or two on each island.

MURANO 🏛️🏛️

For centuries, glassblowers on the island of Murano have turned out those fantastic chandeliers Victorian ladies used to prize so highly. They also produce heavily ornamented glasses so ruby red or so indigo blue you can't tell if you're drinking blackberry juice or pure grain alcohol. Happily, the glassblowers are still plying their trade, though increasing competition (notably from Sweden) has compelled a greater degree of sophistication in design.

Murano remains the chief expedition from Venice, but it's not the most beautiful nearby island (Burano and Torcello are far more attractive).

You can combine a tour of Murano with a trip along the lagoon. To reach Murano, take **vaporetto no. 12 or 13** at Riva degli Schiavoni, a short walk from Piazzetta San Marco. The boat docks at the landing platform at Murano where the first furnace awaits conveniently. It's best to go Monday to Friday from 10am to noon if you want to see some glassblowing action.

On your way to Murano, you can hop off the vaporetto for a look at the cemetery island of **San Michele.** Celebrities buried here include impresario Sergei Diaghilev (1872–1929), who introduced Western Europe to Russian ballet, and composer Igor Stravinsky (1882–1971). Ezra Pound's grave is also here. One of the most influential poets of the 20th century, he was a supporter of Mussolini who remained in Italy during World War II. After the war, he was confined for a time in psychiatric hospitals in lieu of being sent to prison for treason; when he was released, he spent the rest of his life in Italy.

Also on the island is the 15th-century **Church of San Michele,** with its handsome white classical facade and richly decorated

---

Moments **A Special Glass Museum**

For a really special museum, call for an appointment to visit the **Barovier & Toso Museum,** Palazzo Contarini, Fondamenta Vetrai 28, Murano (© **041-739049**). Here Angelo Barovier displays rare glass from his private collection acquired over half a century. The museum is open (providing you call first) during foundry hours Monday to Friday from 9:30am to noon and 2:30 to 5pm.

---

interior. It was the first church in Venice to be built in the Renaissance style.

TOURING THE GLASS FACTORIES & OTHER SIGHTS

As you stroll through Murano, you'll find that the factory owners are only too glad to let you come in and see their age-old crafts. While browsing through the showrooms, you'll need stiff resistance to keep the salespeople at bay. Bargaining is expected. Don't—repeat, *don't*—pay the marked price on any item. That's merely the figure at which to open negotiations.

However, the prices of made-on-the-spot souvenirs aren't negotiable. For example, you may want to buy a horse streaked with blue. The artisan takes a piece of incandescent glass, huffs, puffs, rolls it, shapes it, snips it, and behold—he has shaped a horse. The showrooms of Murano also contain a fine assortment of Venetian crystal beads, available in every hue. You may find some of the best work to be the experiments of apprentices.

While on the island, you can visit the Renaissance palazzo housing the **Museo Vetrario di Murano,** Fondamenta Giustinian 8 (© **041-739586**), which contains a spectacular collection of Venetian glass. From April through October, it's open Monday, Tuesday, and Thursday to Saturday from 10am to 5pm (to 4pm Nov–Mar). Admission is 4€.

If you're looking for something different, head to **San Pietro Martire,** Fondamenta Vetrai (© **041-739704**), which dates from the 1300s but was rebuilt in 1511 and is richly decorated with paintings by Tintoretto and Veronese. Its proud possession is a *Madonna and Child Enthroned* by Giovanni Bellini, plus two superb altarpieces by the same master. The church lies right before the junction with Murano's Grand Canal, about 250 yards from the vaporetto landing stage. It's open daily from 9am to noon and 3 to 6pm; it is closed for Mass on Sunday morning.

Even more notable is **Santa Maria e Donato,** Campo San Donato (*©* **041-739056**), open daily 9am to noon and 4 to 6pm with time variations for Sunday Mass. Dating from the 7th century but reconstructed in the 1100s, this building is a stellar example of Venetian Byzantine style, despite its 19th-century restoration. The interior is known for its mosaic floor (a parade of peacocks and eagles, as well as other creatures) and a 15th-century ship's-keel ceiling. Over the apse is an outstanding mosaic of the Virgin against a gold background from the early 1200s.

BURANO 🎭🎭

Burano became world famous as a center of lace making, a craft that reached its pinnacle in the 18th century. The visitor who can spare a morning to visit this island will be rewarded with a charming fishing village far removed in spirit from the grandeur of Venice but only half an hour away by ferry.

Boats leave from Fondamenta Nuove, overlooking the Venetian graveyard (which is well worth the trip all on its own). To reach Fondamenta Nuove, take **vaporetto no. 12 or 52** from Riva degli Schiavoni. Once you land at Burano, you'll discover that the houses of the islanders come in varied colors: sienna, robin's egg or cobalt blue, barn red, butterscotch, and grass green.

Check out the **Scuola di Merletti di Burano,** "Museo del Merletto," San Martino Destra 183 (*©* **041-730034**), in the center of the village at Piazza Baldassare Galuppi. From November through March, the museum is open Wednesday to Monday from 10am to 4pm (to 5pm Apr through Oct). Admission is 4€. The Burano School of Lace was founded in 1872 as part of a movement aimed at restoring the age-old craft that had earlier declined, giving way to such lace-making centers as Chantilly and Bruges. On the second floor you can see the lace makers, mostly young women, at their painstaking work and can purchase hand-embroidered or hand-made lace items.

After visiting the lace school, walk across the square to the **Duomo** and its leaning **campanile** (inside, look for the *Crucifixion* by Tiepolo). See it while you can, because the bell tower is leaning so precariously it looks as if it may topple at any moment.

TORCELLO 🎭🎭

Of all the islands of the lagoon, Torcello, the so-called Mother of Venice, offers the most charm. If Burano is behind the times,

Torcello is positively antediluvian. You can stroll across a grassy meadow, traverse an ancient stone bridge, and step back into that time when the Venetians first fled from invading barbarians to create a city of Neptune in the lagoon.

To reach Torcello, take **vaporetto no. 12** from Fondamenta Nuova on Murano. The trip takes about 45 minutes.

Warning: If you go to Torcello on your own, don't listen to the gondoliers who hover at the ferry quay. They'll tell you that the cathedral and the *locanda* (inn) are miles away. Actually, they're both reached after a leisurely 12- to 15-minute stroll along the canal.

Torcello has two major attractions: a church with Byzantine mosaics good enough to make Empress Theodora at Ravenna turn purple with envy, and a locanda that converts day-trippers into inebriated angels of praise. Below, the spiritual nourishment; turn to the end of chapter 5, "Dining," for the alcoholic sustenance.

Cattedrale di Torcello, also called **Santa Maria Assunta Isola di Torcello** (© 041-730084), was founded in A.D. 639 and subsequently rebuilt. It stands in a lonely grassy meadow beside an 11th-century campanile. The **Byzantine mosaics** *★★* are the stars here. Clutching her child, the weeping Madonna in the apse is a magnificent sight, and on the opposite wall is a powerful *Last Judgment.* Byzantine artisans, it seems, were at their best in portraying hell and damnation. In their *Inferno,* they've re-created a virtual human stew with the fires stirred by wicked demons. Reptiles slide in and out of the skulls of cannibalized sinners. The church is open daily April through October from 10am to 12:30pm and 2:30 to 6pm (to 5pm Nov through Mar). Admission is 4€.

7

Venice Strolls

You'll spend a lot of your time in Venice walking. You'll probably even get lost once or twice, but that's part of the fun. When you want a little more guidance, though, the two walking tours outlined in this chapter will help you organize your time and link together some of the major sights, while showing you some hidden gems and secret spots along the way.

WALKING TOUR 1	PIAZZA SAN MARCO & THE DOGE'S PALACE

by Thomas Worthen

Start:	Basilica of San Marco.
Finish:	Basilica of San Marco.
Time:	About 3 hours or more.
Best Times:	Mornings (9 or 9:30am).
Worst Times:	Afternoons, when crowds gather.

This is the heart of Venice, and there's enough to keep you busy for a week. Here you'll find the Basilica of San Marco, which was the spiritual heart of Venice, and the Doge's Palace, which was its political center. These are two of the world's great cultural treasures. The other buildings that surround the piazza have much to offer as well.

Piazza San Marco may be the most beautiful plaza in the world. It has always been Venice's ceremonial gathering place. It's a wonderful place to stroll, to window shop, to listen to the cafe orchestras, and to watch pigeons attack visitors. In the height of the tourist season, you may want to ignore our itinerary and just go to what's open and available, because there can be a line just to get into the:

① Basilica of San Marco

It was built in A.D. 832 to house the relics of St. Mark, brought here from Alexandria in Egypt by two Venetian merchants—or grave robbers, depending on your point of view. According to the legend, they took the holy man's body from its shrine in Alexandria with the

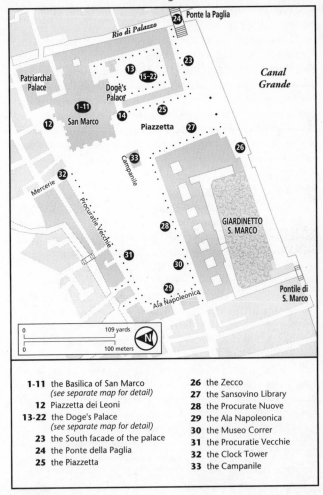

1-11 the Basilica of San Marco
(see separate map for detail)

12 Piazzetta dei Leoni

13-22 the Doge's Palace
(see separate map for detail)

23 the South facade of the palace

24 the Ponte della Paglia

25 the Piazzetta

26 the Zecco

27 the Sansovino Library

28 the Procurate Nuove

29 the Ala Napoleonica

30 the Museo Correr

31 the Procuratie Vecchie

32 the Clock Tower

33 the Campanile

help of some local Christians to prevent the precious relic from being desecrated by the Muslim rulers of Egypt. St. Mark himself was said to have made a few timely appearances to bless and abet the enterprise. The legend inspired many works of art, but it's at least as likely that the ruling doge at the time, Giustiniano Participazio, actually commissioned the theft to enhance his own prestige, and that of Venice. In any event, relics could not be owned but merely possessed, so *robbery* would certainly be too strong a word for this translocation of a spiritual treasure.

The Venetians based the design of their new church on that of the Church of the Apostles in Constantinople (then the richest city in Christendom) in order to announce architecturally that Venice was one of the great cities of the world, with one of the holiest relics. The church, built to honor St. Mark, is the most magnificent in Venice. The basic structure you see today is mainly the result of a rebuilding that took place from around 1063 to 1094. The process of clothing the basilica in marble and mosaic took more than two additional centuries.

Take a moment to look at:

❷ The principal facade

This facade was originally plain brick. The columns, sculpture, and sheets of marble that cover it now are pure show. Since they're mainly spoils from elsewhere, they have a slightly hodgepodge quality, but because of careful attention to symmetry, the variety of colors and shapes is a delight. Venetian sculptors made free copies of some of the imported (or stolen) reliefs to maintain this symmetry. The large Byzantine relief of Hercules carrying a boar on the far left, just past the leftmost portal, is balanced by a Venetian carving of Hercules with a stag, on the far right. The Venetian imitation is less dignified and less classical, but it is also sharper, more energetic, and more decorative, like Venice itself.

Stand just in front of the central doorway, and look up at the **three stone arches,** two below and one above the large mosaic of the Last Judgment. Here the sculptors were at their most original. The inner arch was created first and has the simplest figures carved in the lowest relief. As the sculptors proceeded to the second and third arches they became progressively more confident, and the relief of the carving becomes more pronounced, as well as more complex and naturalistic.

The outer faces of the upper two arches show such pious subjects as virtues and prophets. The insides of the arches—the parts you have to get underneath to see—are most interesting for the scenes they give us of 13th-century Venetian life. In the second arch, the inner face depicts the months, each illustrated with the appropriate zodiac sign and a typical seasonal labor. The inside of the third arch, the one surrounding the mosaic, shows a number of specifically Venetian occupations, such as fishing (in the lower right) and ship-building (in the lower left), just above the seated man with crutches.

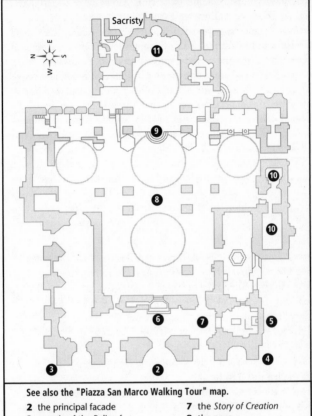

Sacristy

N E S W

See also the "Piazza San Marco Walking Tour" map.

2 the principal facade
3 mosaic of the Relic of
   St. Mark
4 the Pietra del Banda
5 the south facade
6 the narthex

7 the *Story of Creation*
8 the nave
9 sanctuary barrier
   and pulpits
10 the Treasury
11 Pala d'Oro

According to tradition, that seated man was the architect of San Marco; however, he probably represents old age, when men can no longer practice their occupations.

Only around the year 1400 were the standing saints added to the very top of the facade.

Above the central portal, in front of the large window, are statues of four horses, the **Triumphal Quadriga.** These were the most spectacular of the trophies sent from Constantinople by Doge Enrico Dandolo, and when they were installed here they were the only free-standing works of sculpture on the facade. As one of Venice's greatest treasures, they became something of a symbol of the republic's greatness. According to legend, the Four Horses of St. Mark's once stood at the hippodrome in Constantinople, and before that they decorated Nero's arch in Rome. Napoleon had them carted off to Paris after he seized Venice in 1797. In Paris they graced the Triumphal Arch of the Carousel for 18 years, but they were returned to Venice after the Battle of Waterloo. What you see today are actually copies, made in 1982. The originals are in the church's museum.

The four semicircular mosaics above the side doors illustrate the story of the theft of the body of St. Mark, while the four large mosaics on the second story depict the death and resurrection of Jesus Christ. Most of them were made in the 17th century as replacements for the original Byzantine-style mosaics, which were then totally out of fashion.

One 13th-century mosaic mercifully escaped destruction, the one above the doorway on the far left, which shows:

❸ The Relic of St. Mark

This lovely mosaic shows the relic of St. Mark being carried into the church. It depicts San Marco as it was around 1260 when the mosaic was laid and when the topmost part of the facade was much simpler.

Go to the other end of the main facade, where you'll find the:

❹ Pietra del Banda

This is a short red column, really no more than a platform, which was probably brought from Acre late in the period of the Crusades. Officials would announce public decrees while standing upon this perch. It was severely battered in 1902 when the bell tower collapsed and a lot of the rubble slid onto it.

Now go around the corner to the side of the church facing the Doge's Palace and the lagoon to see:

❺ The south facade

The south facade is a showcase for some of the finest loot. The most distinctive piece is the dark-red porphyry relief carving with four grim men, at the corner adjacent to the palace (near no. 15, below). These four are the Tetrarchs, who ruled the Roman Empire around A.D. 300; these sculptures, too, were brought from Constantinople. A Venetian legend says that these are four Muslims who were turned

The Doge's Palace

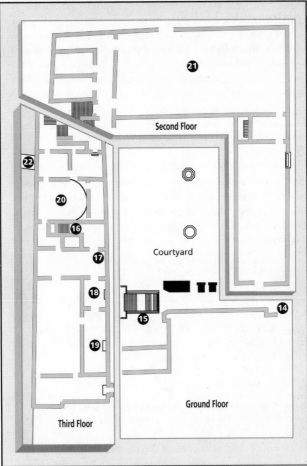

to stone as they tried to carry off the treasury of San Marco, the exterior of which they adorn.

About 15 feet from the south facade are two highly decorated squared shafts. It had always been thought that they were trophies taken from the Genoese at Acre, but recently it has been proved that they came from a 6th-century church in Constantinople, destroyed by the Crusaders.

Return to the main facade and enter the church through the main door. As you do so, admire the 6th-century bronze doors with the lion's heads. (No prizes for guessing where the doors came from.) Inside the doorway is the:

⑥ Narthex

This is the porch of the church. It's a different world—dimmer, more delicately adorned, and with a soft, uncanny glow of golden light coming from the mosaics in the vaults overhead. The low late-afternoon sun shining into the narthex can turn this effect into a glittering blaze. On either side of the entryway into the church are miniature columns framing mosaic niches. These mosaics, from around 1100, the oldest surviving in San Marco, present us with austere but colorful Byzantine saints.

The larger mosaic in the half-dome above the door shows **St. Mark in Ecstasy** (1545). Here is a very different, boldly Renaissance conception of a saint, three-dimensional and energetic. It was designed by Titian, who wisely left the time-consuming and demanding job of inserting little cubes of stone and glass in wet mortar to a professional mosaicist.

The mosaics in the vaults that cap the narthex to the right and left depict scenes from the Old Testament.

Now go to your right (as you entered the narthex), and stand beneath the dome. When you look up into the dome you will see the:

⑦ Story of Creation

Each of the 6 days of creation as described in the Book of Genesis is represented by the appropriate number of dainty little winged women. The reason for this odd bit of symbolism is made clear if, while standing beneath the dome, you face 45° to the right of the door leading back into the piazza and look up at the middle row of scenes in the dome. Here you'll see the Lord blessing the Sabbath Day and making her holy.

A number of threadlike red lines run through the mosaics (you can see them clearly in the scene closest to the door to the church). The red lines outline sections of the mosaic that, because of their ruinous condition, had to be filled in by restorers. You can see similarly outlined areas in many of the other older mosaics.

Now return to the part of the narthex just before the main entrance to the church. If you're up to climbing 44 steep steps, then, with the soft glow of the narthex mosaics fresh in your mind, enter the small door to the left of the central portal and climb up to the **museum** (there's an admission fee of 1.50€), which contains ancient paintings, manuscripts, and fabrics that were used in church services. The unfinished brick vaults in the smaller rooms will help you imagine what the entire building must have looked like before it was covered with mosaics. The museum is especially worthwhile for the views you'll have of the piazza and the interior of the church.

In the room to the right of the top of the stairs you can study fragments of 14th-century mosaics close up. The faces are lined with small squares of reds, greens, and blues as intense as in a painting by Matisse. When seen from across the room, the brilliant colors make the faces vivid, but blend together in such a way that they're hardly visible individually.

Continue still farther into the museum and you'll come to the originals of the *Triumphal Quadriga,* the four magnificent horses brought from Constantinople in 1204, that were once on the facade of the building. In ancient Rome they had been harnessed to a bronze chariot carrying a bronze Roman emperor holding the reins.

If the church is extremely crowded, you might begin your tour from the balcony; otherwise, descend the stairs, go through the main door, and enter the church proper. The first part of the church is the:

8 Nave

If you come in the dead of winter and are very lucky, you may have the entire place to yourself, but more likely you'll find yourself in a dense throng with too many guides. Don't abandon hope (or the building). Find a place to sit (you may have to go well into the church before you find an empty bench), and take time to gaze about.

The church is cross-shaped, covered by five domes. Three of the domes march in succession from the main door to the high altar. Another dome is above each of the arms of the cross (the transepts). The lower part of the church is covered with stone that's flatter and simpler than that in the porch. The alabaster columns are all functional. The walls are covered with sheets of marble, cut and arranged so that their veining creates symmetrical patterns.

In the nave's vaults the Venetian mosaicists created their greatest masterpieces, all surrounded by a golden aura that W. B. Yeats called "God's holy fire." Light is important mainly to illumine and reflect off the mosaics; therefore, the windows were placed at the very bottom of the domes to be as unobtrusive as possible. There's a large circular Gothic rose window in the south transept that seems very out of place in this Byzantine-style building; it was added to provide light for ducal ceremonies and for the display of relics.

The three major domes between the door and the altar depict three forms of interaction between God and humanity. In the large dome immediately above as you enter the church is the Descent of the Holy Spirit, in the form of a dove, on the disciples. The great dome in the center of the church shows the Ascension of Christ into heaven. In the dome above the sanctuary is still another image of Christ, this time with the prophets who foretold his coming.

The arches between the domes and some of the walls have scenes from the life of Christ. On the arch between the first and second domes are some of the most beautiful narrative scenes in San Marco, illustrating Christ's death and resurrection with Byzantine restraint. On the right is the Crucifixion. On the top are the holy women visiting the empty tomb on Easter morning. On the left, opposite the Crucifixion, is Christ's journey to hell to liberate the souls of the righteous of the Old Testament. This last scene was the usual way of illustrating Christ's resurrection in Byzantine art.

The lesser domes, arches, and walls depict various saints and stories connected with St. Mark.

Many of the original mosaics have been replaced in the last 500 years. Sometimes the mosaicist simply copied the composition that had been here before. The apse above the high altar is Renaissance in date (1506) but very Byzantine in style. More often an artist was commissioned to design a new composition of the same subject, and these changes were generally for the worse.

Move on now to the:

❾ Sanctuary barrier and pulpits

The culmination of any church is its sanctuary, the place around the altar reserved for the priests and choir. The rest of the church, where the congregation stands, is focused on it. It's separated architecturally by being raised up and enclosed by a screen. The stone slabs that form the parapet of the screen have, however, been put on hinges so that they can be opened for services (today's congregation has a much better view of the sanctuary than did earlier congregations).

Beneath the sanctuary is a many-columned crypt designed to contain the shrine of St. Mark. It's well below water level and was generally flooded until an impressive job of sealing, completed in

1993, rendered it dry for the first time in centuries. The crypt is accessible only for prayer.

On top of the screen, in the center, is a silver crucifix flanked by statues of Mary and John the Evangelist, and flanking this group are the 12 Apostles. These handsome Gothic figures were installed in 1396.

Immediately in front of the screen on either side are pulpits. The one on the left, the green stone wedding cake topped with a bulging parapet and a canopy, was for reading the Bible. The reddish pulpit on the right was for the presentation of the doge to the people and the display of holy relics. In the 18th century, when the choir of San Marco was world famous, musicians would crowd into it to play for services.

Walk into the transept, beneath the dome, and turn right between the columns. In front of you is the:

⑩ Treasury

The treasury (admission fee 2€) has the world's best collection of Byzantine treasures, together with a number of masterpieces made in Venice itself.

The very best treasure, however, is in the sanctuary, and it requires still another admission fee (1.50€). As you leave the treasury, move toward your right in the direction of the sanctuary, following the signs that say PALA D'ORO. The turnstile just beyond the ticket seller is more or less where the doge's throne would have been placed when the doge attended the service.

After you pay, go around to the back of the high altar to see the:

⑪ Pala d'Oro (Golden Altarpiece)

The altarpiece is a stunning conglomeration of Byzantine enameling, gold, and jewels. According to a 1796 inventory, its decorations include 1,300 pearls, 400 garnets, 300 sapphires, 300 emeralds, 90 amethysts, 75 balases, 15 rubies, 4 topazes, and 2 cameos. Begun around 1105, it reached its present appearance only in 1342, enlarged and enriched through several centuries. It was made to face into the nave, and still does on the major feasts. Generally, however, it's turned in the opposite direction so that you can't look for free.

While you're in the sanctuary, admire the four richly carved alabaster columns that support the stone canopy above the altar. The figures in the arches illustrate the life of Christ. Scholars have argued about whether the columns were made in Constantinople in the 6th century or Venice in the 13th. The latter date is probably correct, but it hardly matters. Like so much else in San Marco, they're unique.

You'll probably leave the church on the side opposite the Doge's Palace, which will bring you to the:

⑫ Piazzetta dei Leoni (Small Square of the Lions)

The square is named for the two battered red Verona stone beasts (1722) that guard the well. Facing it, beneath the large arch (to your right if you left the church through the side door), is the noble tomb of Venice's 19th-century hero, Daniele Manin, who led the short-lived revival of the Venetian Republic from 1848 to 1849.

Now it's time to circle back to the other chief treasure of Venice, the:

⑬ Doge's Palace

The palace was begun in or shortly after A.D. 811 as a castle for the first duke, Agnolo Participazio. It has undergone several rebuildings and expansions, so no traces of the original structure are visible. The gracious Gothic structure you see today was not begun until around 1340 and was constructed in various stages over the next 100 years.

This palace remained the home of the doges (dukes) for almost a millennium, until the fall of the Venetian Republic in 1797; but the doge's actual living quarters were effectively reduced to four rooms. The purpose of the 14th-century rebuilding was to accommodate the various councils, offices, courts, prisons, and armories that were needed to make the palace not merely the town hall of the city of Venice but capital of the Venetian Empire as well. Unlike other medieval Italian governmental buildings, it's not a fortress. Its open loggias, picturesque decorations, and graceful structure bear witness to the security that the Venetian rulers felt here in the center of their stable, prosperous state.

There is sculpture at each corner of the building. On the level of the upper loggia is a protecting archangel. On the lower level are symbolic biblical scenes: *The Judgment of Solomon* is nearest the basilica, and *Adam and Eve* is at the opposite end of the facade near the piazzetta. There are delicate bits of symbolic sculpture on the capitals. Look for the ninth arch from the left on the upper loggia. Between these columns of red stone, death sentences were read.

The principal entrance to the palace is between the palace and the basilica, the:

⑭ Porta della Carta (Paper Door)

The door may have gotten its name from the professional scribes who set up shop near here. It was built under Doge Francesco Foscari (in office 1423–57). Doge Foscari began the series of conquests of the mainland of Venice—conquests that ultimately turned Venice from an aggressive city of merchant gentlemen in the 14th century into a conservative city dominated by a landed aristocracy in the 18th. Foscari built this impressive and elaborate late-Gothic entrance to the Doge's Palace, with a statue of himself kneeling before a winged lion, the symbol of St. Mark and of Venice itself.

After Napoleon conquered Venice in 1797, the French paid the chief stonemason, one Giacomo Gallini, 982 ducats to destroy all the lions of St. Mark in Venice. Though Giacomo took the money, this was one of the few lions his masons got around to chiseling off. It seems appropriate that the effigy of the man who began Venice's mainland empire should have been effaced by order of the man who destroyed it. The lion and the statue of the doge that you see today are 19th-century replacements.

Go through the entrance to the enormous stairway you see before you, the:

⑮ Scala dei Giganti (Stairway of the Giants)

The stairway and the facade of the courtyard on that side were constructed after a fire gutted the east wing of the palace in 1483, to designs by Antonio Rizzo. The project was finished in 1501, but Rizzo didn't get to see it through—he had to flee Venice in 1489 when his overseers suspected that he was keeping about 15% of the construction funds for himself. The carved decoration here is derived from ancient Rome, but it's as delicate and charming—and as expensive and overdone—as the late-Gothic entryway that leads to it.

The magnificent stairway takes its name from the two oversized statues of Neptune and Mars, carved by Jacopo Sansovino in 1554, that symbolize Venice's domination of the sea and the land. The stairway was principally a stage for such ceremonies as the coronation of the doge and the reception of important foreign dignitaries. Curiously, there's a jail cell beneath the stairs.

To go any farther you'll need to pay, but it's well worth it—the council rooms are decorated with some of the best art that Venice produced.

Your tour through the Palazzo Ducale will have to follow the path laid out for you. The following are some of the highlights and are (probably) in the order that you'll encounter them. But be warned that the mandatory path occasionally changes.

You'll first encounter the:

⑯ Scala d'Oro (Golden Stairs)

This is the white-and-gold stairway that rises from the second floor. It was designed by Jacopo Sansovino and added to the palace between 1554 and 1558 to give important dignitaries a splendid access to the major reception and council rooms.

At the top of the stairs, turn right, and you'll be in the:

⑰ Sala dei Quattro Porti (Room of the Four Doors)

This is really a staging area for three of the most important meeting rooms. The best thing in it is the painting on the long wall immediately to your right as you enter, *Doge Antonio Grimani Kneeling before Faith,* begun by Titian around 1555.

The next room on the itinerary is the:

⑱ Antecollegio

This room has the loveliest collection of paintings in the palace. On the walls before you and behind you as you enter the room are four allegories (1577) by Tintoretto, filled with spiraling figures that are at once austere and sensuous. Each allegory combines pagan gods (symbolic of properties particularly propitious for Venice) with the four seasons to suggest that Venice is favored under all seasons and circumstances. If you face the door you came through, you'll see on your left, in winter, Vulcan, god of craftsmen. On your right are the three Graces in spring. Facing the opposite direction on your right is Ceres, goddess of prosperity, harvest, and summertime, separated by Wisdom (Minerva) from the harms of War (Mars). On your left, Bacchus, god of wine and of autumn, is married to Ariadne.

On the wall opposite the windows, on your right, is Jacopo Bassano's *Return of Jacob into Canaan.* To the left of it is Veronese's stunningly elegant and beautiful *Rape of Europa* (1580). We see the Phoenician princess, Europa, climbing in all innocence on the back of a white bull, who is Jupiter in disguise. Then, in several more distant scenes, we see him carrying her to the shore and across the Mediterranean, toward Crete, one of Venice's major possessions.

Next comes the:

⑲ Sala del Collegio

With its richly decorated ceiling and walls, this may well be the single most beautiful room in the palace. On the walls are glorifications of the virtues and piety of various 16th-century doges. Though there's a redundancy of Virgins and Christs, each work separately is quite handsome. As you enter, all the paintings to your right and behind you are by Tintoretto. The painting facing you is by Veronese, celebrating Doge Sebastian Falier and the Battle of Leponto (1581–82). Veronese also painted the allegorical scenes in the ceiling (1575–78); the large painting above the raised tribune is *Venice Enthroned, Honored by Justice and Peace.* The smaller figures in the ceiling represent the virtues of Venice. The woman knitting a spider web on your right, in the second ceiling panel from the entrance wall, for instance, is Dialectic, weaving (allegorically) a web of words.

The next room is a larger hall for the senate. The paintings (1585–95) are more extensive, if not necessarily of higher quality.

The exit returns you to the Room of the Four Doors. The painting on the easel is *Venice Honored by Neptune* (1745–50), by Tiepolo, one of the more recent paintings in the palace; the version above the windows is a copy. Next follows the:

⓴ Sala del Consiglio dei Dieci (Room of the Council of Ten)

The most powerful committee in Venice once met in this room. This council actually consisted of 17 people: the Council of Ten itself, the doge, and the doge's six counselors. The room's ceiling would be even more spectacular if the central painting hadn't been carted off to Paris during the Napoleonic occupation and replaced by a copy.

After this room, the tour can vary. You'll probably pass through the armory, and you may see fragments of some of the older works of art in the building, if that section is open. The two following sites are among the most memorable parts of the palace, though you may or may not see them in this order.

㉑ Sala del Maggior Consiglio (Room of the Great Council)

This room was originally constructed between 1340 and 1355, but after being gutted by fire in 1577, it was completely rebuilt. It needed to be big, because it had to seat every enfranchised citizen of Venice—all noblemen over the age of 25. Their average number was around 1,500, and their primary function was to elect the officials in the other councils. There were nine double rows of seats, arranged back-to-back and running lengthwise down the hall. (The specific arrangement of seats can be seen in a display at the far end of the room.)

The ensemble of the decoration may be more spectacular than its parts, but two of the paintings are wonderful. The enormous scene on the end wall is *Paradise* (1588–94), by Tintoretto, one of the largest paintings on canvas in the world. The oval painting on the ceiling above it is the *Triumph of Venice,* by Paolo Veronese, the perfect embodiment of Venice's self-conception—elegant, wealthy, aristocratic, and most serene.

On the walls immediately beneath the ceiling are portraits of the doges. The most famous is the one who isn't here. Opposite

Paradise, on the left, one of the portraits seems to be covered with a veil, and a text reads: "Here is the place of Marin Falier, beheaded for his crimes." In 1355, after a year in office, Doge Marin Falier attempted to overthrow the republic in an effort to replace his ceremonial power with real power, but he underestimated the efficiency of the Venetian bureaucrats.

After passing through small barren corridors, you'll come to the:
㉒ Bridge of Sighs and the New Prisons (1566–1614)
The bridge served as the link between the court and torture rooms in the Doge's Palace and the prisons on the other side of a small canal. The name "Bridge of Sighs" was a 19th-century romantic invention, but it's certainly appropriate and evocative.

The prisons continued to be used until 1919. The most famous prisoner here was Daniele Manin, the Venetian patriot, who was imprisoned here by the Austrians and later released in the 1848 rebellion. The famous and daring escape of another prisoner, Casanova, was made from an older prison, under the roof of the palace.

Much has been written about the evils of the Venetian judicial system, its use of secret denunciations and trials, political imprisonment, and torture. The piazzetta in front of the Doge's Palace was the traditional spot for state executions, and even in the republic's eminently civilized later centuries, these spectacles were gruesome. In 1595, Fynes Moryson, an Elizabethan traveler, witnessed the execution of two young men who were the sons of senators. Their hands were cut off and their tongues ripped from their throats before they were beheaded. Their crime had been a night of public drunkenness and wild behavior—their sentence may have had more to do with their failure to uphold standards expected of patricians than with their actual crimes. William Lithgow, a Scottish visitor to Venice in 1610, reported seeing a friar "burning quick [that is, alive] at St. Mark's pillars for begetting 15 young noble nuns with child, and all within one year."

Still, similar methods were standard for the period, and the rulers of Venice instinctively avoided fanaticism. For its time, Venice had one of the world's more equitable judicial systems. In the 18th century, the republic became the second country in the world to outlaw judicial torture.

At the end of your tour of the palace, you'll find yourself in the large courtyard. Note the two fantastically elaborate wellheads (1556 and 1559), made of expensive bronze, not cheap stone.

After you leave the palace, you'll be beside the:

㉓ South facade of the palace

This was built before the facade near the basilica, and the sculptural details are even better. Each capital is elaborately carved, and each is different.

The bridge next to this corner is the:

㉔ Ponte del Paglia (Bridge of Straw)

It was named not for the building material but for the cargo that was brought here. It offers a fine view of the Bridge of Sighs. Drowned bodies used to be placed nearby for relatives to claim, or, if unclaimed, to be buried by a charitable institution.

The sculpture at this corner of the Doge's Palace is the *Drunkenness of Noah,* whose three sons are just around the corner. Since those sons were supposed to have been the ancestors of all the races on the earth, this scene may suggest the breadth of Venetian trading enterprises.

Now go to the opposite end of the palace, to the two enormous columns, and you'll be in:

㉕ Piazzetta San Marco

This is the sea entrance to San Marco and the palace, with the two columns forming its gateway. This was the site of a variety of ceremonies and celebrations. From here the doge entered his ceremonial boat, *Bucentoro,* for his annual Marriage with the Sea ceremony on Ascension Day. During Carnevale, acrobats used to form huge human pyramids and some daredevil would slide down a rope to the piazzetta from the top of the campanile.

The enormous monolithic columns were trophies brought from the eastern Mediterranean in the 12th century and dedicated to Venice's patron saints. The one with the winged lion on the top is the **Column of St. Mark.** The lion was probably made around 300 B.C. in what is today southeastern Turkey, but the wings are Venetian additions. The other column supports St. Theodore, the pre-Mark patron saint of Venice; it's a hodgepodge of antique fragments standing on a Venetian dragon. Executions took place between the two columns, and to this day, some Venetians are reluctant to walk between them.

The large building opposite the Doge's Palace is the library designed by Jacopo Sansovino, beginning in 1536, and called, appropriately, the Sansovino Library (see no. 27, below). It's a glorious building. Using nothing but white stone and shadows, Sansovino achieved an effect as rich and lush as that of its polychromed neighbors. No surprise that it was influential—and you'll see echoes of it along the Grand Canal.

If you go around the library, along the water and away from the Doge's Palace, the next building you'll come to is the:

26 Zecco (mint)

The shiny gold coins minted here were called *zecchini*, which gives us our word *sequin*. The facade of this knobby building is radically different from that of the library; strangely, the two were designed by the same man, Sansovino. The ponderous and rough stones suggest that the building is so strong that the gold within is safe. Originally it had only two stories, but because the furnaces made it intolerably hot, a third story was added in 1554 to help with ventilation.

The next part of the tour is a stroll alongside and through the porticoes that surround the Piazzetta and Piazza San Marco. Begin in the nearest one, the portico beneath the:

27 Sansovino Library

At no. 7 Piazzetta San Marco is the entrance to the library itself, which is also called the Biblioteca Marciana, or Library of St. Mark. Its greatest treasure is its collection of books printed in Venice; until the end of the republic, Venice was the most important book-printing center in Italy, at one time producing more books than the rest of the world combined. Its most famous press was that of Aldus Manutius, known especially for his beautiful and scrupulously correct editions of Greek and Latin classics.

No. 13A is the entrance to the **old library,** generally opened only for special exhibits. If the door is open, by all means go up, if only to see the richly decorated rooms with paintings by Veronese, Tintoretto, and Titian, among others. With a place this beautiful for study, it's surprising that Venice didn't produce more great writers.

No. 17 is the entrance to the **Museo Archeologico,** which has an excellent collection of sculpture from ancient Greece (the Venetian Empire included many possessions in what is today Greece) and Rome.

Shortly after, the portico takes a left-hand turn, then you'll be in the:

28 Procuratie Nuove

Built after 1586, it was conceived as a sort of extension of the Sansovino Library, with one floor too many. It served as the residence for the procurators, the most honored officials in Venice after the doge. Today it houses some of the city's more elegant shops and, on the upper floors, the Correr Museum (see below).

No. 52 leads into a courtyard with the best collection of well-heads in Venice and with an excellent explanatory text in English, just inside the door from the portico. If a doorkeeper should question your purpose, indicate that you want to see the *vere da pozzo* (wellheads).

TAKE A BREAK

A few doors down is the **Caffè Florian**, Piazza San Marco 56–59 (© 041-5205641), a coffee shop that has been here since the middle of the 18th century. Casanova claimed to have stopped here for coffee after breaking out of his cell in the Doge's Palace, before fleeing Venice. From 1815 to 1866, during the years of the Austrian occupation, the Caffè Florian was a bastion of Venetian patriots. During the rebellion against Austria from 1848 to 1849, the Florian for a time called itself the Manin, in honor of the leader of the insurrection. Later in the century, according to author John Ruskin, it was a place where "the idle Venetians of the middle classes lounge, and read empty journals." It's a real pleasure to sit at an outdoor table or in one of the hyperdecorated rooms and while away an hour, but it's a pleasure that doesn't come cheap.

Now turn into the portico that runs at a right angle to the one you've been in, the:

29 Ala Napoleonica (Napoleonic Wing)

This is the wing opposite the basilica. It was rebuilt (1808–14) under Napoleon to make a formal entrance and a ballroom for the royal residence that he had constructed into the Procuratie Nuove. In the middle of this wing is a large passageway named for the Church of San Gimignano, torn down in 1808 for the greater glory of the French ruler. A representation of the facade of the church is set in the pavement in the middle of the passageway.

A grand, though chilly, neoclassical stairway rises from the passageway to the second floor and the:

30 Museo Civico Correr

This is really several connected museums. There are temporary exhibition galleries, with tickets sold at the foot of the stairs in the tourist season. This part is almost always worthwhile since the Correr hosts some of the finest temporary exhibitions in Venice. The first room of the exhibition hall is a magnificent neoclassical ballroom of 1822, designed by Lorenzo Santi, with pieces of sculpture by Venice's great neoclassical sculptor, Antonio Canova.

The main floor of the Correr Museum is dedicated to Venetian civilization, in both its more stately and its more intimate forms.

Objects range from battle standards to zoccoli, the foot-high shoes that many upper-class women and prostitutes once tottered about in. Painted scenes range from ducal processions to battles between rival Venetian mobs.

The museum continues on the next floor with the **Picture Gallery (Quadreria),** which features an excellent collection of earlier Venetian art, including what may be the earliest surviving Venetian panel painting (on a chest from around 1250). It's especially strong in paintings of the 14th and 15th centuries, and includes not only works by such Venetian artists as the Bellinis (Jacopo, Gentile, and Giovanni) and Carpaccio, but also some small masterpieces by their northern European contemporaries.

The last wing bordering the piazza is the:

㉛ Procuratie Vecchie

Built between 1514 and 1526, this was the older residence of the procurators. Now there are elegant shops on the ground floor.

Shortly after you turn into this wing you'll come upon two arches on your left that open into the **Bacino Orseolo,** which has probably the largest conglomeration of gondolas in the city, so if you're interested in hiring one (and can afford it) this is a good staging point.

TAKE A BREAK
Continuing down the portico of the Procuratie Vecchie, you'll pass several cafes with their orchestras, including **Quadri**, Piazza San Marco 120–124 (© **041-52289299**), which the occupying Austrians patronized in the first half of the 19th century, while Venetian patriots were at Florian, across the piazza. Now the bands occasionally seem at loggerheads, but not the clientele.

At the end of the portico is the:

㉜ Torre dell'Orologio (Clock Tower)

The tower was designed by Mauro Codussi and constructed between 1496 and 1499, with the two side wings added at a later time. It tells the time (to within 5 min.), the phases of the moon, and the place of the sun in the zodiac. The clock is the city's most wondrous and beloved timepiece. At the top of the tower is a balustraded terrace from which two mechanical bronze statues, called "Moors" because of the dark color of the bronze, faithfully strike the hour on a massive bell. Just below, against a field of golden stars, a winged lion of St. Mark looks out over the piazza and lagoon with his book open to the words "Peace unto you . . . ." Below the lion, a niche contains a statue of the Madonna and Child. On Epiphany (Jan 6) and during the Feast of the Ascension, the clock's hourly pageant expands to include the Magi, led by an angel, who emerge from the doors on either side of the niche and bow before the figure of the Madonna. Legend has it that the eyes of the creators of the clock, Paolo and Carlo Rainieri, were put out to prevent them from ever matching this achievement for other patrons, but in actuality the two master clockmakers received only solid praise and very solid pensions.

The arch beneath the tower marks the beginning of the Mercerie, the main shopping drag that connects San Marco and the Rialto.

Now that you've seen the piazza from the ground, you may want to see it from above. Return to the:

🕉 Campanile (Bell Tower)

It collapsed on July 14, 1902, harming no one or nothing, apparently, but the watchman's cat. In the reconstruction, the original design (1511–14, by Bartolomeo Bon) was followed faithfully, but with a much more sophisticated understanding of building principles. It's unlikely to fall again soon.

At the base of the tower is a loggia that was begun in 1538 by Jacopo Sansovino, flattened in 1902, and carefully reconstructed by piecing together the original fragments as much as possible. It's a real jewel box and is decorated with some of Sansovino's finest statues. Originally it was a sort of clubhouse for nobles; now it's the entrance to the elevator going up the tower.

This is one of the two great tower views in Venice (the other is across the water at San Giorgio Maggiore). If the line here isn't too long, you can complete your tour of the piazza with a different perspective on what you've seen.

WALKING TOUR 2	THE ACCADEMIA BRIDGE TO PIAZZA SAN MARCO

by Robert Ullian

Start:	Accademia Bridge.
Finish:	Piazza San Marco.
Time:	Two or more hours, depending on time spent exploring museums or galleries.
Best Times:	Weekday mornings or late afternoons.
Worst Times:	Midday or Sunday, when most places are closed.

Much of this walk avoids the parts of San Marco that visitors generally see anyway. Instead, it leads down side streets that take you into hidden neighborhoods and enclaves of interesting shop windows and galleries. The walk includes a visit to one church with a wonderful interior and a quick look at the exterior of another, but basically this is an odyssey of twisting explorations and small, unusual discoveries.

To start this tour, take vaporetto no. 1 to the Accademia stop and climb to the top of the:

❶ Accademia Bridge

This wooden structure was built in the 1930s (and redone in the 1980s) to replace the first Accademia Bridge, an iron span constructed by the Austrians in 1854. For both patriotic and aesthetic reasons, Venetians seem not to have fond memories of the original, which was demolished when traffic on the Grand Canal needed higher clearance. Most Venetians envision a permanent stone bridge here someday, but in recent years a proposal for a transparent plastic bridge that wouldn't obstruct the vistas has gained some attention.

Coming from the Accademia side of the bridge, the view to the right is spectacular. Looking back toward the Dorsoduro side of the Grand Canal, the vista includes the white domes and towers of Longhena's baroque masterpiece, the Church of Santa Maria della Salute (completed in 1681).

Ahead, on the invitingly gardened San Marco side of the Grand Canal, the first building to the right of the bridge is the 15th-century:

❷ Palazzo Franchetti

This palazzo is adorned with lavish Gothic tracery and a large, beautifully tended canal-side garden. Heavily renovated in 1896 by the same Baron Franchetti who restored the Ca' d'Oro, the Palazzo Franchetti, though sumptuous, is not admired by purists.

The next two buildings to the right of the palazzo, separated from it by a narrow side canal, compose the:

❸ Palazzo Barbaro

This was once the home of the family whose portraits appear on the baroque facade of the nearby Church of Santa Maria Zobenigo. The older, closer part dates from 1425. The second part of the house, added in 1694, included a much-needed ballroom. In 1882, the upper two floors of Palazzo Barbaro were bought by Mr. and Mrs. Daniel Curtis of Boston, noted patrons of the arts. Robert Browning was invited to give recitations in the library. Henry James stayed while writing *The Aspern Papers;* he also used the palazzo as a setting for *The Wings of the Dove.* Claude Monet and John Singer Sargent each had a studio in the palazzo, and Whistler did a residence there. Cole Porter visited in 1923 before moving to a floating nightclub moored outside the Salute.

From the left side of the Accademia Bridge, the first house on the San Marco side of the Grand Canal is the:

❹ Palazzo Marcello

This is now the German Consulate, with a lush, overgrown garden to its side.

The large white palazzo immediately beyond is the:

❺ Palazzo Giustiniani-Lolin

The architect Longhena completed this palazzo in 1623, when he was in his early twenties. The sculptural baroque extravagances (like those on the Salute church) that later became Longhena's hallmark are scarcely evident in this restrained, classic facade.

The next house to the left (if you stretch your neck to look and step back a bit toward the Dorsoduro side of the bridge) is the:

❻ Palazzo Falier

Though the two roofed terrace wings might seem to be a modern addition, they're actually rare surviving examples of an old architectural form the Venetians called a *liago.* Such structures appear in Carpaccio's *Miracle of the Holy Cross* (in the Accademia), which depicts the busy area of the Rialto Bridge as it looked approximately 500 years ago. A branch of the Falier family produced Marin Falier, who, in 1355, became the only doge in the history of the republic to be executed (he plotted to overthrow the republic and seize complete power). Palazzo Falier was built in the early 15th century.

Directly ahead as you proceed across the bridge, you'll see the campanile of the Church of San Vidal, the parish church originally built in the 9th century by the Falier family, whose connection to this part of town is very ancient. Follow the way around to the right and then left, past the imposing pseudo-Palladian facade of the deconsecrated Church of San Vidal, and enter the spacious, sunny:

❼ Campo Santo Stefano

Also called Campo Francesco Morosini, this is the heart of the area this walk will explore. For now, we'll stay near the wellhead at the end of the *campo* (square) closest to the Accademia Bridge.

This fashionable campo, surrounded by a number of Venice's most unusual palazzi, was inhabited by some of the republic's

Walking Tour 2: The Accademia Bridge to San Marco

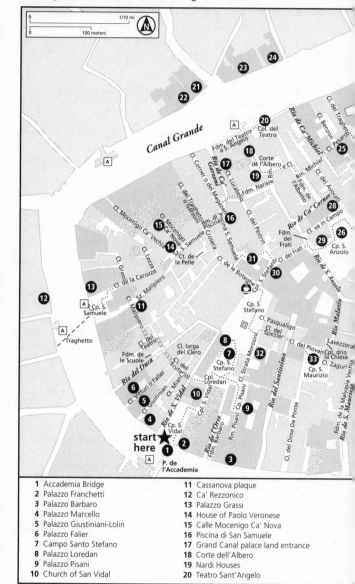

1 Accademia Bridge
2 Palazzo Franchetti
3 Palazzo Barbaro
4 Palazzo Marcello
5 Palazzo Giustiniani-Lolin
6 Palazzo Falier
7 Campo Santo Stefano
8 Palazzo Loredan
9 Palazzo Pisani
10 Church of San Vidal

11 Cassanova plaque
12 Ca' Rezzonico
13 Palazzo Grassi
14 House of Paolo Veronese
15 Calle Mocenigo Ca' Nova
16 Piscina di San Samuele
17 Grand Canal palace land entrance
18 Corte dell'Albero
19 Nardi Houses
20 Teatro Sant'Angelo

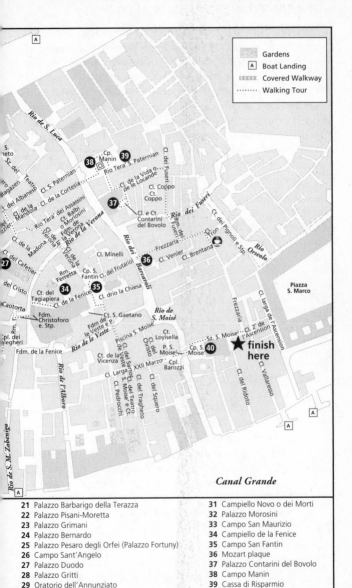

21 Palazzo Barbarigo della Terazza	**31** Campiello Novo o dei Morti
22 Palazzo Pisani-Moretta	**32** Palazzo Morosini
23 Palazzo Grimani	**33** Campo San Maurizio
24 Palazzo Bernardo	**34** Campiello de la Fenice
25 Palazzo Pesaro degli Orfei (Palazzo Fortuny)	**35** Campo San Fantin
26 Campo Sant'Angelo	**36** Mozart plaque
27 Palazzo Duodo	**37** Palazzo Contarini del Bovolo
28 Palazzo Gritti	**38** Campo Manin
29 Oratorio dell'Annunziato	**39** Cassa di Risparmio
30 Church of Santo Stefano	**40** Church of San Moisè

Gardens
Boat Landing
Covered Walkway
Walking Tour

noblest families. It was also the address of some notable courtesans. For centuries, Venice's vast community of prostitutes was one of its main tourist attractions. In the late 16th century, a directory for visitors was published, listing the names, addresses, and specialties of more than 11,000 such professionals (a copy can be seen at the Marciana Library). The campo was also the scene of bull-baiting spectacles; in 1802 the collapse of a grandstand here caused many injuries and led to the banning of this "sport" throughout Venice. A statue in the center of the campo commemorates Nicolo Tommaseo, who, along with Daniele Manin, led the insurrection against Austria from 1848 to 1849.

From the wellhead, you are opposite the very long, low-slung Renaissance facade of the:

⑧ Palazzo Loredan

After the fall of the republic in 1797, the palazzo was used to house a number of public institutions. Since 1892 it has been the home of the Veneto Institute of Science, Letters, and Arts. Check out the lavish Neptune door knocker on the main entrance, just beneath the central second-story row of eight balconied windows.

In the corner of the campo opposite the Palazzo Loredan is the immense:

⑨ Palazzo Pisani

Palazzo Pisani was begun in 1614 and continued to grow until the mid-18th century. With its formal, Romanesque-baroque style, this palazzo is unusual because its principal facade has always faced the campo rather than a canal, and because of its interior arcades, courtyards, and vast wings, which threatened to slowly encompass the entire neighborhood. Note the palazzo's own entrance *campiello*, sometimes used for outdoor performances, and the few small houses nearby that didn't get swallowed up as the palazzo grew. The palazzo now houses the Venice Conservatory of Music, as well as a banking house. Visitors are not generally welcome, but at times it's possible to see a bit of the interior during recitals, or, with luck, by sneaking in and asking about the school or concert programs when someone stops you.

From this side of the campo, look across to the:

⑩ Church of San Vidal (San Vitale)

This former church now houses an art gallery. Notice how the monumental facade, an imitation of Palladio's San Giorgio Maggiore, seems misplaced against a building with so little depth. Inside, Carpaccio's *San Vitale and Other Saints* survives from earlier times.

TAKE A BREAK
At the far end of the campo you'll see the austere wall of the side of the Church of Santo Stefano; to the left, across the calle from the entrance to the church, you'll find the **Gelateria Paolin**, Campo San Stefano, San Marco 2962A (☎ **041-5225576**), one of the best ice-cream places in Venice, with flavors that are very rich and alive. You may not be in the mood to carry a cone or sherbet now, but we'll cross this campo a number of times, and, especially on a hot day, this is an option to keep in mind.

We'll leave the palaces and facades behind for a while and enter another world via the narrow Calle de Fruttarol, which starts between the side of the Church of San Vidal and the Palazzo Loredan. Follow this narrow passageway as it continues relatively straight (though it changes names), under a soto-portego and over a canal (check the view each way as you cross the small bridge). Just after the end of the second sotoportego, turn left onto Calle dei Theatro, and then immediately onto the first right (Calle Malpiero), which goes under another sotoportego. At the end of the street, just before the intersection with Salizzada Malpiero, you'll find the:

⓫ Casanova plaque

It was on this street, once called Calle della Commedia, that Giovanni Giacomo Casanova (1725–98), the son of two actors in the nearby Theatro San Samuele, was born. The plaque conforms to the information in Casanova's autobiography, although no one can be certain in which house he was born or even if the events he recorded in his picaresque memoirs are in any way close to the truth. He became known as a libertine, spy, economist, philosopher, satirist, tax expert, and iconoclast, and we can only assume that Casanova's early years were spent planning how to escape to the glittering palaces and ballrooms only meters away from the world of his childhood.

At Salizzada Malpiero, look right at the flower boxes that adorn the buildings, but turn left, past the little-used Church of San Samuele, with its 12th-century campanile, and pass the vaporetto stop at Campo San Samuele, where you have a good view across the canal to:

⓬ Ca' Rezzonico

Look for the large white palazzo to the right of the Ca' Rezzonico vaporetto stop. Designed by the baroque master Baldasare Longhena in 1657, it was not completed until 1750; its top two floors were designed by Giorgio Massari. The Rezzonico family was legendary for its lavish entertainment; in 1758 they reached new heights of prestige when one of their members became Pope Clement XIII. He was the fifth Venetian to serve as pope.

In 1889, Robert Barrett Browning (known as "Pen"), the son of the poet Robert Browning, bought Ca' Rezzonico with the help of his wife, an American heiress, and together they refurbished the interior and built a chapel dedicated to Pen's mother, Elizabeth Barrett. They also installed a central heating system. Pen and his wife invited the 77-year-old Robert Browning, who had already spent much time in Venice, to join them in the palazzo, which the poet modestly described as "a quiet corner for my old age." Despite the heating system, Browning caught a chill and died there in December 1889. Ca' Rezzonico is now a museum of 18th-century Venetian art and furnishings (culled from many palaces) that gives you a sense of being in a still-functioning late-baroque palazzo. The attic houses a puppet theater and a period pharmacy.

In case you haven't already noticed the vast palazzo overpowering the far side of Campo San Samuele, you're facing Giorgio Massari's restrained, neoclassical:

⓭ Palazzo Grassi

Built between 1748 and 1772, this was the last of the great houses to be constructed on the Grand Canal; the Grassi family, latecomers to Venetian high society, didn't buy their way into patrician status until 1718. After the fall of the republic, the palazzo became a hotel for a time, and later a public bathhouse. In 1984 Fiat bought and refurbished the palazzo and converted it into a dazzling center for cultural and art exhibitions. The Palazzo Grassi's exhibits are beautifully mounted, often mobbed, and always worthwhile.

From Campo San Samuele, turn right onto Calle de le Carroze, and continue straight until it becomes the wider Salizzada San Samuele, which contains a number of interesting shops and galleries, some good for a quick glance, others worth further inspection.

At no. 3338 is the comfortable but nonpalatial:

⓮ House of Paolo Veronese

Veronese (1528–88) was the last great painter of the Venetian Renaissance and a master of the use of illusion in decorative art. Among Veronese's early triumphs are the lighthearted trompe l'oeil wall paintings of Villa Barbaro at Maser that create optical illusions of servants coming through nonexistent doorways, children peering through elaborate windows, and beautiful women gazing down from balconies. Venice adored his magic and showered him with commissions. For a Dominican friars' refectory, Veronese painted *The Last Supper* in the form of a lively and lavish Renaissance banqueting scene that some inside the church regarded as irreverent. Summoned before the Inquisition and ordered to change the painting, Veronese quickly complied by renaming the work *Banquet in the House of Levi*. Although (as his name indicates) Veronese was not a native Venetian, his work embodied the spirit of Venice at the height of its power—serenely joyful, poetic, and materially splendid.

Just past the house of Veronese, you might care to wander down the narrow:

🟊 Calle Mocenigo Ca' Nova

It doesn't look very interesting, but this was the land entrance to the Palazzo Mocenigo, a quadruple palace on the Grand Canal that was rented by British poet Lord Byron in 1817, two years after the final defeat of Napoleon. The more spectacular entrances would have been made directly from the Grand Canal—and not merely by gondola. At times the romantic Byron would swim from the Lido up the Grand Canal to his house, with members of the foreign community perched at various locations en route to admire his sagging but still heroic spirit and figure. The comings and goings at the rear entrance were interesting as well. Byron's household consisted of a wolf, a fox, and a number of dogs, cats, birds, and monkeys; it also included a mistress who was the wife of a Venetian draper. Later on another mistress was added, called La Fornarina ("the little oven") because she was the wife of a baker. The fiery La Fornarina, whom he described as "energetic as a python," attacked Byron with a knife and then threw herself into the Grand Canal after being banished from the palazzo.

Another important British poet, Percy Bysshe Shelley, would also have trod this alleyway. He and his wife, Mary (author of *Frankenstein*), visited Byron in 1818, accompanied by Mary Shelley's stepsister, Claire Clairmont, who was Byron's former mistress. The 19-month-old Clara Allegra, Byron's daughter by Claire Clairmont, had already been in residence for some time, under the care of La Fornarina. There's much more (when Byron finally decamped from the palazzo, he did so in the company of a new 19-year-old mistress, Countess Teresa Guiccioli), but perhaps this will be enough to entice you to detour down this alleyway with its walled gardens and hidden mysteries. Byron completed several cantos of *Don Juan* while in Venice; he died in 1824 at the age of 36.

The next part of this walk will explore the beauty and eccentricity of this hidden part of San Marco. Continue straight up Salizzada San Samuele, which narrows to become Ramo di Piscina, and ends at:

🟊 Piscina di San Samuele

The name *piscina* indicates that this was once a pool or sleeve of water leading into a canal that has long since been filled in with earth. In earlier times a piscina would have been used for bathing, or for sheltering boats. Now it is a long, colorful courtyard.

Walk to the left. At the end of Piscina San Samuele, the way diverges into three possibilities. Take the small stairway with the iron banisters on the extreme right. Follow the narrow bridgeway to the first cross passageway, and turn left into the Corte Lucatello, which is a worthwhile dead end leading to a:

⓱ Palazzo land entrance

Now that private gondolas are history, this is the kind of daily route most modern-day palazzo dwellers must take, though not every palazzo is so pleasantly landscaped. Look through the gate into a secret garden, and beyond that, the *androne*, or water-level lobby. In this palazzo, you can see straight through the androne to the Grand Canal at the front of the building.

Retrace your steps, and walk a bit past the sotoportego on the left, then turn and look back. Roof gardens abound in this neighborhood—there's even one over the sotoportego. Go back and turn right under the sotoportego, which leads onto the canal-side Fondamenta Narisi. At the end you must turn left, and suddenly this traditional neighborhood has vanished. You're in:

⓲ Corte dell'Albero

This used to be a neighborhood of narrow canals and calles.

Walk a bit to the left and you'll see what has swallowed up much of this neighborhood, the massive:

⓳ Nardi Houses

The Veneto-Byzantine and Art-Nouveau touches on this rare example of a 20th-century Venetian apartment building (built 1909–14) help it blend into the architectural fabric of the city. The building is interesting, but it reminds me how fortunate it is that large parts of Venice were not demolished to create more such complexes.

As you face the Nardi Houses, turn right and follow the corte as it narrows and leads to the Grand Canal. Here you'll find a tiny campiello beside the Sant'Angelo vaporetto stop, and to the left, a rare walkway along the Grand Canal in front of the site of the former:

⓴ Teatro Sant'Angelo

We probably owe the existence of this small *fondamenta* (walkway) to the need for a landing spot to accommodate the many gondolas that once delivered the audience. The theater that once stood here produced many of Vivaldi's 40 operas.

Walk to your left, to the end of the fondamenta. The views from spots along the Grand Canal are always interesting. Directly across the Grand Canal, bordered by a rio, is the:

㉑ Palazzo Barbarigo della Terrazza

You can recognize this palazzo by its long side terrace with a white stone balustrade. Much of its famed art collection eventually came into the possession of Czar Nicolas II.

To the left of this palazzo is the large 15th-century:

㉒ Palazzo Pisani-Moretta

Note the elaborate Gothic windows. This house still remains in the hands of the descendants of the Pisani family and retains much of its original furnishing and interior decoration.

If you walk to the far right end of the fondamenta, beside the vaporetto stop, and look across the canal to the right, you'll notice a white three-story palazzo with triple-arched windows. This is the:

㉓ Palazzo Grimani

Built in about 1520, this is one of the first Renaissance houses in Venice.

The second Gothic house to the right beyond that, with two Gothic water entrances and two floors of six Gothic central windows adorning its *piani nobili,* (main floors) is the 15th-century:

㉔ Palazzo Bernardo

If you look carefully, you can see that the two floors of central windows are out of line. Nonetheless, this is one of the most beautiful Gothic facades on the Grand Canal.

Retrace your steps to the Nardi Houses, turn left, and continue straight to the tiny short calle at the far end of the corte. When you reach the canal, turn right onto Fondamenta de l'Albero, then take a left on the first bridge you come to, which leads to Ramo Michiel. The way jogs slightly to the left as it crosses the next calle to become Calle Pesaro. As you come to the next short bridge, look to the right across the rio and you'll see the canal facade of the Palazzo Fortuny. Continue straight along the side of the palazzo, then turn right into Campo San Benedetto, and at no. 3958 is the:

㉕ Palazzo Pesaro degli Orfei

Also called the Palazzo Fortuny, it was bought at the end of the 19th century by the Spanish-born couturier, fabric designer, and photographer Mariano Fortuny y Madrazo (1871–1949). The palazzo now houses a museum of Fortuny's varied works and is also a venue for temporary exhibitions. At the turn of the century, Fortuny invented and patented a method of pleating silk ("Fortuny-pleated" skirts are still produced today), from which he created diaphanous gowns popularized by Isadora Duncan, Eleanora Duse, Sarah Bernhardt, and other romantic heroines of that age. The wide-ranging private collection of Fortuny is interesting but uneven; the studio and living quarters of this versatile genius, as well as the unrestored Gothic palazzo with its courtyard, ancient staircase, and wooden loggia, are all fascinating. During popular exhibits, the number of people allowed to enter the building must be limited because of the palazzo's fragile structure.

Exit the museum and enter Campo San Benedetto. From Campo San Benedetto, follow Calle a Fianco Ca' Pesaro to the right turn at the corner of the palazzo; at the sotoportego, turn left onto Rio Terrà de la Mandola until you reach the intersecting main thoroughfare, Calle dei Spezier, where you turn right. You'll quickly enter the bright, open:

26 Campo Sant'Angelo

Pause on this square to take in a view of the Chiesa di Santo Stefano, with the most oblique of the many leaning towers of Venice. The former convent of Santo Stefano fills one entire side of this square.

The first palazzo on the left side of the square is the:

27 Palazzo Duodo

This palazzo is privately owned and can't be visited, but you can admire its facade. Look for the numbers 3584 to identify this palace. It was once the Locando Tre Stelle, a historic inn that attracted many composers and writers in its 18th- and 19th-century heyday. The composer Cimarosa died at this inn in 1801.

Directly across, on the right side of the campo, is the:

28 Palazzo Gritti

This palazzo is unusual for its off-center doorway. Because they face onto dry land, these magnificent Gothic houses offer an unusual chance to study their carved stone ornamentation close up.

To the right, in the center of the campo, is the tiny 12th-century:

29 Oratorio dell'Annunziato

Here you'll find an *Annunciation* by Antonio Triva.

Walk straight across the campo, cross the Ponte dei Frati (enjoying views both ways), and continue straight. On your left, you'll come to the Gothic doorway of the:

30 Church of Santo Stefano

This church was built in the 14th and 15th centuries. The interior of the church is filled with rich patterning—gold and pale silver paneled squares on the ship's-keel ceiling, peach and maroon brickwork design on the upper walls, floral frescoes on the arches dividing the naves, delicately carved and painted beam work crossing the central nave, and a garden of red and white marble columns leading to the Gothic tracery of the apse. The space is lit by high windows recessed into the sides of the roof. In the sacristy you'll find three late works by Tintoretto: *The Washing of the Feet, The Agony in the Garden,* and *The Last Supper;* behind the altar, you can see the elaborately carved 15th-century monks' choir. In the center of the nave is the tomb of Francesco Morosini, who was doge from 1688 to 1694. One of the republic's great leaders, he reversed Venice's sagging fortunes by briefly reconquering the Peloponnese in Greece (see no. 32, below). The far door in the left aisle leads into the cloister, once covered with frescoes by Pordenone.

Exit the church, and turn left toward the campo. Just as you enter the campo, turn right onto Calle de le Botteghe, take the first right, and climb the steps into:

③ Campiello Novo o dei Morti (New Campiello or Campiello of the Dead)

Today this spot is a pleasant discovery: a secluded plaza with gardens overhanging one wall and a terraced, vine-covered *locanda* (small hotel) at the right. The campiello's name, however, betrays a catastrophic history. The area was a mass grave for victims of the great plague of 1630, which accounts for its higher elevation. Until 1838 the site was closed to the public for health reasons.

Retrace your steps and enter Campo Santo Stefano. On the left side of the campo, just before it narrows, is the vast:

③ Palazzo Morosini

Palazzo Morosini has its own courtyard in the corner of the campo. This was the family palace of Francesco Morosini (1619–94), who, during the Turkish invasion of Crete in 1669, held off 17 sorties and 32 assaults before finally surrendering his besieged garrison to overwhelmingly superior forces. Morosini returned to Venice and was relieved of his command, but he refused to accept defeat. Fifteen years later, sailing into battle with his beloved cat at his side (in the true spirit of Venetian eccentricity), Morosini led the republic in the last successful military campaign of its history, the reconquest of the Peloponnese. Morosini is known to the rest of the world chiefly for lobbing a shell into the Parthenon, where the Turks were unfortunately storing gunpowder. Although the Parthenon had survived relatively intact until then, the explosion turned it into the ruin we know today. Morosini's bad luck with the Parthenon continued. Like Doge Enrico Dandolo, who had sent the *Triumphal Quadriga* back to Venice to adorn the Basilica of San Marco after the sack of Constantinople in 1204, Morosini envisioned sending home a spectacular trophy to mark his triumph. He chose the horses and chariot of the goddess Athena, which formed the western pediment of the Parthenon. In the attempt to dislodge the sculpture, however, it fell to the ground and was smashed beyond repair. Morosini was elected doge upon his return to Venice in 1688, and in 1694 he sailed off once more to fight the Turks. Again like Doge Enrico Dandolo, who had led a similar expedition in his old age 500 years earlier, Morosini died in the effort; within a few years, his conquests were recaptured by the Turks. Although Venice never made a cult of its leaders, this last hero of the republic was gratefully revered. To commemorate Morosini's naval triumphs, a sculptured sea horse and various marine motifs adorn the main entrance of the palazzo. In 1894 the contents of the house were sold at auction. The embalmed body of his beloved cat is among the many Morosini possessions on display at the Museo Correr in Piazza San Marco.

One building to the left, as you face the Palazzo Morosini, is Calle dei Spezier, through which we'll exit the campo. The shops on this street bespeak the neighborhood's elegance. As you cross the small bridge, look left and you'll see that the apse of the Church of Santo Stefano has been built over the canal and that only low canal traffic can pass beneath it. A few feet beyond, is the reserved, patrician:

33 Campo San Maurizio

The campo's neoclassical church was rebuilt from 1806 to 1828. We're in the antique-gallery district of Venice, and this campo hosts occasional outdoor antique markets; check with the Tourist Information Office if you're interested.

As you face the Church of San Maurizio, enter the narrow passageway to the right, which leads to a rabbit hole of twists and turns. Bear to the right, and take a right at Calle Lavezzera; at the sotoportego at the end of the calle, turn left onto Fondamenta de la Malvasia Vecchia, which ends at an angled bridge. Proceed straight into Campiello dei Caligari (the shoemakers' campiello), and exit through the ramp on the far right at the opposite side of the campiello. From this street, turn onto the first right, Fondamenta Cristoforo, which becomes a bridge. At the end of the bridge, a sotoportego takes you to the left. Turn right onto Calle de la Fenice. Turn left into the second corte you pass, the delightful, vine-trellised:

34 Campiello de la Fenice

At the left corner of the far end of the campiello, an interesting sequence of sotoportegos eventually leads back toward Campo Sant'Angelo. The building at the end of the campiello bears a plaque dedicated to the memory of those who died in the insurrection against Austria from 1848 to 1849. The Hotel La Fenice et des Artistes is on the left side of the campiello.

A right turn at the end of the campiello, and then the next right turn, will lead you to:

35 Campo San Fantin

On your right, you'll see the remains of the legendary Fenice Theater, built in 1792 during the very last days of the republic and destroyed by fire in January 1996. (Controversy over its rebuilding is still going on.) Venice was the first city to have public perform-ances of opera, and the jewel-like 1,500-seat oval interior of the Fenice saw the world premieres of Verdi's *Rigoletto, La Traviata,* and *Simon Boccanegra,* as well as Stravinsky's *Rake's Progress* (in 1951) and Benjamin Britten's *Turn of the Screw.* During the years of the Austrian occupation (and especially during productions of works by Verdi), the Fenice was a rallying point for patriotic fervor.

The **Church of San Fantin,** opposite the site of the theater, con-tains a beautiful Renaissance dome by Sansovino over its apse. At the head of the campo is the Venetian Athenium, formerly the Scuola della Buona Morte, a confraternity that comforted prisoners condemned to death.

As you face the Church of San Fantin, exit the campo via the street to the left of the church, Calle dei Fruttarol, which is home to a number of the city's most stylish and personal shops and galleries. As you cross the bridge, look to the right across the rio at the:

36 Mozart plaque

This plaque declares that "the city of Vivaldi and Goldoni" wished to record that the young Salzburger, Wolfgang Amadeus Mozart, festively sojourned during the Carnevale of 1771.

Beyond the bridge, the name of the calle changes to Frezzeria (street of the arrow makers).

> **TAKE A BREAK**
> We're almost at the end of the walk, but if you'd like to stop for a fast, inexpensive meal, **Le Chat Qui Rit**, Calle Frezzeria 1131 (© **041-5229086**), a self-service cafeteria, is a good bet for soup or a quick bite. Follow Frezzeria until it makes a 90° turn; turn right and then immediately left. The restaurant is just on that corner. There are lots of rustic dining areas from which to choose, but they can be mobbed at mealtimes or when a tour group comes through.

To continue the tour, retrace your steps, and take a right onto the upmarket Ramo Fusieri. Continue over the bridge, along the narrowing but busy calle; opposite no. 4460, turn right onto Calle de la Vida o de Locanda (Street of Life or of the Small Inn); continue until you turn left onto Calle de Contarini del Bovolo. On the left side of this narrow calle, you'll see the:

37 Palazzo Contarini del Bovolo

This palazzo, constructed in 1499, is known for its spiral-staircase tower and airy arcaded loggia. The large Contarini family built many palaces in Venice, each with its own identifying nickname—in this case, Bovolo comes from the Venetian word for "snail shell."

Outdoor staircases were the rule in older palaces, but the Bovolo is unique. During the 19th century the palace changed hands a number of times and even served as a hotel for a time; it now houses an educational foundation. The ivy-covered garden has become a repository for architectural fragments and carved wellheads and is home to many local cats. The canal facade of this palace is unremarkable.

Retrace your steps to the intersection with Calle de la Vida, but at that point turn left. Then take the first right turn, which will lead you into the bustling:

38 Campo Manin

This campo was named for Daniele Manin, leader of the 1848 to 1849 insurrection against Austria (his house was on this plaza; looking from the statue of Manin, it's next to the left of the two bridges at the end of the campo).

The opposite end of the campo is graced by one of the city's few prominently placed modern buildings, the:

39 Cassa di Risparmio bank offices

Built in 1964, the offices were designed by noted architects Angelo Scattolin and Pier Luigi Nervi.

Exit Campo Manin by the left bridge as you face away from the statue of Manin. Continue straight on Calle de la Cortesia, a busy shopping street, which changes its name to Calle de la Mandola. Make a right turn onto Calle de la Verona, which will lead you back to Campo San Fantin. Continue straight across the campo, exit on Calle del Cafetier, and keep straight until this sequence of calles ends at Calle Larga XXII Marzo, a broad pedestrian street built in the 1870s and named for the date of the establishment of Manin's new republic in 1848. Turn left onto this important shopping calle. The dominant feature of this street, of course, is the:

40 Church of San Moisè

This church was founded in the 8th century. The current church building dates from 1632, with its facade designed by Alessandro Tremignon in 1668 and many sculptural decorations added by Heinrich Meyring in the 1680s to create a wildly rococo presence. You either love this extravaganza or hate it. Inside, Meyring created an extraordinary sculptural altarpiece in the form of Moses receiving the Ten Commandments on Mount Sinai. Venice had an unusual tradition of naming some of its churches for Old Testament figures. Not quite like anything else in Venice, San Moisè might well be translated as "Holy Moses."

To the left of San Moisè is Salizada San Moisè, which will lead you back to Piazza San Marco and the end of this stroll.

8

Shopping

In a city that for centuries has thrived almost exclusively on tourism, there's certainly no lack of places to exercise your credit cards. On second thought, make that "exercise your *platinum* cards"—just as the hotel and restaurant prices in Venice are some of the highest in Italy, so are the price tags in most of its retail stores. However, there's a lot here to buy that's truly lovely and unique— and strolling and browsing just doesn't get much more enjoyable in any other city in the world.

1 The Shopping Scene

All the main shopping streets, even the side streets, are touristy and overrun. The greatest concentration of shops is around Piazza San Marco and around the Rialto. Prices are much higher at San Marco, but the quality of merchandise is also higher.

There are two major **shopping strolls** in Venice.

First, from **Piazza San Marco** you can stroll toward spacious **Campo Morosini.** You just follow one shop-lined street all the way to its end (though the name will change several times). You begin at Salizzada San Moisè, which becomes Calle Larga XXII Marzo, and then Calle delle Ostreghe, before it opens onto Campo Santa Maria Zobenigo. The street then narrows and changes to Calle Zaguri before widening once more into Campo San Maurizio, finally becoming Calle Piovan before reaching Campo Morosini. You can take a detour down Calle Vallaressa, between San Moisè and the Grand Canal, which is one of the major shopping arteries with some of the biggest designer names in the business.

The other great shopping stroll wanders from Piazza San Marco to the Rialto in a succession of streets collectively known as the **Mercerie.** It's virtually impossible to get lost because each street name is preceded by the word *merceria,* like Merceria dell'Orologio, which begins near the clock tower in Piazza San Marco. Many commercial places, mainly shops, line the Mercerie before it reaches the Rialto, which then explodes into one vast shopping emporium.

Venice Shopping

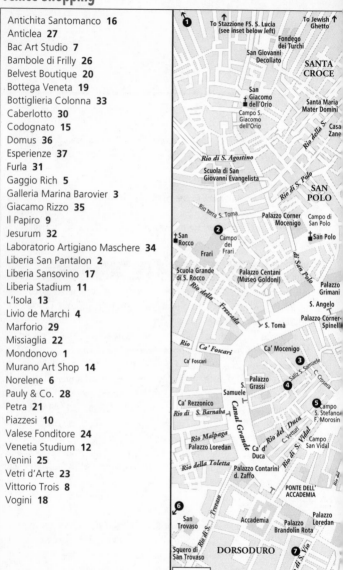

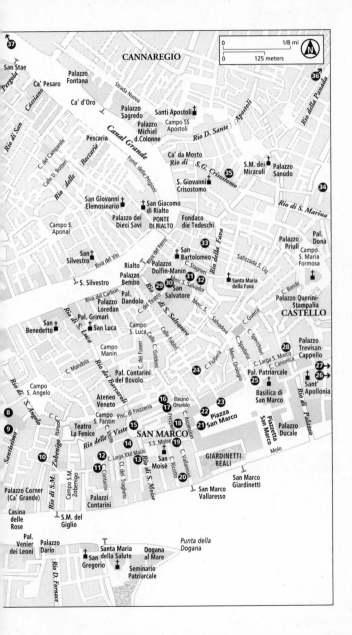

CANNAREGIO

Palazzo Fontana
Ca' Pesaro
San Stae
Ca' d'Oro
Palazzo Sagredo
Palazzo Michiel d.Colonne
Santi Apostoli
Campo SS Apostoli
Pescaria
Canal Grande
Rio di San Cassiano
Calle D. Botteri
C. del Campanile
Calle delle Beccarie
Fond. delle Prigioni
Rio di S.G. Crisostomo
Ca' da Mosto
Rio di S.G. Crisostomo
S. Giovanni Crisostomo
Rio D. Sante
Rio della Panada
S.M. dei Miracoli
Palazzo Sanudo
Rio di S. Marina
Palazzo Priuli
Pal. Donà
Campo S. Maria Formosa
San Giovanni Elemosinario
San Giacomo di Rialto
PONTE DI RIALTO
Palazzo dei Dieci Savi
Fondaco die Tedeschi
Campo S. Aponal
San Bartolomeo
Rio della Fava
Santa Maria della Fava
Salizzada S. Liq.
C. Bande
Palazzo Querini-Stampalia
CASTELLO
San Silvestro
Riva del Vin
Rialto
Palazzo Dolfin-Manin
Merc. S. Salvador
Santa Maria della Fava
C. Stagneri
S. Silvestro
Palazzo Bembo
Pal. Dandolo
Riva del Carbon
Palazzo Loredan
Pal. Grimani
San Luca
Campo S. Luca
San Salvatore
Merc. S. Salvatore
Calle Fabbri
C. Guerra
C. Specchieri
C. Spadaria
Merc. Ortologo
Palazzo Trevisan-Cappello
San Benedetto
Rio di S. Luca
Riva del Teatro
Rio di S. Salvatore
Campo Manin
Calle Goldoni
Calle C. Fuseri
Pal. Contarini del Bovolo
C. Frubera
C. Larga S. Marco
Pal. Patriarcale
Sant' Apollonia
Campo S. Angelo
C. Mandola
Rio dei Barcaroli
C. del Teatro
Ateneo Veneto
Campo S. Fantin
Pisc. di Frezzeria
Bacino Orseolo
Piazza San Marco
Basilica di San Marco
Rio di Palazzo
Canonica
Santissimo
Rio di S. Angelo
Rio di S.M. Zobenigo
Teatro La Fenice
Frezzeria
C. Ascension
C. Vallaresso
Piazzetta San Marco
Palazzo Ducale
Rio delle Veste
SAN MARCO
S.S. Moisè
San Moisè
C. Larga XXII Marzo
Cl. del Traghetto
Rio di S. Moisè
C. Ricotto
GIARDINETTI REALI
Molo
Palazzo Corner (Ca' Grande)
Casina delle Rose
Contarini
Campo S.M. Zobenigo
San Marco Giardinetti
San Marco Vallaresso
Palazzi Contarini
S.M. del Giglio
Pal. Venier dei Leoni
Palazzo Dario
San Gregorio
Santa Maria della Salute
Dogana al Mare
Punta della Dogana
Rio D. Fornace
Seminario Patriarcale

TAX REFUNDS   As a member of the European Union, Italy imposes a **value-added tax (IVA)** on most goods and services sold within its borders. If you're a resident of any country that's not a member of the European Union and spend more than 150€ at any one store (regardless of how many individual items are involved), you're entitled to a refund of the IVA.

At the time of your purchase, be sure to get a receipt and an official IVA refund form from the vendor. When you leave Italy, find an Italian Customs agent at the airport (or at the point of your exit from the country if you're traveling by train, bus, or car). The agent will want to see the item you've bought, confirm that it's physically leaving Italy, and then stamp the IVA refund form.

In some cases, including leaving Italy via one of the larger airports, you can receive a cash refund directly on the spot. If the point of departure you've selected doesn't offer this (many highway and border crossings don't), you should mail the stamped form (keeping a photocopy for your records) back to the address indicated on your IVA refund form. Sooner or later, you'll receive a refund of the tax you paid at the time of your purchase. Reputable stores view this as a matter of ordinary paperwork and are very businesslike about it. Less honorable stores might lose your dossier or be unwilling to provide the forms you'll need. It pays to deal with established vendors, especially if you're making a large purchase. You can also request the refund be credited to the credit card with which you made the purchase.

SHOPPING HOURS   Most stores open at 9 or 10am, many closing for lunch around 1 or 1:30pm and reopening from 3 to 7:30pm. Many also close on Monday morning and reduce winter hours when business is bad.

2 Tips on Shopping for Glass & Lace

Venetian glass and Venetian lace are known throughout the world. However, there are so many shoddy imitations that selecting quality products of either craft requires a shrewd eye. Some of the glassware hawked isn't worth the cost of shipping it home. Yet other pieces represent some of the world's finest artistic and ornamental glass. Murano is the island where glass is made, and the women of Burano put in painstaking hours turning out lace. If you're interested in some little glass souvenir, perhaps an animal or a bird, you'll find such items sold in shops all over Venice.

SHOPPING FOR GLASS   Venice is crammed with glass shops: It's estimated there are at least 1,000 in San Marco alone. Unless you go to a top-quality dealer, you'll find most stores sell both shoddy and high-quality glassware, and often only the most trained eye can tell the difference. A lot of "Venetian glass" isn't from Venice at all but from the Czech Republic. (Of course, the Czech Republic has some of the finest glassmakers in Europe, so that may not be bad either.) Buying glass boils down to this: If you like an item, buy it. It may not be high quality, but then high quality can cost thousands.

If you're looking for an heirloom, stick to such award-winning houses as Pauly & Co. and Venini. Even buyers of glassware for distribution outlets in other parts of the world have been fooled by the vast array of glass in Venice. If even a buyer can be tricked, the layperson has only his or her own good instincts to follow.

SHOPPING FOR LACE   Most of the lace vendors are centered around Piazza San Marco. Although the price of Venetian lace is high, it's still reasonable considering the painstaking work that goes into it. A small handkerchief with a floral border can sell for as little as 3€; however, for large items like an heirloom-quality hand-worked tablecloth, the sky's the limit.

The catch is that a lot of imitation, shoddily made lace is also sold, and you have to check carefully to make sure you're getting the real thing. If you think you're getting a deal that's too good to be true, it's probably because what you're looking at really isn't Venetian lace, but machine-made in who knows what country.

The name in Venetian lace is Jesurum, which has stood for quality since the 19th century. It has its own lace makers and, to guarantee its future, even has a school to teach apprentices how to make lace. Jesurum offers the most expensive, but also the highest quality, lace in Venice. At other places you take your chances. The lace shops are like the glassware outlets. They sell the shoddy, the machine-made, and the exquisite handmade pieces. Sometimes only the trained eye can tell the difference. Again, the best advice is to buy what you like, if you think the price is reasonable. However, even if a piece is handmade, you can never be sure exactly where it was handmade. Maybe China.

3 Shopping A to Z
ANTIQUES
Antichita Santomanco   This store is for the specialist only—particularly the well-heeled specialist. It deals in antique furniture, books, prints, and coins. Of course, the merchandise is ever-changing, but you're likely to pick up some little heirloom item in the midst

of the clutter. Many of the items date from the Venetian heyday of the 1600s. Calle Frezzeria, San Marco 1504. ✆ 041-5236643. Vaporetto: Vallaresso.

BOOKSTORES

Libreria San Pantalon   Known to Venetians as the bookshop with the cat in the window, this is a kind of store where you might browse for hours. It's known for its good selection of books on Italian music, especially opera, and it also carries beautiful arts and crafts books, gifts, games, children's books, and greeting cards. Dorsoduro 3950, Salizzada Pantalon. ✆ 041-5224436. Vaporetto: San Tomà.

Libreria Sansovino   This store is centrally located to the north of Piazza San Marco. It carries both hard- and softcover books in English as well as books on art, literature, and history. Bacino Orseolo, San Marco 84. ✆ 041-5222623. Vaporetto: Vallaresso.

Libreria Stadium   Located behind St. Mark's Basilica, this two-room shop has a wide selection of books on Venice, assorted travel books, and novels in English. The back room is devoted to special studies such as theology. Unless that interests you, the good stuff is up front. San Marco 337C. ✆ 041-4222382. Vaporetto: Vallaresso.

BRASS OBJECTS

Valese Fonditore   Founded in 1913, Valese Fonditore serves as a showcase for one of the most famous of the several foundries that make their headquarters in Venice. Many of the brass copies of 18th-century chandeliers produced by this company grace fine homes in the United States. Many visitors to Venice invest in these brass castings, which eventually become family heirlooms. If you're looking for a brass replica of the sea horses decorating the sides of gondolas, this shop stocks them in five or six styles and sizes. A pair of medium-size ones, each about 11 inches tall, begins at 150€. Calle Fiubera, San Marco 793. ✆ 041-5227282. Vaporetto: Vallaresso.

CARNEVALE MASKS

Venetian masks, considered collectors' items, originated during Carnevale, which takes place the week before the beginning of Lent. In the old days there was a good reason to wear masks during the riotous Carnevale—they helped wives and husbands be unfaithful to one another and priests break their vows of chastity. Things got so out of hand that Carnevale was banned in the late 18th century. But it came back, and the masks went on again.

You can find shops selling masks practically on every corner. As with glass and lace, however, quality varies. Many masks are great artistic expressions, while others are shoddy and cheap. The most sought-after mask is the *Portafortuna* (luck bringer), with its long nose and birdlike visage. *Orientale* masks evoke the heyday of the Serene Republic and its trade with the Far East. The *Bauta* was worn by men to assert their macho qualities, and the *Neutra* blends the facial characteristics of both sexes. The list of masks and their origins seems endless.

Mondonovo   Here, talented artisans labor to produce copies of both traditional and more modern masks, each of which is one-of-a-kind and richly nuanced with references to Venetian lore and traditions. Prices range from 25€ for a fairly basic model to 1,500€ for something you might display on a wall as a piece of sculpture. Rio Terrà Canal, Dorsoduro 3063. ✆ 041-5287344. Vaporetto: Ca' Rezzonico.

DOLLS

Bambole di Frilly   This studio/shop offers dolls with meticulously painted porcelain faces (they call it a "biscuit") and hand-tailored costumes, including dressy pinafores. The reasonably priced smaller dolls are made with the same painstaking care, offering a real souvenir value. Fondamenta dell'Osmarin, Castello 4974. ✆ 041-5212579. Vaporetto: Mto. Vittorio Emanuele.

FABRICS

Select outlets in Venice sell some of the greatest fabrics in the world.

Gaggio Rich   This emporium offers unique items, the most stunning of which are velvets and artistic fabrics with filigree, all inspired by the deep colors and designs of fabled designer Mariano Fortuny. It's all very Venetian and very decadent. You can purchase these fabrics by the meter, or they can be fashioned into clothing, shawls, cushions, or whatever. San Marco, San Stefano 3451-3441. ✆ 041-5228574. Vaporetto: Accademia.

Norelene   This legendary store features lustrous hand-printed silks, velvets, and cottons, plus wall hangings and clothing. Calle della Chiesa, Dorsoduro 727. ✆ 041-5237605. Vaporetto: Accademia.

Venetia Studium   For years, Lino Lando worked to crack the secret of fabled designer Mariano Fortuny's *plissé* (finely pleated silk). Eventually he found the secret. The result can now be yours in his selection of silk accessories, scarves, Delphos gowns, and even silk lamps. There's also a newer shop at Mercerie, San Marco 723 (✆ 041-5229859). Calle Larga XXII Marco, San Marco 2403. ✆ 041-5229281. Vaporetto: Santa Maria del Giglio or San Marco.

Vittorio Trois   Trois was selected to receive a priceless legacy. The great Mariano Fortuny revealed his exquisite printing techniques to a friend of Trois, the late Contessa Gozzi, and she passed them on to Trois, who made a business of them. Today you can buy the same Fortuny patterns that stunned your grandparents on their visit to Venice decades ago. The radiant designs look like brocade and are sold by the yard. Campo San Maurizio, San Marco 2666. ✆ 041-5222905. Vaporetto: Santa Maria del Giglio.

FASHION

Belvest Boutique   This is one of the finest boutiques, specializing in clothing for women and men, both handmade and ready-to-wear. Fabric from some of the world's leading cloth makers is used in the designs. Linked with Vogini, the famous purveyor of leather work, the boutique is a bastion of top-quality craftsmanship and high-fashion style. Calle Vallaresso, San Marco 1305 (near Harry's Bar). ✆ 041-5287933. Vaporetto: Vallaresso.

Caberlotto   By accident we stumbled on Caberlotto, with a stunning collection of classic apparel for both women and men, all in jewel-like colors. Head here to see the rich collection of Loro Piana shawls, cashmere sweaters, scarves, and other apparel. San Salvador, San Marco 5114. ✆ 041-5229242. Vaporetto: San Marco.

FOOD PRODUCTS

Giacamo Rizzo   For packaged food products, many from the surrounding Veneto, this is one of our favorite stores in Venice. On our most recent visit, we counted 30 different types of pasta alone, with excellent selections in ravioli and tortellini. Sometimes the pasta is imaginatively shaped into Venetian symbols such as carnival hats or even a gondola. Flavors include zucchini, spinach, and beet. Other Italian specialties such as balsamic vinegar, all kinds of sauces, and refined olive oils are also sold. The location is northeast of the Rialto Bridge. Cannaregio 5778 (Calle San Giovanni Grisostomo). ✆ 041-5222824. Vaporetto: Rialto.

GLASS

Anticlea   This shop offers scores of antique and reproduction glass beads, strung or unstrung, in many sizes, shapes, and colors. Campo San Provolo, Castello 4719. ✆ 041-5286949. Vaporetto: San Zaccaria.

Domus   On the island of Murano, home of the actual glassworks, this shop offers a good selection of designs by the island's top artisans, concentrating on smaller objects like jewelry, vases, bowls, bottles, and drinking glasses. Here you'll find designs by Carlo Moretti. Fondamenta dei Vetrai 82, Murano. ℭ 041-739215. Vaporetto: 12 or 13 to Murano.

Galleria Marina Barovier   This isn't just another store stocking the Murano-style glass trinkets found by the thousands throughout Venice—it's the repository for some of Italy's most creative modern glass sculptures. Since it was opened in the early 1980s by its namesake, Marina Barovier, in the unlikely Venetian suburb of Mestre, it has grown in stature. Especially sought after are sculptures by master glassmakers Lino Tagliapietra and Dale Chihuly, whose chandeliers represent amusing and/or dramatic departures from traditional Venetian forms. Don't despair if you're on a budget; some simple items begin as low as 10€. Anything can be shipped. Salizzada San Samuele, San Marco 3216. ℭ 041-5226102. Vaporetto: San Samuele.

L'Isola   This is the shop of Carlo Moretti, one of the world's best-known contemporary artisans working in glass. You'll find all his signature designs in decanters, drinking glasses, vases, bowls, and paperweights. Campo San Moisè, San Marco 1468. ℭ 041-5231973. Vaporetto: Vallaresso.

Pauly & Co   One of the oldest (founded in 1866) and largest purveyors of traditional Venetian glass is Pauly, with a labyrinth of more than two dozen showrooms. Part of the premises is devoted to something akin to a museum, where past successes (now antiques) are displayed with pride. Antique items are only rarely offered for sale, but they can be copied and shipped to virtually anywhere, and chandeliers can be wired to work with the electricity back home. Ponte dei Consorzi, San Marco 4392. ℭ 041-5209899. Vaporetto: San Zaccaria.

Venini   Venini's art glass has caught the attention of collectors from all over the world. Many of their pieces, including extraordinary lamps, bottles, and vases, are works of art and represent the best of Venetian craftsmanship. Along with the previously recommended Pauly & Co., Venini represents the master craftspeople of Venetian glassmakers. Its best-known glass has a distinctive swirl pattern in several colors, called a *venature*. This shop is known for the refined quality of its glass, some of which appears almost transparent. Much of it is very fragile, but they learned long ago how to ship it anywhere safely. To visit the furnace, call ℭ **041-739955.** Piazzetta Leoncini, San Marco 314. ℭ 041-5224045. Vaporetto: San Zaccaria.

Vetri d'Arte   Here you can find moderately priced glass jewelry for souvenirs and gifts, as well as a selection of pricier crystal jewelry and porcelain bowls. Piazza San Marco, San Marco 140. ℂ 041-5200205. Vaporetto: Vallaresso.

GRAPHICS

Bac Art Studio   This studio sells paper goods, but it's mainly a graphics gallery, noted for its selection of engravings, posters, and lithographs of Venice at Carnevale time. Items for the most part are reasonably priced; care and selection obviously went into the gallery's choice of merchandise. Campo San Vio Dorsoduro 862. ℂ 041-5228171. Vaporetto: Accademia.

Petra   Head here for that just right, and light, souvenir. Osvaldo Böhm has a rich collection of photographic archives specializing in Venetian art as well as original engravings and maps, lithographs, watercolors, and Venetian masks. You can also see modern serigraphs by local artists and some fine handcrafted bronzes. San Marco 2424. ℂ 041-5231815. Vaporetto: Vallaresso.

HANDCRAFTS

Murano Art Shop   Not the friendliest shop in Venice, this small, well-stuffed store is nonetheless a repository of some of the city's best crafts. Much of the merchandise is whimsical and creative, with a wide array of porcelain, Venetian dolls, pictures, frames, puppets, marionettes, costume jewelry, and even music boxes. This is also one of the best places to shop for those famous Venetian masks used during Carnevale. Shop carefully, though. Prices aren't always to our liking. San Marco 1232. ℂ 041-5233851. Vaporetto: San Marco.

JEWELRY

Codognato   For antique jewelry, there's no shop finer than Codognato. Some of the great heirloom jewelry of Europe is sent here when estates are settled. Calle Ascensione, San Marco 1295. ℂ 041-5225042. Vaporetto: San Marco.

Esperienze   The owner personally designs the jewelry here, crafting it from the famous Murano glass. A wide selection of necklaces, one-of-a-kind pins, and assorted jewelry is sold. The shop is especially noted for its earrings, which could contain anything from a Venetian pearl to a typically Venetian scene on glass in the middle. Cannaregio 326B (Ponte delle Guglie). ℂ 041-721866. Vaporetto: Ponte delle Guglie.

Missiaglia   Since 1846, Missiaglia has been the private supplier to rich Venetians and savvy shoppers from around the world seeking the best in gold and jewelry. Go here for that special classic piece. But, because the family keeps a sharp watch on the latest developments in international jewelry design, something a little more cutting edge might catch your eye. Their specialty is colored precious and semiprecious gemstones set in white or yellow gold settings. Piazza San Marco, San Marco 125. ✆ 041-5224464. Vaporetto: Vallaresso.

LACE

Jesurum   For serious purchases, Jesurum is the best place. This elegant shop, a center of noted lace makers and fashion creators, is located in a 12th-century palazzo. You'll find Venetian handmade or machine-made lace and embroidery on table, bed, and bath linens, plus hand-printed swimsuits. Quality and originality are guaranteed and special orders are accepted. The exclusive linens are expensive, but the inventory is large enough to accommodate any kind of budget. Staff members insist that everything sold is made in or around Venice in traditional patterns. Merceria del Capitello, San Marco 4857. ✆ 041-5206177. Vaporetto: San Zaccaria.

LEATHER

Bottega Veneta   Bottega Veneta is primarily known for its woven leather bags. These bags are sold elsewhere too, but you'll get the best deals here at the company's flagship outlet. The shop also sells shoes for men and women, suitcases, belts, and everything made of leather. There's also an array of high-fashion accessories. Calle Vallaresso, San Marco 1337. ✆ 041-5202816. Vaporetto: Vallaresso.

Furla   Furla is a specialist in women's leather bags. It also sells belts and gloves for women. Many of the bags are stamped with molds, making them appear to be alligator, lizard, or some other exotic creature. They come in a varied choice of colors, including what Austrians call "Maria Theresa ochre." Furla also displays a varied selection of costume jewelry and an array of belts, silk scarves, briefcases, and wallets. Merceria del Capitello, San Marco 4954. ✆ 041-5230611. Vaporetto: Rialto.

Marforio   Marforio is in the heart of the city. Founded in 1875, it's the oldest and largest leather-goods retail outlet in Italy. The company, run by the same family for five generations, is known for the quality of its leather products, and this outlet has an enormous assortment. You'll find all the famous European labels—Valentino, Armani, Cerruti, and Cardin, among others. Campo San Salvador, San Marco 5033. ✆ 041-5225734. Vaporetto: Rialto.

Vogini   Every kind of leather work is offered here, especially women's handbags, which are exclusive models. There are also handbags in petit-point embroideries and crocodile as well as men's and women's shoes. Brand names include Armani, Mosquino, Versace, and products designed and manufactured by Vogini itself. The travel-equipment department contains a large assortment of trunks and both hard- and soft-sided suitcases and makeup cases. Calle dell'Ascensione, San Marco 1291, 1292, and 1301 (near Harry's Bar). ✆ 041-5222573. Vaporetto: Vallaresso.

MARKETS

If you're looking for some bargain-basement buys, head not for any basement but to one of the little shops lining the **Rialto Bridge** (Vaporetto: Rialto). The shops there branch out to encompass fruit and vegetable markets as well. The Rialto isn't the Ponte Vecchio in Florence, but for what it offers it isn't bad, particularly if your euros are running short. You'll find a wide assortment of merchandise, from angora sweaters to leather gloves. The quality is likely to vary widely, so keep your eyes open.

PAPER & STATIONERY

Florence is still the major center in Italy for artistic paper—especially marbleized paper. However, craftspeople in Venice still make marble paper by hand, sheet by sheet. The technique of marbling paper originated in Japan as early as A.D. 1000, spreading through Persia and finally reaching Europe in the 1400s. Except for France, marbling had largely disappeared with the coming of the Industrial Revolution, but it was revived in Venice in the 1970s. Each sheet of handmade marbleized paper is one of a kind.

Il Papiro   If you never considered paper and stationery a high art form, think again. Thinking of sending off a handwritten proposal of marriage? Pen it on something from Il Papiro, and it will certainly look a lot more impressive. In addition to absolutely gorgeous stationery, you'll also find beautiful photo albums, address books, picture frames, diaries, and boxes covered in artfully printed paper. Campo San Maurizio, San Marco 2764. ✆ 041-5223055. Vaporetto: San Maria del Giglio.

Piazzesi   Stylish Piazzesi claims to be the oldest purveyor of writing paper in Italy (it opened in 1900). Some of its elegant lines of stationery require as many as 13 artisans to produce. Most of the production here is hand-blocked, marbleized, stenciled, and/or accented with dyes that are blown onto each sheet with a small breath-operated tube. Also look for papier-mâché masks and commedia dell'arte–style statues representing age-old professions like architects, carpenters, doctors, glassmakers, church officials, and notaries. We also like the whimsically decorated containers for CDs and computer diskettes. Campiello della Feltrina, San Marco 2511. ✆ 041-5221202. Vaporetto: Santa Maria del Giglio.

WINE

Bottiglieria Colonna   The best selection of wines from the Veneto but also from other wine-growing regions of Italy are found here. Feast your eyes on an array of Chianti, Brunelli, Varoli, and other wines. The selection from the north of Italy, obviously, is the strongest. Gift packages of six wines can be made up for you. Castello 5595 (Calle della Fava). ✆ 041-5285137. Vaporetto: Rialto.

WOOD SCULPTURES

Livio de Marchi   This is a unique outlet in Venice. De Marchi and his staff can take almost any item, from cowboy boots to a Vespa to a woman's handbag, and sculpt it in wood in hyper-real detail. Even if you don't buy anything, just stop in to take a look at these stunning items sculpted from wood. San Samuele, San Marco. ✆ 041-5285694. Vaporetto: Vallaresso.

9

Venice After Dark

For such a fabled city, Venice's nightlife is pretty meager. Who wants to hit the nightclubs when strolling the city at night is more interesting than any spectacle staged inside? Ducking into a cafe or bar for a brief interlude, however, is a nice way to break up your evening walk. Although it offers gambling and a few other diversions Venice is pretty much an early-to-bed town. Most restaurants close at midnight.

The best guide to what's happening in Venice is *Un Ospite di Venezia,* a free pamphlet (part in English, part in Italian) distributed by the tourist office. It lists any music and opera or theatrical presentations, along with art exhibitions and local special events.

At least 10 of Venice's historic churches host **concerts,** with a constantly changing schedule. These include the Chiesa di Vivaldi, the Chiesa della Pietà, and the Chiesa Santa Maria Formosa. Many concerts are free; others charge an admission that ranges from 15€ to 25€. For information about what's on, call ℂ **041-5208722.**

1 The Performing Arts

In January 1996, a dramatic fire left the fabled **Teatro de La Fenice** at Campo San Fantin, the city's main venue for performing arts, a blackened shell and a smoldering ruin. Opera lovers around the world, including Luciano Pavarotti, mourned its loss. The Italian government has pledged $12.5 million for its reconstruction, but restoration efforts have proceeded at the proverbial snail's pace. Who can predict when it will be done? However, the theater's neo-classical facade survived the blaze and is the subject of sightseeing interest today.

Despite the tragic loss of La Fenice, cultural events have continued in a temporary theater built as a short-term substitute. Designed in the form of a big circus-style tent, within walking distance of Piazzale Roma, is the **Teatro Temporaneo de La Fenice (aka PalaFenice),** Isola Tronchetto (ℂ **041-786511**). For a list of other cultural performances in Venice, contact either the tourist office or City Hall, the **Municipio Comunale di Venezia,** at ℂ **041-2748200.**

This is the city of Vivaldi, and if you're lucky, you might catch a performance of *The Four Seasons* at the **Chiesa di Vivaldi** (© **041-5231096**), officially known as the Chiesa della Pietà. There are Vivaldi performances at other churches, but this church, where the "red priest" (nicknamed because of his red hair, not his politics) was once choral director, is the main venue. Tickets are sold at the church's box office on the Riva degli Schiavoni or at the desk of the next-door Metropole Hotel, and cost around 25€ for adults and 13€ for students.

Teatro Goldoni   This theater, close to the Ponte di Rialto in the San Marco district, honors Carlo Goldoni (1707–93), the most prolific Italian playwright. The theater presents a changing repertoire of productions, often plays in Italian, but musical presentations as well. The box office is open Monday to Saturday from 10am to 1pm and 4:30 to 7pm. Calle Goldoni (near Campo San Luca). © **041-2402011**. Tickets 14€–25€. Vaporetto: Rialto.

2 The Bar Scene

Want more in the way of nightlife? All right, but be warned: The Venetian bar owners may sock it to you when they present the bill.

Bar ai Speci   This charming corner bar is only a short walk from St. Mark's Basilica. Its richly grained paneling is offset by dozens of antique mirrors, each different, whose glittering surfaces reflect the rows of champagne and scotch bottles and the clustered groups of Biedermeier chairs. In the Hotel Panada, Calle dei Specchieri, San Marco 646. © **041-5209088**. Vaporetto: Vallaresso.

Bar Ducale   Bar Ducale occupies a tiny corner of a building near a bridge over a narrow canal. Customers stand at the zinc bar facing the carved 19th-century Gothic-reproduction shelves. Mimosas are the specialty here, but tasty sandwiches are also offered. The ebullient owner learned his craft at Harry's Bar before going into business for himself. Today his small establishment is usually mobbed every day of the week. It's ideal for an early evening cocktail as you stroll about. Calle delle Ostreghe, San Marco 2354. © **041-5210002**. Vaporetto: Vallaresso.

Devil's Forest   Set a stone's throw from the Rialto Bridge, this is an authentic Irish pub where you'll find a good balance between the English- and Italian-speaking worlds. You'll find a comforting roster of beers and ales on tap here (Guinness, Harp, Kilkenny, and a line of German beers), and platters of food that average between 4.20€

and 8€. Don't expect bangers and mash—things are more Mediterranean than that, with lots of emphasis on sandwiches, pastas, and simple grills. Calle Stagneri, San Marco 5185. ✆ 041-5200623. Vaporetto: Rialto.

Do Leoni The interior is a rich blend of scarlet-and-gold carpeting with a lion motif, English pub–style furniture, and Louis XVI–style chairs, along with plenty of exposed mahogany. While sipping your cocktail, you'll enjoy a view of a 19th-century bronze statue, the lagoon, and the foot traffic along the Grand Canal. In the Londra Palace Hotel, Riva degli Schiavoni, Castello 4171. ✆ 041-5200533. Vaporetto: San Zaccaria.

Fiddler's Elbow Five minutes from the Rialto Bridge in the Cannaregio district, this Irish-style pub is run by the same people who operate equally popular Fiddler's Elbows in both Florence and Rome. Since its opening late in 1992, it has become one of Venice's most popular watering holes, complete with satellite TV. In the summer, there is live outdoor music. Corte dei Pali, Cannaregio 3847. ✆ 041-5239930. Vaporetto: Ca' d'Oro.

Guanotto From bustling premises one floor above street level, this bar and cafe has attracted neighborhood locals since it was established in 1884. Within either of two old-fashioned rooms, you can order such drinks as whiskey, an array of coffees, hot chocolate, and a house specialty (spritz) that combines white wine with seltzer waters and bitters. Toast, pastries, and ice cream are the only food served. Except during busy days in midsummer, many visitors find it a bit more soothing, and less frenetic, than many of the ground-floor cafes nearby. Ponte del Lovo, 4819. ✆ 041-5208439. Vaporetto: Rialto.

Harry's Bar The single most famous of all Ernest Hemingway's watering holes, Harry's Bar is known for inventing its own drinks and exporting them around the world. It's also said that carpaccio, the delicate raw-beef dish, was invented here. Fans say that Harry's makes the best Bellini in the world. (Even Hemingway ordered a Bellini here once, though later he called it a drink for sissies and suggested it might be ideal for Fitzgerald.) Harry's Bar is found around the world, from Munich to Los Angeles, from Paris to Rome, but this is the original. Except for a restaurant, Harry Cipriani in New York City, the other bars are unauthorized knockoffs. In Venice, the bar is a Venetian tradition and landmark—not quite as famous as the Basilica di San Marco, but almost. Celebrities frequent the place during the various film and art festivals. Calle Vallaresso, San Marco 1323. ✆ 041-5285777. Vaporetto: Vallaresso.

Martini Scala Club   Martini Scala Club is an elegant restaurant with a piano bar. It has functioned as some kind of inn in one manifestation or another since 1724. You can enjoy its food and wine until 3:30am—it's the only kitchen in Venice that stays open late. The piano bar gets going after 10pm. Campo San Fantin, San Marco 1980. ☎ 041-5224121. Vaporetto: Vallaresso or Santa Maria del Giglio.

Paradiso Perduto   Early every evening except Wednesday, this authentic inn functions as a likable tavern, serving well-prepared platters of seafood to locals who live close to Venice's train station, far from the congestion around St. Mark's Square. If you're interested in dining (the *frittura mista* of fish, served with polenta, is wonderful), main courses are quite cheap; dinner is served Thursday to Tuesday from 7 to 10:30pm. But the place is at its best after 11pm, when a mixture of soft recorded music and live piano music creates a backdrop for conversation until at least 2am. Fondamenta della Misericordia, Cannaregio 2540. ☎ 041-720581. Vaporetto: San Marcuola.

3 Wine Bars

Cantina do Spade   This historic wine bar beneath an arcade near the main fish and fruit market dates from 1475. It was once a hangout of Casanova's. It's completely rustic and bare bones, but regulars come here to order *cicchetti* (equivalent to Spanish tapas), of which there are 250 varieties. Seasonal game dishes, including boar, deer, and reindeer, are served. Venetians delight in the 220 different wines, beginning at 1.75€ per glass. The place is a local favorite, and has been for centuries. Calle do Spade, San Polo 860. ☎ 041-5210574. Vaporetto: Rialto.

Mascareta   This wine bar was established in 1995. The focus is on Italian wines, many from the Veneto region, with affordable vintages available by the glass. There's only room for 20 people, seated at cramped tables in an old Venetian building, but if you're hungry, you can order simple, cheap platters of snack-style food (prosciutto, cheese plates, and other dishes). Calle Lunga Santa Maria Formosa, Castello 5138. ☎ 041-5230744. Vaporetto: Rialto.

Vino Vino   You can choose from more than 250 Italian and imported wines here. Vino Vino attracts a varied clientele: It wouldn't be unusual to see a Venetian countess sipping Prosecco near a gondolier eating a meal. This place is loved by everyone from snobs to young people to almost-broke visitors. It offers wines by the bottle or glass, including Italian grappas. Popular Venetian dishes are also served, including pastas, beans, *baccalà* (codfish), and polenta. The two rooms are always jammed like a vaporetto at rush hour, and there's take-out service if you can't find a table. Ponte della Veste, San Marco 2007. ℂ **041-2417688.** Vaporetto: Vallaresso.

4 The Cafe Scene

All of the cafes on Piazza San Marco offer a simply magical setting, several with full orchestras playing in the background. But you'll pay shockingly high prices (plus a hefty music charge) to enjoy a drink or a snack while you soak in this setting. Prepare yourself for it, and splurge on a beer, a cappuccino, or an ice cream anyway. It'll be the most memorable 15€ or 20€ (yep, that's *per person*) you'll drop on your trip.

Caffè Chioggia   Although it isn't the only cafe whose entrance opens onto the Piazza San Marco, it's the only one with a view of the Venetian lagoon (off to one side), and the only one offering live music that continues in one form or another throughout the day and evening. Starting around 10am and continuing, with reasonable breaks, until 1:30am, piano bar music might begin the day, eventually terminating with a jazz trio. Chioggia has been flourishing here since the 1930s. There's not a full-fledged menu, but you can order light platters and sandwiches. Piazza San Marco, San Marco 8–11. ℂ **041-5285011.** Vaporetto: Vallaresso.

Caffè Florian   This is Venice's most famous cafe. The Florian was built in 1720, and it remains romantic and elegant—a pure Venetian salon with red plush banquettes, intricate murals under glass, and art-nouveau lighting and lamps. The Florian has hosted everyone from Casanova and Lord Byron to Goethe. In the afternoon, you can even get an English tea from 3 to 6pm, when you can select from a choice of pastries, ice cream, and cakes. Piazza San Marco, San Marco 56–59. ℂ **041-5285338.** Vaporetto: Vallaresso.

Cips   The hippest cafe in Venice today is funky little Cips, on Isola della Giudecca, run by the owners of Harry's Bar and the Cipriani hotel. Pronounced "chips" (as in potato), this cafe with its summer terrace frames one of the grandest views of Piazza San Marco. If you arrive between May and August, ask for a Bellini, made from Prosecco and white-peach purée, or perhaps a *sgroppino,* a slushy mix of lemon gelato and vodka whisked over ice. You can also order the best bitter chocolate gelato in Venice here. Cip's also serves terrific international and Venetian dishes. Isola della Giudecca 10. ℂ **041-5207744.** Vaporetto: Zitelle.

Gran Caffè Lavena This popular but intimate cafe under the arcades of Piazza San Marco was once frequented by Richard Wagner when he stayed in Venice. It has some of the most beautifully ornate glass chandeliers in the city. They hang from the ceiling between the iron rails of an upper-level balcony. The most interesting tables are near the plate-glass window in front, although there's plenty of room at the stand-up bar as well. Piazza San Marco, San Marco 133–134. ℂ 041-5224070. Vaporetto: Vallaresso.

Quadri Quadri stands on the opposite side of the square from the Florian. It, too, is elegantly decorated in antique style. It should be— it was founded in 1638. Wagner used to drop in for a drink when he was in Venice working on *Tristan and Isolde*. Its prices are virtually the same as at the Florian, and it, too, imposes a surcharge on drinks ordered during concert periods. The bar was a favorite with the Austrians during their long-ago occupation (Venetian patriots went to Florian's). Piazza San Marco, San Marco 120–124. ℂ 041-5289299. Vaporetto: Vallaresso.

5 Ice Cream & Pastries

Gelateria Paolin For many, strolling to the Gelateria Paolin (set in a large colorful square) and ordering some of the tastiest gelato in Venice is nightlife enough. That's the way many a Venetian spends a summer evening. This gelateria has stood on the corner of this busy square since the 1930s, making it the oldest ice-cream parlor in Venice. You can order your ice cream to eat at one of the sidewalk tables (which costs more) or order it to go. Many interesting flavors are offered. Your best bet is one of the ice creams made with fresh fruit from the Veneto. Campo San Stefano, San Marco 2962A. ℂ 041-5225576. Vaporetto: Santa Maria del Giglio.

Pasticceria Marchini If you'd like to escape the throngs of visitors that overrun Venice in the early evening, head here, have a pastry and a coffee, and contemplate your evening plans. This is where your Venetian friend (if you have one) would take you for the most delectable pastries served in the city. The small pastries are made according to old recipes—ask for their *bigna* or *cannolo*. Campo San Maurizio, San Marco 2769. ℂ 041-5229109. Vaporetto: Accademia.

6 Dance Clubs

Il Piccolo Mondo This pub, near the Accademia, is open during the day, but it comes alive with dance music at night, drawing a young crowd. It's open Thursday to Tuesday from 10pm to 4am, but the action actually doesn't begin until after midnight. Calle Contarini Corfu 1056A. ℂ **041-5200371.** Cover (including the first drink) 7€ Thurs–Fri, 9€ Sat; otherwise free. Vaporetto: Accademia.

Casanova   Since the real Casanova is no longer seen around town, this dance club, one of the few in Venice, still carries on his name with its allure of romance. In the vicinity of the rail station, the place is a bar and Internet cafe (charging 1€ per hour) until 10pm, when it becomes a disco. The club attracts a scattering of Venetian youth in their 20s and 30s who mingle with an international coterie of foreign visitors. Often Casanova stays open until 4am. Different nights are devoted to a different type of music—salsa on Wednesday; pop, rock, and indie on Thursday; dance music on Friday; and a progressive DJ plays Saturday night. Cannaregio 158A. ℂ **041-2750199.** Cover (including the first drink) 10€ Fri–Sat. Vaporetto: Lista di Spagna.

7 Casinos

Venice is home to two casinos. The larger and busier of the two, the Casino Municipale, lies beside the flat, sandy expanses of the Lido; it's almost deserted in winter and mobbed in summer. As cold winds descend on Venice from the Alps in winter, the action moves back to the center of town, to a cozier venue known as the Vendramin-Calergi Palace.

Regardless of where you might happen to drop your euros, know in advance that a jacket (but not a tie) is requested for men, and that sneakers and shorts are forbidden. Both casinos contain slot machines, but more interesting are the roulette wheels, where minimum bets are 5€ and maximum wagers 200€.

Casino Municipale   If you want to risk your luck and your euros, take a vaporetto ride on the Casino Express, which leaves from stops at the railway station, Piazzale Roma, and Piazzetta San Marco, and delivers you to the landing dock of the Casino Municipale. The Italian government forbids its nationals to cross the threshold unless they work here, so bring your passport. The building itself is foreboding, almost as if it could have been inspired by Mussolini-era architects. However, the action gets hotter once you step inside. You can try your luck at blackjack, roulette, baccarat, or whatever. You can also dine, drink at the bar, or enjoy a floor show. Open June through September daily from 4pm to 2:30am. Calle Bedramin Calergi Cannaregio 20–40. ℂ **041-5297111.** Admission 10€. Vaporetto: San Marcuola.

Vendramin-Calergi Palace   From October through May, the
casino action moves to the Vendramin-Calergi Palace. Incidentally,
in 1883 Wagner died in this house, which opens onto the Grand
Canal. Open daily from 3pm to 2:30am. Strada Nuova, Cannaregio 2040.
© 041-5297111. Admission 10€. Vaporetto: San Marcuola.

8 Gay & Lesbian Clubs

There are no gay bars in Venice, but you'll find some in nearby
Padua, a lovely old city about 35 minutes from Venice by train.
However, Venice does have a local division of a government-
affiliated agency, **ArciGay ArciLesbica,** Campo San Giacomo
dell'Orio, Santa Croce 1507 (© **049-8762458**). It serves as a kind
of home base for the gay community, with info on gay-friendly
accommodations and such. The best hours to call (it's hard to find)
are Monday 9 to 11:30pm, and Thursday from 6 to 8pm.

Index

See also Accommodations and Restaurant indexes below.

ACCOMMODATIONS

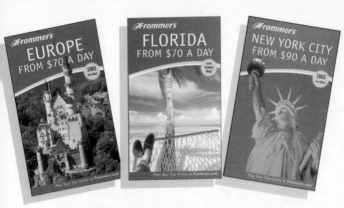

FROMMER'S® COMPLETE TRAVEL GUIDES

Alaska
Alaska Cruises & Ports of Call
Amsterdam
Argentina & Chile
Arizona
Atlanta
Australia
Austria
Bahamas
Barcelona, Madrid & Seville
Beijing
Belgium, Holland & Luxembourg
Bermuda
Boston
Brazil
British Columbia & the Canadian
  Rockies
Budapest & the Best of Hungary
California
Canada
Cancún, Cozumel & the Yucatán
Cape Cod, Nantucket & Martha's
  Vineyard
Caribbean
Caribbean Cruises & Ports of Call
Caribbean Ports of Call
Carolinas & Georgia
Chicago
China
Colorado
Costa Rica
Denmark
Denver, Boulder & Colorado
  Springs
England
Europe
European Cruises & Ports of Call
Florida

France
Germany
Great Britain
Greece
Greek Islands
Hawaii
Hong Kong
Honolulu, Waikiki & Oahu
Ireland
Israel
Italy
Jamaica
Japan
Las Vegas
London
Los Angeles
Maryland & Delaware
Maui
Mexico
Montana & Wyoming
Montréal & Québec City
Munich & the Bavarian Alps
Nashville & Memphis
Nepal
New England
New Mexico
New Orleans
New York City
New Zealand
Northern Italy
Nova Scotia, New Brunswick &
  Prince Edward Island
Oregon
Paris
Philadelphia & the Amish Country
Portugal
Prague & the Best of the Czech
  Republic

Provence & the Riviera
Puerto Rico
Rome
San Antonio & Austin
San Diego
San Francisco
Santa Fe, Taos & Albuquerque
Scandinavia
Scotland
Seattle & Portland
Shanghai
Singapore & Malaysia
South Africa
South America
South Florida
South Pacific
Southeast Asia
Spain
Sweden
Switzerland
Texas
Thailand
Tokyo
Toronto
Tuscany & Umbria
USA
Utah
Vancouver & Victoria
Vermont, New Hampshire &
  Maine
Vienna & the Danube Valley
Virgin Islands
Virginia
Walt Disney World® & Orlando
Washington, D.C.
Washington State

FROMMER'S® DOLLAR-A-DAY GUIDES

Australia from $50 a Day
California from $70 a Day
Caribbean from $70 a Day
England from $75 a Day
Europe from $70 a Day

Florida from $70 a Day
Hawaii from $80 a Day
Ireland from $60 a Day
Italy from $70 a Day
London from $85 a Day

New York from $90 a Day
Paris from $80 a Day
San Francisco from $70 a Day
Washington, D.C. from $80 a Day

FROMMER'S® PORTABLE GUIDES

Acapulco, Ixtapa & Zihuatanejo
Amsterdam
Aruba
Australia's Great Barrier Reef
Bahamas
Berlin
Big Island of Hawaii
Boston
California Wine Country
Cancún
Charleston & Savannah
Chicago
Disneyland®
Dublin
Florence

Frankfurt
Hong Kong
Houston
Las Vegas
London
Los Angeles
Los Cabos & Baja
Maine Coast
Maui
Miami
New Orleans
New York City
Paris
Phoenix & Scottsdale

Portland
Puerto Rico
Puerto Vallarta, Manzanillo &
  Guadalajara
Rio de Janeiro
San Diego
San Francisco
Seattle
Sydney
Tampa & St. Petersburg
Vancouver
Venice
Virgin Islands
Washington, D.C.

FROMMER'S® NATIONAL PARK GUIDES

Banff & Jasper
Family Vacations in the National
  Parks
Grand Canyon

National Parks of the American
  West
Rocky Mountain

Yellowstone & Grand Teton
Yosemite & Sequoia/ Kings Canyon
Zion & Bryce Canyon

FROMMER'S® MEMORABLE WALKS

Chicago	New York	San Francisco
London	Paris	Washington, D.C.

FROMMER'S® GREAT OUTDOOR GUIDES

Arizona & New Mexico	Northern California	Vermont & New Hampshire
New England	Southern New England	

SUZY GERSHMAN'S BORN TO SHOP GUIDES

Born to Shop: France	Born to Shop: Italy	Born to Shop: New York
Born to Shop: Hong Kong, Shanghai & Beijing	Born to Shop: London	Born to Shop: Paris

FROMMER'S® IRREVERENT GUIDES

Amsterdam	Los Angeles	San Francisco
Boston	Manhattan	Seattle & Portland
Chicago	New Orleans	Vancouver
Las Vegas	Paris	Walt Disney World®
London	Rome	Washington, D.C.

FROMMER'S® BEST-LOVED DRIVING TOURS

Britain	Germany	Northern Italy
California	Ireland	Scotland
Florida	Italy	Spain
France	New England	Tuscany & Umbria

HANGING OUT™ GUIDES

Hanging Out in England	Hanging Out in France	Hanging Out in Italy
Hanging Out in Europe	Hanging Out in Ireland	Hanging Out in Spain

THE UNOFFICIAL GUIDES®

Bed & Breakfasts and Country Inns in:	Southwest & South Central Plains	Mid-Atlantic with Kids
California	U.S.A.	Mini Las Vegas
Great Lakes States	Beyond Disney	Mini-Mickey
Mid-Atlantic	Branson, Missouri	New England and New York with Kids
New England	California with Kids	New Orleans
Northwest	Chicago	New York City
Rockies	Cruises	Paris
Southeast	Disneyland®	San Francisco
Southwest	Florida with Kids	Skiing in the West
Best RV & Tent Campgrounds in:	Golf Vacations in the Eastern U.S.	Southeast with Kids
California & the West	Great Smoky & Blue Ridge Region	Walt Disney World®
Florida & the Southeast	Inside Disney	Walt Disney World® for Grown-ups
Great Lakes States	Hawaii	Walt Disney World® with Kids
Mid-Atlantic	Las Vegas	Washington, D.C.
Northeast	London	World's Best Diving Vacations
Northwest & Central Plains		

SPECIAL-INTEREST TITLES

Frommer's Adventure Guide to Australia & New Zealand
Frommer's Adventure Guide to Central America
Frommer's Adventure Guide to India & Pakistan
Frommer's Adventure Guide to South America
Frommer's Adventure Guide to Southeast Asia
Frommer's Adventure Guide to Southern Africa
Frommer's Britain's Best Bed & Breakfasts and Country Inns
Frommer's Caribbean Hideaways
Frommer's Exploring America by RV
Frommer's Fly Safe, Fly Smart
Frommer's France's Best Bed & Breakfasts and Country Inns
Frommer's Gay & Lesbian Europe

Frommer's Italy's Best Bed & Breakfasts and Country Inns
Frommer's New York City with Kids
Frommer's Ottawa with Kids
Frommer's Road Atlas Britain
Frommer's Road Atlas Europe
Frommer's Road Atlas France
Frommer's Toronto with Kids
Frommer's Vancouver with Kids
Frommer's Washington, D.C., with Kids
Israel Past & Present
The New York Times' Guide to Unforgettable Weekends
Places Rated Almanac
Retirement Places Rated

You Need A Vacation.

700 Airlines, 50,000 Hotels, 50 Rental Car Companies, And A Million Ways To Save Money.

Travelocity.com
A Sabre Company
Go Virtually Anywhere.